INDONESIA AND THE ASIAN DEVELOPMENT BANK

FIFTY YEARS OF PARTNERSHIP

Peter McCawley

ADB

Notes:
In this publication, "$" refers to United States dollars and "Rp" refers to Indonesia rupiah, unless otherwise stated.
ADB recognizes "China" as the People's Republic of China, "Holland" as the Netherlands, "Korea" as the Republic of Korea, and "Vietnam" as Viet Nam.

On the front cover, from top left, clockwise: Lady farmers transporting crops beside an irrigation canal in Yogyakarta (Photo by Ariel Javellana for ADB); Neighbors helping each other pull a fishing net in Gorontalo (Photo by Ariel Javellana for ADB); A student at Batam State Polytechnic's teaching factory work to mass-produce microchips (Photo by Lester Ledesma for ADB); Aerial view of Hotel Indonesia roundabout in Jakarta with the background of the Plaza Office Tower, in which the ADB Indonesia Resident Mission is located (Photo by ximagination © 123RF.com); Electricity grid in Sumba (Photo by Sean Crowley for ADB); Batam State Polytechnic students learn work with metal at the welding and plasma cutting lab (Photo by Lester Ledesma for ADB). Cover design by Edith Creus.

All photos are by ADB, unless otherwise stated.

ABOUT THE AUTHOR

Peter McCawley is an economist from the Arndt-Corden Department of Economics at the Australian National University (ANU) in Canberra, who has worked on development issues in Asia and the Pacific for many years.

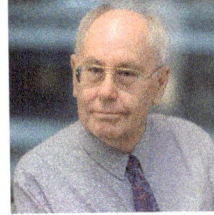

He has a PhD in economics (1972) from the ANU. He later taught at Gadjah Mada University in Yogyakarta in the early 1970s before becoming head, Indonesia Project, at the ANU. In 1986, he joined Australian Aid as a deputy director general.

Much of his work in Asia has been with the Asian Development Bank (ADB). Between 1992 and 1996, he was a member of the ADB Board of Directors. Later, in 2003–2007, he became dean of the ADB Institute in Tokyo.

He was also cochair and chair of Asian Development Fund negotiations between 1999 and 2008.

He has numerous publications about development issues in Asia and the Pacific.

CONTENTS

About the Author   iii
Tables, Figures, and Boxes   vii
Foreword   x
Acknowledgments   xiii
Abbreviations   xv
Executive Summary   xviii

Chapter 1—Introduction   1
  A Multilateral Agency   2
  Development Activities   3
  Finance   5
  ADB in Indonesia   7
  Overall Assistance to Indonesia   9

Chapter 2—Indonesia in the Region   15

Chapter 3—Early Years (1967–1976)   21
  The Inter-Governmental Group on Indonesia   23
  Next Steps for Indonesia   24
  Growing International Support   26
  ADB Begins Work   29
  Changes in Indonesia   37
  Delivery of Aid   38
  Next Steps for the Bank   42
  Annual Meeting in Indonesia   44
  Ten Years Old   45

Chapter 4—A Widening Role (1977–1986)   51
  New Challenges   52
  External Shocks   53
  Donor Programs 1977–1980   55
  ADB Programs   56
  Changes in Approach   62
  Economic Changes   64
  Donor Activities in the Early 1980s   68
  ADB in the Early 1980s   71
  Into a Third Decade   76

Chapter 5—Adjustment in Indonesia (1987–1996) — 81
Adjustment — 81
The October 1988 Package — 84
Changes for Donors — 88
ADB in the Third Decade — 91
Adjustment Continues — 102
Donor Activities in the 1990s — 108
ADB Programs — 112
Calm Before the Storm — 122

Chapter 6—Asian Financial Crisis (1997–1998) — 127
Before the Crisis — 128
The Crisis Erupts — 130
Donors and the Crisis — 136
ADB Response — 139
Issues from the Crisis — 142
Causes of the Crisis — 142
Policy Responses — 144
Mitigating the Social Impact — 145
Views in the Region — 146
Lessons for ADB — 148

Chapter 7—Recovery (1999–2006) — 151
Aftermath of the Crisis — 151
Difficulties of Recovery — 152
Strengthening Economy — 153
The Donor Community — 155
Differences with the Donor Community — 156
A Changing Mood — 160
ADB's Role — 164
ADB Programs — 168
New Strategy — 174
Tumult Through the Decade — 184

Chapter 8—Middle-Income Country Issues (2007–2019) — 191
Strengthening Recovery — 191
New Era for Donors — 199
Place of ADB — 209

ADB Activities　　　　　　　　　　　　　　　　　215
Beyond 50 Years: 2017–2019　　　　　　　　　229
Relations with Donors　　　　　　　　　　　231
ADB Looking Ahead　　　　　　　　　　　232
Reviewing the Decade　　　　　　　　　　239

Chapter 9—Lessons and Challenges　　　　**245**
Indonesia and the International Community　　　245
Asian Development Bank　　　　　　　　　246
Four Efforts　　　　　　　　　　　　　251
Challenges Ahead　　　　　　　　　　257

Bibliography　　　　　　　　　　　　**258**

Appendixes　　　　　　　　　　　　**275**
1　　Indonesia: Overview Charts and Tables　　276
2　　Asian Development Bank and Indonesia: Charts and Tables　278

Index of Names　　　　　　　　　　**288**

TABLES, FIGURES, AND BOXES

Tables

ES 1	Summary of Notable Events, 1966–2018	xix
ES 2	Main Phases in ADB Assistance to Indonesia	xlvii
1.1	Total International Official Flows to Indonesia, 1967–2016	10
1.2	Total Official Gross Flows to Indonesia, 1967–2016	13
2.1	Selected Regional Institutions and Indonesia	18
3.1	Notable Events, 1966–1976	33
3.2	ADB Early Lending to Indonesia, 1969–1973	35
3.3	ADB Lending to Indonesia, 1974–1976	43
4.1	ADB Lending to Indonesia, 1977–1981	60
4.2	Notable Events, 1977–1986	63
4.3	Planning Investment and Government Receipts and Spending as a Share of GDP, Various Years	67
4.4	IGGI Commitments and Disbursements, 1974–1981	69
4.5	ADB Lending to Indonesia, 1982–1986	72
5.1	Chronology of Adjustment Programs in Indonesia, 1983–1990	86
5.2	Notable Events, 1987–1996	91
5.3	ADB Lending to Indonesia, 1987–1991	93
5.4	ADB Cofinancing in 1989 and 1990	101
5.5	ADB Lending to Indonesia, 1992–1996	113
5.6	ADB Approved Lending to Indonesia by Sector, 1969–1994	117
5.7	ADB Approved Lending and Technical Assistance to Indonesia, 1969–1994	118
5.8	ADB Approved Lending to Indonesia by Mode, 1969–1994	118
5.9	Advisory Technical Assistance for the Financial Sector, 1990–1996	120
6.1	Main Crisis-Related Loans provided by ADB to Indonesia during the Asian Financial Crisis	149
7.1	Total Pledges at IGGI and CGI Meetings, 1967–2003	163
7.2	Pledges at IGGI and CGI Meetings by Share, 1967–2003	164
7.3	Notable Events, 1997–2006	165
7.4	ADB Lending to Indonesia, 2000–2006	169
7.5	Decentralization Support Loans to Indonesia, 1998–2009	179

8.1   Notable Events, 2007–2018   210
8.2   Disbursements by Sector during the 2006–2009   216
      CSP Period
8.3   ADB Lending to Indonesia, 2007–2016   217
8.4   Proposed ADB Spending by Sector, 2016–2019   233
8.5   ADB Lending to Indonesia, 2017–2018   234
8.6   Selected ADB-Supported Private Sector Loans,   236
      2013–2018
9.1   Main Phases in ADB Assistance to Indonesia   247
9.2   ADB Cumulative Lending, Grants, and Technical   250
      Assistance Commitments, 1967–2018
9.3   Capital Stock Per Capita, Selected Countries, 2014   253

Figures
1.1   Per Capita Gross Domestic Product in the People's   5
      Republic of China, India, Indonesia, and Japan,
      1900–2010
1.2   ADB Approvals for Indonesia as % of GDP, 1969–2016   8
1.3   Total Official Gross Flows as % of GDP, 1967–2016   11
7.1   Government of Indonesia Development Spending   176

Boxes
3.1   ADB's First Technical Assistance Grant: Food Supply   31
      Issues in Indonesia
3.2   Tajum Irrigation Project   31
4.1   Summary of Recommendations from the Second Asian   58
      Agricultural Survey, 1978
4.2   ADB Operational Strategy in Indonesia, 1986   77
5.1   Reasons for and Path of Economic Reform in 1985   82
5.2   ADB's Operational Strategy for Indonesia, 1987   97
5.3   Northeast Indonesia: Development through Cooperation   123
6.1   Asian Financial Crisis in Indonesia: Key Dates   131
6.2   World Bank's View on the Need for Aid to Indonesia   137
      in Mid-1997
6.3   Social Safety Net Programs   145
7.1   Bappenas' 2003 Recommendations on Indonesia's   161
      Relations with the CGI and the Donor Community

7.2	Strategic Focus of ADB's Country Strategy and Program, 2003–2005	174
7.3	Government's Views on How ADB Can Become More Relevant	177
8.1	The National Medium-Term National Development Plan 2010–2014	195
8.2	Masterplan for the Acceleration of Indonesian Economic Development	197
8.3	Seven Lessons for Disaster Reconstruction	212
8.4	Development Policy Support Loans to Indonesia	219
9.1	Evaluation of ADB's Work in Indonesia	249

FOREWORD

In 1966, when Indonesia became one of the founding members of the Asian Development Bank (ADB), the country faced daunting socioeconomic challenges. Production was stagnating, inflation was skyrocketing, and there was an urgent need to rebuild relations with the international community. At the time, ADB had just been established and was beginning to prepare its first programs in developing countries in Asia, including in Indonesia.

In the five decades since then, both Indonesia and ADB have evolved in remarkable ways. Indonesia, having experienced rapid development that spanned three decades, faced a difficult adjustment after the 1997–1998 Asian financial crisis, before resuming another long period of sustained growth until today. With this growth, Indonesia has made significant development strides, including the reduction of the poverty rate to single digits, expansion of public services, improvements to the investment climate, and increased investments in infrastructure. ADB, for its part, has widened its operations from a project-oriented development bank into a broad-based development institution. ADB currently offers tailor-made financial, policy, and knowledge solutions to help its developing country members, including Indonesia, address a multitude of development challenges.

In 2016, ADB celebrated its 50th anniversary. This book has been prepared to mark 50 years of partnership between Indonesia and ADB. It reviews the way that the relationship between Indonesia, ADB, and the international community has evolved during these five decades.

Looking back over the past 50 years, the partnership between Indonesia and ADB, and the international development partner community more broadly, has been one of the most substantial—and successful—longer-term development cooperation efforts in post-war history. It is a striking example of effective cooperation between one of the largest developing countries in the world and the international community.

One of the keys to this successful development cooperation has been a will on both sides to work well together. On the Government of Indonesia's side, senior officials work effectively with the international community, both responding to concerns from development partners and taking care to clearly communicate Indonesia's development priorities. On the ADB side, there is a well-judged and long-term relationship with policymakers and demonstrated responsiveness to the needs and priorities of the government.

A second central element in the partnership between Indonesia and ADB has been the country's strong ownership of the development cooperation program. The government determines the broad directions of national development policy and sets out sector strategies. It allocates projects and programs for international cooperation and monitors the implementation of related activities.

A third key to success has been the flexibility of the cooperation. As the situation changed in Indonesia, international partners also changed the way they worked to respond to the country's evolving needs. During the 1970s, ADB mainly provided support for investment projects in Indonesia. Later, during the 1980s, the government began to give increasing attention to the need for economic reforms, so the international community supported activities to promote reform programs. In 1997–1998, large-scale fast-disbursing financial support was provided to help Indonesia adjust during the Asian financial crisis. More recently, the bank introduced flexible forms of financing, such as the results-based lending modality, which has been responsive to Indonesia's evolving development priorities especially in infrastructure sectors.

There was much flexibility, too, in the priority that Indonesia and the international community gave to activities in different sectors at different times. In the 1970s, the need to strengthen food security was a central goal of development policy in Indonesia. ADB supported many agricultural projects and activities to promote the Green Revolution in the rice sector. Later, there was an increased focus on bank programs in sectors such as health and education, and for new social protection policies. There has been growing awareness, too, of the need to strengthen the capacity to deal with natural disasters and other risks that local communities encounter across Indonesia. In 2005, one of the world's largest international emergency response efforts was organized when the Asian tsunami struck Aceh and Nias, and spread outward across the Indian Ocean, with a death toll amounting to nearly 230,000 people across the region. The challenges of environmental sustainability and climate change are now recognized as key issues that need to be addressed across all development sectors in Indonesia.

Today, Indonesia is an emerging upper-middle income country that aspires to achieve high-income status by 2045. Toward this end, Indonesia faces a complex set of development challenges: advancing productivity and competitiveness, developing a sophisticated workforce to support the future economy, and addressing increasing climate costs. At the same time,

Indonesia must successfully navigate emerging megatrends including rapid urbanization, climate change, demographic changes, technological disruptions, and shifting economic powers.

The government recognizes these challenges. The policy priorities set out by President Joko Widodo at the beginning of his second term in 2019 address these most pressing issues. Specifically, policy priorities include a continued focus on infrastructure development and improving connectivity, human capital development, investment and job creation, structural and regulatory reform, and the improvement of public service delivery.

Looking to the future, Indonesia and ADB will continue to be steadfast partners, as they have been over the past 50 years, in advancing inclusive and sustainable development. ADB is well-positioned and remains committed to supporting Indonesia in delivering its development priorities and achieving its vision of becoming a high-income economy by 2045.

Sri Mulyani Indrawati
Minister of Finance, Republic
of Indonesia and Governor
for Indonesia, Asian Development
Bank

Masatsugu Asakawa
President and Chair of the
Board of Directors, Asian
Development Bank

ACKNOWLEDGMENTS

I have been generously assisted by many people in Indonesia, the Philippines, Australia, and elsewhere in writing this book. Indonesian colleagues include one of Indonesia's most senior policymakers Anwar Nasution, former Minister of Finance M. Chatib Basri, ADB Vice-President for Knowledge Management and Sustainable Development Bambang Susantono, Edimon Ginting and Ari Perdana from ADB headquarters in Manila, and Arianto Patunru, former head of the Institute for Economic and Social Research at the University of Indonesia and now a colleague at the Australian National University (ANU).

I have drawn extensively on published materials from the Indonesian National Development Planning Agency (Bappenas) in drafting the text. I learned much about Bappenas policies and relations with international donor agencies while working with the agency in Jakarta for over two years between 2011 and 2013. I would like to make special mention of help from Pungky Sumadi and Wismana Adi Surya, both senior officials in Bappenas, as well as generous assistance from staff of the Bappenas library.

Numerous current and former ADB colleagues also provided help in numerous ways. These include Jade Tolentino, who worked with me on our earlier book *Banking on the Future of Asia and the Pacific*, as well as ADB Secretary Eugenue Zhukov, and staff of his office, Walter Kolkma and Kori Emzita. The range of former ADB staff who offered advice and pointed to useful sources of information includes Robert Boumphrey, Paul Dickie, John Eyers, David Green, Chris MacCormac, Khaja Moinuddin, Pieter Smidt, and Robert Wihtol.

From ADB's Indonesia Resident Mission in Jakarta, Country Director Winfried Wicklein, and my former bank colleague in Jakarta, Sona Shrestha, encouraged me to begin to work on this study. Emma Allen, Meity Tanujaya, and Cahyadi Indrananto provided ongoing support while the text was being prepared. Amr Qari, David Donovan, and Juliette Leusink supplied up-to-date information about ADB's private sector operations in Indonesia.

A number of academic colleagues who have worked on Indonesian economic affairs for many years also provided comments and advice. These include Anne Booth, Chris Manning, Stephen Grenville, Hal Hill, and Pierre van der Eng.

The book was produced to a very tight deadline. Hannah Maddison-Harris provided excellent editorial support. The ADB Department of Communications in Manila helped ensure that the production process was completed on time.

Finally, I should mention that the views set out here are my own. They are not the official views of ADB. Mistakes and errors of judgment that readers may identify are mine.

Peter McCawley

ABBREVIATIONS

ADB	Asian Development Bank
ADBI	Asian Development Bank Institute
ADF	Asian Development Fund
AFIC	Asian Finance and Investment Corporation
AMRO	ASEAN+3 Macroeconomic Research Office
ANU	Australian National University
APEC	Asia-Pacific Economic Cooperation
ARIC	Asia Regional Integration Center
ASEAN	Association of Southeast Asian Nations
ASEAN+3	ASEAN, Japan, the People's Republic of China, and the Republic of Korea
ATF	Asian Tsunami Fund (of ADB)
Bapindo	*Bank Pembangunan Indonesia* (Indonesian Development Bank)
Bappenas	*Badan Perencanaan Pembangunan Nasional* (National Development Planning Agency)
Bimas	*Bimbingan Massal* (mass guidance in the rice sector)
BIMP-EAGA	Brunei Darussalam–Indonesia–Malaysia–Philippines East ASEAN Growth Area
BIS	Bank for International Settlements
BPK	*Badan Pemeriksa Keuangan* (Supreme Audit Board)
BRR	*Badan Rehabilitasi dan Rekonstruksi* (Rehabilitation and Reconstruction Agency)
CAPE	country assistance program evaluation
CERD	Community Empowerment for Rural Development Project
CGI	Consultative Group on Indonesia
CIDA	Canadian International Development Agency
CFS	complementary financing scheme
CMI	Chiang Mai Initiative
CMIM	Chiang Mai Initiative Multilateralization
COS	country operational strategy (of ADB)
CPS	country program strategy (also country partnership strategy)
CSF	countercyclical support facility
CSP	country strategy and program (also country strategic plan)
CSS	country safeguard system
DFI	development finance institution
DPD	*Dewan Perwakilan Daerah* (Regional Representative Council)
DPSP	Development Policy Support Program

EA	executing agency
EAS	East Asia Summit
ECAFE	United Nations Economic Commission for Asia and the Far East
EDP	external development partner
EMEAP	Executives' Meeting of East Asia-Pacific Central Banks
ETESP	Earthquake and Tsunami Emergency Support Project
FAO	Food and Agriculture Organization of the United Nations
FDI	foreign direct investment
FGSSR	Financial Governance and Social Security Reform program
FPEMP	Fiscal and Public Expenditure Management Program
FSPL	Financial Sector Program Loan
GDP	gross domestic product
GTZ	*Deutsche Gesellschaft für Technische Zusammenarbeit* (German Technical Cooperation Agency)
G20	Group of 20
HNSDP	Health and Nutrition Sector Development Program
IBRA	Indonesian Bank Restructuring Agency
IBRD	International Bank for Reconstruction and Development
IDA	International Development Association
IED	Independent Evaluation Department (of ADB)
IGGI	Inter-Governmental Group on Indonesia
IIP	irrigation improvement program
ILO	International Labour Organization
IMF	International Monetary Fund
IMT-GT	Indonesia–Malaysia–Thailand Growth Triangle
IRM	Indonesia Resident Mission (of ADB)
LGFGR	Local Government Finance and Governance Reform program
LNG	liquefied natural gas
LOI	letter of intent
MDG	Millennium Development Goal
MOU	memorandum of understanding
MPRS	*Majelis Permusyawaratan Rakyat Sementara* (Provisional People's Consultative Assembly)
MP3EI	*Masterplan Percepatan dan Perluasan Pembangunan Ekonomi Indonesia* (Masterplan for the Acceleration and Expansion of Indonesian Economic Development)
MW	megawatt
NGO	nongovernment organization

NTB	non-tariff barrier
OECD	Organisation for Economic Co-operation and Development
OECD-DAC	OECD Development Assistance Committee
OCR	ordinary capital resources
ODA	official development assistance
OJK	*Otoritas Jasa Keuangan* (Financial Services Authority)
OOF	other official flows
Pakto	*Paket Oktober* (October Package)
PBA	program-based approach
PDAM	*Perusahaan Daerah Air Minum* (government-owned water company)
PFF	Precautionary Financing Facility
PLN	*Perusahaan Listrik Negara* (State Electricity Company)
PPP	public–private partnership
PRC	People's Republic of China
PROPENAS	*Program Pembangunan Nasional* (National Development Program)
PRPA	Poverty Reduction Partnership Agreement
PSM	public sector management
RBL	results-based lending (also results-based loan)
REMU	Regional Economic Monitoring Unit
Repelita	*Rencana Pembangunan Lima Tahun* (Five-Year Development Plan)
RPJMN	*Rencana Pembangunan Jangka Menengah Nasional* (National Medium-Term Development Plan)
RPJPN	*Rencana Pembangunan Jangka Panjang Nasional* (National Long-Term Development Plan)
SBY	President Susilo Bambang Yudhoyono
SIEP	Sustainable and Inclusive Energy Program
SIGAP	Stepping Up Investments for Growth Acceleration Program
SMEs	small and medium enterprises
SPSDP	Social Protection Sector Development Program
TA	technical assistance
UK	United Kingdom
UNCTAD	United Nations Conference on Trade and Development
US	United States
USAID	United States Agency for International Development

EXECUTIVE SUMMARY

In the late 1960s, the international community began to support a new and rapidly expanding program of assistance to Indonesia. The aim was to promote economic recovery in Southeast Asia's largest country after a long period of political and economic difficulties since independence in 1945.

Over the next five decades to 2016, the flow of assistance to Indonesia became one of the largest sustained programs of foreign aid supported by the international donor community in the post-World War II period (Table 1.1). The total amount of support reached around $340 billion (2016 constant prices), made up of around $130 billion of official aid—gross official development assistance (ODA)—and almost $210 billion of other flows, mainly provided as loans—gross other official flows (OOF).[1] Much of the assistance was provided as grants. Many loans were also approved, both by bilateral national agencies and by international organizations such as the World Bank, the International Monetary Fund (IMF), and ADB.

This book outlines the experiences of ADB in Indonesia since the late 1960s. During these five decades, ADB worked closely with partners in Indonesia including the rest of the donor community and the Government of Indonesia (Table ES 1). The account of ADB's activities is set within the broader context of the programs of the international donor community and of the development effort led by the government.

Early Years (1967–1976)

When the new Soeharto government began the task of economic rehabilitation in 1967, the first priority was to restore economic stability. A looming debt crisis needed urgent attention. To discuss debt rescheduling, meetings of creditor countries were convened in late 1966 and 1967. A range of meetings was held including with Eastern Bloc countries and with other debtors under the auspices of the Paris Club. One outcome of the meetings was that a new aid group—the Inter-Governmental Group

---

[1] Official development assistance (ODA) and other official flows (OOF) are measures of official flows agreed to for development purposes recorded by the Development Assistance Committee (DAC) of the Organisation for Economic Co-operation and Development (OECD). ODA mainly refers to official flows provided on concessional terms, often as grants. OOF are official flows that do not meet the conditions for eligibility as ODA, either because they are not primarily provided for development purposes or because they have a grant element of less than 25%. Definitions of ODA and OOF may be found in the DAC Glossary of Key Terms and Concepts on the OECD website.

Table ES 1: Summary of Notable Events, 1966–2018[a]

Item	Comment
1966	
Indonesia joins ADB	As a founding member in Tokyo
1967	
Agricultural mission	First ADB TA to any member country
IGGI established	Donor group for aid coordination
1969	
Tajum Irrigation	First ADB loan to Indonesia
1976	
ADB annual meeting	Ninth Annual Meeting of ADB held in Central Jakarta
1980	
First ADB sector loan	Small Towns Water Supply Sector project approved for Indonesia was ADB's first sector loan
1984	
TA program loan for multisectoral feasibility studies	First ADB loan of this kind in any country
1987	
Indonesia Resident Mission	Opened in Jakarta
1988	
Financial Sector Program Loan	ADB began to give increasing attention to issues in the financial sector supporting policy reform
1992	
Consultative Group on Indonesia	New CGI group replaced IGGI for aid coordination
Power XXII Loan ($350 million)	Largest ADB loan ever approved for any country

continued on next page

Table ES 1 *continued*

Item	Comment
1994	
ADB country strategy 1994	The 1994 *Country Operational Strategy*, the first formal ADB strategy for Indonesia, set out a major review of the bank's work in Indonesia for the 1990s
1997–1998	
Asian financial crisis	ADB responded to coordinated efforts to respond to the crisis in late 1997
Asian financial crisis loans	ADB approved a series of crisis-related loans
2004–2005	
Asian tsunami in December	The international community began to mount a major relief effort in response to the tsunami
Asian Tsunami Fund established	First ADB fund established to focus on disaster relief
2006	
Bantul earthquake loan	ADB's expanded support for assistance after disasters continued following a large earthquake in the Yogyakarta region in Java
2007	
CGI dissolved	Full ownership of the coordination of international assistance taken over by Indonesia
2009	
ADB annual meeting	42nd Annual Meeting of ADB held in Bali
2012–2013	
ADB Precautionary Financing Facility approved for Indonesia	The facility was part of ADB's participation in a contingent $5 billion donor package to provide liquidity support

continued on next page

Table ES 1   *continued*

Item	Comment
2015	
Electricity grid strengthening in Sumatra	ADB's first results-based lending loan in Indonesia
2017	
First Indonesia rupiah-linked bond issued	ADB raised about $74 million from a new issue of offshore Indonesia rupiah-linked bonds
2018	
Major response to natural disasters	ADB provided assistance following large-scale disasters in Lombok and in Palu, Sulawesi
Private sector lending	ADB lending to the private sector in Indonesia reached a record lending level

ADB = Asian Development Bank, CGI = Consultative Group on Indonesia, IGGI = Inter-Governmental Group on Indonesia, TA = technical assistance.

ᵃ For additional details, see "Notable Events" tables in the chapters below.

on Indonesia (IGGI)—was established. Meetings of the IGGI, chaired by the Government of the Netherlands, were held annually, and sometimes more frequently, throughout the 1970s and 1980s. Later, in 1992, a new aid consortium, the CGI chaired by the World Bank, was formed to continue the aid coordination activities of the IGGI.

In 1969, Indonesia's First Five-Year Development Plan (Repelita I), for 1969–1974, was adopted. Early concerns about food policy came to the fore in 1972 when a severe drought led to fears of rice shortages and to sharp increases in rice prices. No sooner had rice prices been stabilized than other inflationary pressures emerged: In late 1973, there was a sharp rise in the world price of oil following instability in the Middle East. Indonesia, as an oil-exporting country at that time, benefited from a huge windfall following the oil boom. But the rapid expansion in the oil sector brought troubles as well: In 1975, a financial crisis in the state-owned oil company Pertamina, caused by ambitious foreign borrowings, attracted widespread publicity and was of major concern both to the Government of Indonesia and the international donor community.

ADB: Early Work

When ADB began work in Indonesia in 1967, stabilization of domestic food markets was one of the government's top priorities. The bank's first technical assistance (TA) activity in Indonesia, which was the first TA grant approved by ADB for an individual member country, was for a study of ways to improve food supplies. The bank also aimed to expand its investment activities so that a pipeline of project lending would build up. The first ADB loan, agreed to in 1969 on concessional low-interest terms, was to support the Tajum Irrigation Project in Central Java. During the next few years, the international assistance program to Indonesia expanded and ADB, too, broadened the range of activities it supported.

In 1971, ADB began what was to become a large bank program in the power sector in Indonesia. Loans were approved for projects in Pontianak in Kalimantan and in West Sumatra. During the next few years, more loans for the power sector were approved. ADB provided support for other sectors as well. Finance was agreed to for improvements at several of Indonesia's main ports and for loans in the sugar industry and for the fisheries sector in the province of Irian Jaya (later Papua). In the mid-1970s, ADB's loan pipeline broadened to include activities in the manufacturing sector.

In 1976, Indonesia hosted the Ninth Annual Meeting of the bank in Jakarta. The event signaled Indonesia's growing national confidence as a member of the international community. In his speech to the conference, President Soeharto outlined Indonesia's views on a range of key aspects of international relations at the time.

At the end of the first decade of ADB's work in Indonesia, from one point of view the activities of the bank were still largely responsive to requests from Indonesia and lacked strategic direction. But already, and less noticeably, the bank was beginning to strengthen a long-term program focused on the provision of basic infrastructure across the country.

A Widening Role (1977–1986)

As the second decade of ADB's work in Indonesia began, the immediate prospects for the country's economy were somewhat uncertain. On one hand, the worst of the difficulties posed by the Pertamina crisis had largely been overcome, improvements in the international economy were encouraging, and the major investment surge in Indonesia made possible by the 1973–1974 boom was fueling growth. On the other hand, it was unclear how long the revenues from the oil windfall would continue to hold up.

New Challenges

By early 1977 there were signs that the main stimulus from the 1973–1974 oil boom was beginning to wane. Policymakers accepted that major economic adjustments would be needed. As one step toward adjustment, in late 1978 a large devaluation of the rupiah was announced.

No sooner had economic adjustment measures been introduced than a second oil shock occurred. Once again, oil prices rose sharply. For a second time, Indonesia experienced a boost to growth. Nevertheless, the benefits were somewhat mixed because, as a response to global economic difficulties partly caused by the second oil boom, United States (US) monetary policy was sharply tightened. As a result, international interest rates began to rise steeply.

Throughout this period, international donors, especially Japan, continued to provide strong support to Indonesia. Some donor countries were inclined to take the view that although Indonesia had benefited from the two oil booms, the additional resources that had become available were modest compared with the development challenges that Indonesia still faced.

ADB Program

ADB's program in the late 1970s included a range of activities in the agriculture sector. Expected increases in rice production from the Green Revolution in Indonesia had not materialized. Disquiet about the trends was reflected in the Second Asian Agricultural Survey, a major study of trends sponsored by the bank in 1977. During the next few years, ADB adopted the main recommendations from the survey to guide the bank's program in Indonesia (Box 4.1 below).

As well as supporting projects in agriculture, the bank continued to expand its activities in infrastructure. Projects in power, roads, and ports were approved, and earlier support for education was extended to a number of new activities. ADB also began to encourage other agencies to cofinance bank-sponsored programs. By expanding cofinancing arrangements, ADB was aiming to strengthen its role as a financial intermediary and to promote expanded flows of external capital into Indonesia. As part of these steps toward broadening its financing role, ADB began to explore ways of improving operations in domestic financial markets in Indonesia. In Indonesia, as well as in other borrowing countries, the bank began to work with local development financial institutions to channel long-term capital to the private sector. In Jakarta, the Indonesian Development Bank (Bapindo) appeared to be a promising partner. Later, Bapindo failed and was merged with three other banks to form a new institution, Bank Mandiri.

The relationship between Indonesia and ADB broadened throughout this period. During the 1970s, Indonesia's borrowing portfolio with ADB had continued to grow. By 1980, Indonesia had surpassed the Republic of Korea to become the largest borrowing country from the bank. Over 1967–1980, Indonesia's borrowings amounted to over 15% of total bank lending, ahead of lending to the Republic of Korea (14.6% of the total) and the Philippines (14%).

Economic Changes

At the beginning of 1981, economic conditions in Indonesia appeared promising. A boom in 1980, supported by high levels of oil-financed public spending and a record rice harvest, encouraged confidence. However, the optimism was largely dependent on international oil prices. When global oil prices began to fall in late 1981, the mood changed quickly. During the next few years, Indonesian policymakers introduced a bold range of economic reforms. A 28% devaluation of the rupiah was announced in March 1983. Later that year, wide-ranging tax changes were introduced.

During the next few years, a range of policy measures was implemented to open the Indonesian economy to international markets. A devaluation of the rupiah in 1986 helped improve Indonesia's international competitiveness. These reforms quickly led to a marked surge in growth in the manufacturing sector. During the rest of the 1980s, the non-oil manufacturing sector grew at an average rate of over 11% per year. For the first time in Indonesia's history, the pattern of economic growth began to resemble that in other rapidly growing neighboring Asian countries.

Donor Programs

By the early 1980s, there was some questioning in the donor community about the role of foreign aid in Indonesia. In 1980, as revenues from the second oil boom flowed into Indonesia, the country's foreign exchange reserves rose quickly. Some observers began to wonder whether Indonesia really needed continuing support from donors.

Others argued that a temporary boom did not weaken the case for a sustained aid program to Indonesia. The case for continued significant aid flows was strengthened by World Bank reports which discussed the possibility of a reemergence of resource gaps, both in terms of foreign exchange and domestic savings. Indonesian policymakers, for their part, helped bolster confidence in the donor community by speaking frankly about the economic reforms still needed.

ADB Support

During the first half of the 1980s, ADB maintained support for mainstream projects in such areas as agriculture, energy, and roads. At the same time, in response to requests from the government to venture into new areas, loans were approved for innovative activities such as an investment in a project to support small-scale fishpond farmers. Another new activity was an agriculture credit loan to support village cooperatives in Java and Bali. However, throughout the 1980s and into the 1990s, it often proved difficult to support the rural cooperative sector.

The program in the electricity sector remained a priority for the bank. Both the World Bank and ADB had provided much support to the State Electricity Company (PLN) during the 1970s. Numerous additional projects were approved during the 1980s. The bank also provided loans for projects in other sectors such as roads, ports, and irrigation.

Nevertheless, although ADB had established a well-developed pipeline of activities in Indonesia, the increasingly difficult economic climate in the early 1980s made it harder for Indonesian agencies to work effectively with international donor partners. As the price of oil fell, curbs on government spending were introduced. Government departments were obliged to cut back on many activities. The pace of implementation of ADB-assisted projects began to slow. Delays became a matter of concern for both the government and the bank.

Some of the problems reflected the administrative and regulatory requirements of the government. Others arose because ADB's procedures were not flexible enough to respond to the changed circumstances. Delays occurred, for example, because the usual processes that the bank followed in the preparation of high-quality projects took time. In response to these problems of program implementation, Indonesian agencies and ADB worked together to design improved procedures.

By the mid-1980s, as ADB's largest borrower, Indonesia had received over 20% of the bank's loans during the second decade of ADB's work. The scope of ADB's work had broadened as well. At the beginning of the decade in 1977, it was still mainly a project-oriented bank. However, as its activities across Asia and in Indonesia became more diverse, there was a growing need to pay attention to the strategies underpinning ADB's work. By the end of the decade, the bank had adopted the practice of setting out an operational strategy for work in each borrowing country.

Adjustment in Indonesia (1987–1996)

At the beginning of the third decade of ADB's work in Indonesia, economic prospects remained as uncertain as they had been since the early 1970s. The two oil booms had come and gone. The central economic challenge in the mid-1980s was how to adjust to the new post-oil boom era that Indonesia appeared to be facing. Two important steps were taken in this direction in late 1986 and early 1987 when trade policy packages were announced. Both packages removed non-tariff barriers, replacing the barriers with tariffs.

Concerns for Policymakers

Several main issues took up much of the attention of policymakers at the time. One was the level of foreign debt. The level of foreign debt was, paradoxically, seen as a matter of policy concern and yet, in fact, was not really a problem. A careful analysis of debt levels indicated that the level of national debt was comfortably contained within reasonable limits. In the 1984 annual report prepared for the IGGI, for example, the World Bank reported that "Indonesia has been following a very prudent borrowing strategy despite substantial improvements in its creditworthiness…The rate of growth of debt has been moderate."[2]

The need to encourage structural adjustment was a second concern. Essentially, the debate was about the best way to promote development

---

[2]   World Bank, 1984, *Indonesia Policies and Prospects*, 111.

in the post-oil boom period. "Economic nationalists" believed that the state needed to play a leading role to promote technologically advanced industrial growth. "Economic technocrats" were more cautious, arguing that all large national investment projects needed to be analyzed carefully.

The first of a series of key reforms in the financial sector was introduced in October 1988. These reforms, as it turned out, led to dramatic structural changes in the banking industry. They later had the unintended effect of contributing to the factors that led to the financial crisis in Indonesia in 1997–1998.

The 1988 October Package introduced a sweeping liberalization of the banking sector. Other policy reforms were also announced. The overall effect of the reforms was that the number of banks expanded far more quickly than authorities had expected. In response, in March 1991 monetary policy was tightened sharply. However, the increased controls on domestic monetary policy, including higher rates of interest within Indonesia, encouraged many Indonesian firms to increase their overseas borrowings. During the 1990s, therefore, almost unnoticed, the Indonesian corporate sector accumulated significant international debts. The repayment of this debt caused major problems when the value of the rupiah collapsed during the 1997–1998 financial crisis.

Changes in Donor Programs

The third ADB decade was eventful for the donor community in Indonesia. At the beginning of the decade, donor programs, coordinated through the IGGI, were designed to be supportive of the adjustment policies that the government was implementing. Fiscal policy, both in 1986 and in 1987, had been conservative and had restrained national development expenditures. On the Indonesian side, the pragmatic decision was taken to accept that as the oil boom was over, it would be best to look to donors for more support.

One strategy adopted was to maximize concessional loans from creditors such as Japan, the World Bank, and ADB. The availability of new concessional loans during 1987–1991 along with the increase in non-oil exports significantly improved the overall maturity and term structure of Indonesia's external debt.

A second strategy supported by donors was to increasingly provide loan funds for rupiah-denominated spending. At IGGI meetings in 1988 and 1989, donors endorsed these and other steps to ensure that the international aid program was supportive of Indonesia's continuing reform program.

ADB in the Third Decade

Three features marked ADB's activities at the beginning of the third decade of the bank's work in Indonesia:

(i) support for the government's structural adjustment program;

(ii) an expanding capacity to deliver the bank's program in Indonesia;

(iii) greater attention to issues in the financial sector.

In support of these programs, over 40 loans and a wide variety of TA activities were approved during the first five years of the decade.

To help promote structural adjustment, ADB agreed to provide funding for a series of program loans. The Non-Oil Export Promotion Program loan for Indonesia approved in 1987 was the first program loan agreed to by the bank under a new program loan policy. A second feature of ADB's work in Indonesia was the strengthening of the bank's capacity to deliver programs. One step in this direction was the opening of a permanent ADB Indonesia Resident Mission in 1987.

Meanwhile, marked changes to economic policy were being implemented. Growth had strengthened and manufactured exports and employment received a strong boost for several years. There was even talk of Indonesia becoming an "Asian Tiger." Indonesia was included in a select group of countries sampled in a much-publicized World Bank study *The East Asian Miracle* in 1993. To bolster development policy, policymakers in Jakarta gave attention to three main priorities during the 1990s: the need to promote further structural reform; the implications of moving toward a more market-oriented approach to economic management; and the risks arising from the rapid changes taking place in the financial sector. For a time, this approach was successful. But later, managing capital flows became a major issue during the Asian financial crisis.

Donor Programs in the 1990s

At the beginning of the 1990s, the international community remained confident in its donor relationship with Indonesia. Nevertheless, the role of foreign aid in Indonesia was changing. First, there were signs that a two-level system of assistance was developing between the larger donors and a group of smaller donors. A second change was that the level of concessionality of donor support was tending to decline. A third change which led to significant shifts in relations between donor countries and partners over time was that the international donor community began to set a revised and expanded set of priorities for the provision of aid to developing countries. Following the fall of the Berlin Wall and the collapse of communism, Organisation for Economic Co-operation and Development (OECD) donor countries began to become more prescriptive in their approach to aid policies across a range of issues. This important change on the donor side was reflected in the relationship between the international community and Indonesia.

At the same time, Indonesia was becoming more confident. It was not evident at the time, but the aim of Indonesian policymakers was to move toward reducing Indonesia's dependence on foreign aid.

These issues underpinned Indonesia's decision in late March 1992 to announce that it was time for the IGGI, as an international aid coordination group chaired by the Netherlands, to be disbanded. In making the announcement, the government indicated that it would welcome the opportunity to continue to meet with donors on a regular basis. Following the disbandment of the IGGI, a new international consultative group, the CGI chaired by the World Bank, was established.

Despite these changes, donor support for Indonesia remained strong. Donors agreed to over $4.9 billion in pledges at the first meeting of the CGI in 1992. At CGI meetings during the next few years, the donor community pledged similar levels of support. Thus, by 1996, the relationship between Indonesia and donors had developed into a strong partnership. Both Indonesia and the international community remained committed to the relationship.

ADB's Work

Into the mid-1990s, ADB continued to design its program in Indonesia to support the priorities set out by the government in its Fifth Five-Year

Development Plan (Repelita V) for 1989–1994. Earlier, agriculture had been important. But over time, as the structure of the economy changed, the share of agriculture in total output slowly declined. This structural change was reflected in ADB's lending program. In the early years, agriculture had received the largest share of bank assistance (Table 5.6 below). However as Indonesia moved toward industrialization, manufacturing and parts of the service sectors became increasingly important. During the 1980s and 1990s, there was a shift in the focus of ADB programs toward investment in such sectors as transport, energy, finance, urban development, and education.

The bank's traditional approach had been to provide assistance through support for specific projects. Especially since the mid-1980s, however, sector and program lending approaches had been agreed to. A new ADB country operational strategy (COS) in 1994 noted that "both the Government and the Bank found important advantages in the program and sector lending approaches, which warrant their continued use in the country program." Looking ahead, the 1994 COS recommended that ADB's approach in Indonesia should emphasize three objectives: support for economic growth, for human resource development, and for the sustainable use of natural resources.

The 1994 COS also emphasized the advantages of promoting the private sector. Indonesia's Sixth Five-Year Development Plan for the 1994–1999 period (Repelita VI) had noted the need to promote the private sector. The COS suggested that the bank should look for ways to support this goal. In the electric power sector, ADB policy dialogue had focused on issues such as the commercialization of activities of PLN and the expansion of private sector involvement in the supply of electricity. Measures to strengthen the finance sector were also seen as steps toward promoting the private sector.

Despite this emphasis on promoting the private sector, ADB's experience in encouraging private sector growth in Indonesia was at best a mixed success. More broadly, attempts by other agencies including the World Bank and the Government of Indonesia to promote the private sector were only partially successful. In retrospect, it can be seen that the institutional framework for the rapid development of a strong private sector—reflected in such things as a robust legal framework and strong financial markets—in Indonesia was lacking.

While the main focus of the work of the Indonesia Resident Mission was on programs within Indonesia, the bank was also supporting regional activities that Indonesia was participating in. In 1993, the Indonesia–Malaysia–Thailand Growth Triangle was established as a subregional activity to promote economic cooperation. In 1995, the Brunei Darussalam–Indonesia–Malaysia–Philippines East ASEAN Growth Area (BIMP-EAGA) was launched to address inequalities in development.

The Asian Financial Crisis (1997–1998)

At the beginning of 1997, the broad economic outlook for Indonesia seemed encouraging. Appearances were misleading. By the end of the year, policymakers in Indonesia, the Republic of Korea, and Thailand were swept up in the expanding Asian financial crisis.

The Crisis Erupts

The crisis, it is generally agreed, began in Thailand. Speculative pressures against the Thai baht began to mount during the first half of 1997. In early July, in response to the mounting pressures, the baht was devalued. This triggered an unexpected chain of contagion in Southeast Asia which spread into Indonesia in late 1997.

The initial response of Indonesian authorities and the IMF was designed to restore confidence across markets and stabilize movements in the rupiah. But despite a series of policy packages, the crisis rapidly worsened. By the end of December 1997, market confidence had evaporated in Indonesia. In January, the rupiah collapsed, falling quickly through an exchange rate of Rp10,000 to the US dollar and eventually reaching a floor of around Rp17,000.

During the next few months, the economic and political situation in Indonesia deteriorated further. In May 1998, amid political turmoil, nationwide social unrest, and student protests, President Soeharto resigned after 32 years in office. The new president, B.J. Habibie, quickly announced a wide series of political and economic reforms. This early post-Soeharto period became known as the *Reformasi* (Reform Era) period, stretching through the successive presidencies of Abdurrahman Wahid and Megawati Soekarnoputri to 2004.

Donors and the Crisis

The international donor community was unprepared for a serious financial crisis in Asia and found it difficult to respond to the evolving situation in Indonesia. On the eve of the Asian financial crisis in early 1997, the international donor community did not have any plans to introduce significant changes to the established programs of assistance to Indonesia. Indeed, there was some discussion as to whether it was not time to scale back the level of assistance to Indonesia.

As events unfolded in late 1997 and early 1998, most bilateral donor agencies relied almost entirely on the multilateral financial institutions to restore economic stability. The main response to the crisis, therefore, was coordinated by the IMF along with the World Bank and ADB, supported by additional funds from Japan, the US, and a number of other partner countries. The problem for most bilateral donor agencies was that the crisis was unfolding in financial markets. However the management of financial markets was not an area of economic activity that most bilateral agencies had experience of. It was only later, toward the end of 1998 and in 1999, that donor agencies began to consider the need to give attention to the widening social impacts of the crisis.

ADB Response

ADB, like the rest of the international community, was unprepared for the crisis. And like the other two major multilateral institutions, the IMF and the World Bank, ADB needed to respond both rapidly and in a flexible way.

ADB played an active role during the crisis, providing both funds and technical advice. However, the task proved difficult and the bank's program was delayed. Problems arose because, first, the international community itself was divided on important issues of policy and, second, there were disagreements within the Government of Indonesia which were exacerbated by the rapidly deteriorating political situation. Despite these difficulties, the three multilateral organizations worked as well as possible with each other and with the government to prepare programs of assistance.

During 1998 and 1999, ADB approved five fast-disbursing loans for a total of $2.8 billion. These crisis-support loans were regarded as part of the initial IMF package of $23 billion, underpinned by a letter of intent (LOI), agreed to in October 1997. Particular features of ADB's approach were a focus on measures to improve the operations of capital markets and on loans to provide social protection to the poor. Apart from specific objectives for each of the five loans, a common purpose underpinning all of the loans was to provide liquidity and budgetary support to Indonesia.

As the crisis unfolded, it became clear that the economic and social consequences of the crisis would be severe. Unemployment rose and social impacts, such as the growing numbers of children dropping out of school and the rising levels of malnutrition, began to attract attention. The international community quickly realized that programs would be needed to help.

ADB made special attempts to address issues of poverty during the crisis. A range of safety net programs were designed including a Social Protection Sector Development Program and a Health and Nutrition Sector Development Program, totaling $600 million.

Lessons for ADB

There were lessons for ADB from the experience of the Asian financial crisis. These were discussed in some detail in several bank evaluation reports including the *Special Evaluation Study of the Asian Development Bank's Crisis Management in Indonesia* released in 2001.

It was clear from the experience of the crisis that ADB needed to be better prepared to respond to financial crises in the region. Dealing with the Asian financial crisis was a new challenge for ADB. The bank was not at all prepared to deal with a crisis of such proportions, nor did it have ready the financial and policy tools that were needed. A second lesson was that the complexity of large-scale financial crises requires that there be highly effective coordination across numerous international and national institutions.

A third lesson for ADB was that it is necessary to address longer-term issues as well as immediate priorities. On one hand, the short-term priorities were extremely urgent. On the other hand, longer-term social costs such as growing unemployment and marked increases in poverty needed to be addressed as well.

A fourth lesson for ADB was the need to expand efforts to strengthen the region against crises of this kind. ADB responded both by supporting the development of new policies, and by establishing new programs within the bank. Following the crisis there was much consideration among policymakers in the region as to what had gone wrong. ADB supported this region-wide process of reflection by sponsoring seminars and by promoting the publication of books and articles and numerous other activities.

Recovery (1999–2006)

The Asian financial crisis delivered a deep blow to Indonesia. The slow recovery occupied much of the attention of senior Indonesian economic policymakers for most of the rest of the fourth decade of ADB's work in Indonesia.

Difficulties of Recovery

Three effects of the crisis, especially, left a mark. One was the fall in investment as a share of gross domestic product (GDP) from around 30% in the decade before the crisis to about 24% between 2000–2006. This sharp drop in investment hampered efforts to stimulate recovery. Second, the need to reduce the level of national debt as a share of GDP was seen as an urgent priority. Third, relations between Indonesia on one hand, and the IMF and the World Bank on the other, became strained.

Throughout 2003 and into 2004 the economy strengthened. Nevertheless, numerous commentators noted that the growth rate, which was moving up toward an annual rate of 5%, was still well below the precrisis average of over 7% per year. By 2004, real income per capita had still not recovered to precrisis levels.

Strengthening Economy

The election of Susilo Bambang Yudhoyono (widely known as SBY) as president in 2004 boosted hopes for improved governance and economic management. But attention to the policies of the new Yudhoyono administration was overtaken by other events. On 26 December 2004, a massive tsunami struck Aceh. Over 230,000 people died in Aceh and across the Indian Ocean region. During much of 2005 and into 2006, Indonesia's relationship with the international community was focused on responses to the tsunami.

While recovery in Aceh was attracting much attention, the Indonesian economy was strengthening. By 2006, at the end of ADB's fourth decade of work in Indonesia, the overall economic picture was encouraging. The key goal of economic recovery from the Asian financial crisis which had occurred almost a decade earlier had largely been attained.

The Donor Community

In the meantime, much of the recovery period after the Asian financial crisis (a period which, broadly speaking, covered the five years from 1999–2004) was marked by changeable relations between Indonesia and the donor community. Both Indonesia and the international community tried to maintain mutually effective programs. There was, however, a range of factors that made these years a difficult time for the delivery of international assistance.

One complicating factor was political uncertainty. During 2000 and into 2001, for much of the period of the presidency of Abdurrahman Wahid, political controversies complicated the management of government. The relationship between Indonesia and the international donor community became more confident when Megawati became president in July 2001.

A second issue was the concern in Indonesia about the influence that international agencies, especially the IMF, had over key policy issues following the Asian financial crisis. A third element was the way that the changing international environment complicated the delivery of aid to Indonesia. International attention to terrorism and security issues became more pronounced during 2002 in the wake of the September 11 terrorist attacks in the US in 2001 and the Bali bombing in October 2002. Following these events, a number of Western countries issued warnings about travel to Indonesia and scaled back aid activities. Multilateral agencies also began to restrict travel by staff to Indonesia.

There were stops and starts to the programs supported by both the World Bank and IMF in 1998 and 1999 and during the next few years. The relationship between the government, and the IMF and the World Bank, became challenging in September 1999. The rapid deterioration in the security situation in Timor-Leste following the vote in favor of independence at the end of August 1999 attracted worldwide attention. Indonesia faced much international criticism as a result of the Timor-Leste crisis.

Despite the difficulties, both the Government of Indonesia and international donors were keen to ensure that wherever possible, aid programs continued to be delivered. Following the Asian financial crisis, it had become clear that the social impacts of the crisis were severe and that a social safety net system of some kind needed to be established. The international community supported this approach so, during the next few years, numerous partner agencies including ADB worked to design programs to establish new social safety net systems.

However, despite donor support for recovery programs such as social security, by 2003 there was an emerging consensus both on the Indonesian side and among donors that it would be best if Indonesian authorities took greater control of their own affairs. As a step in this direction, Indonesia made advance payments to reduce debts owing to the IMF. By October 2006, Indonesia had paid off the final amounts owed to the fund. The next year, in early 2007, the government decided that it would no longer be necessary to rely on the CGI for the coordination of international assistance to the country.

ADB's Role

ADB's program in Indonesia changed markedly after the 1997–1998 financial crisis. The years between 2000 and 2004 were a transition period for both Indonesia and for development partners such as ADB, the World Bank, and other international donors. It took until around 2005 for ADB's activities to return to a more normalized country program—and, even then, the priorities of the donor community in Indonesia were largely influenced by the effort of responding to humanitarian needs in Aceh following the 2004 tsunami.

Beginning in 2000, ADB's program in Indonesia reflected a new approach designed to respond to priorities that had become clear following the financial crisis. The revised approach focused on reducing poverty and regional inequalities and supporting steps toward better governance. The following year, in 2001, ADB released a full COS for Indonesia. The COS gave increased emphasis to long-term development challenges. For the bank, this was a step toward moving beyond a short-term focus on responses to the 1997–1998 financial crisis.

The bank's 2001 COS set out, for the first time, themes that would guide ADB's approach in Indonesia in the post-crisis transition period. The COS listed five priorities for the bank's work:

(i)   reducing poverty and improving governance;

(ii)   supporting decentralization;

(iii) protecting the environment;

(iv)   promoting human development; and

(v)   strengthening the economy through infrastructure investment and private sector development.

These themes were carried forward in the ADB Country Strategy and Program (CSP) 2003–2005 issued the following year.

But during the next several years, it proved difficult for the bank to sustain a higher level of lending. In terms of expanding the level of operations, this was a challenging period for both ADB and other agencies in the international community. There were underlying difficulties affecting the operations of both ADB and numerous other international agencies in this post-crisis period. Significant changes were taking place which affected both the demand for, and supply of, foreign assistance.

On the demand side, the government had introduced sharp cuts in development spending. These reductions had the flow-on effect of reducing Indonesia's capacity to participate in foreign assistance activities where donors expected that matching rupiah funds would be available. Further, public commentary within Indonesia had become less accepting of the benefits of foreign aid after the financial crisis when the national debt had risen sharply.

The problems were not only on the demand side. International agencies, including ADB, were finding it difficult to supply assistance to Indonesia. Summarizing problems that many international agencies were trying to deal with at the time, ADB's CSP noted that higher levels of lending would only be possible if certain conditions were met: if the government introduced a workable on-lending policy to support local governments; if implementation problems were eased; if the government facilitated investments to reduce poverty; and if structural reforms were accelerated.

Natural Disasters

The usual operational activities of the donor community were overturned when, at the end of 2004, the Asian tsunami struck the province of Aceh. ADB joined with the Government of Indonesia and the rest of the international community to respond quickly to the disaster at both regional and national levels. At the regional level, the Asian Tsunami Fund (ATF) was established.

In Indonesia, ADB's main contribution to the tsunami response effort was through the provision of a grant, the Earthquake and Tsunami Emergency Support Project, a $320 million program approved in April 2005. The project covered five sectors including livelihood restoration, physical infrastructure, and social services. The initial ADB response, given the nature of the disaster, was prepared quickly. The project was implemented over the next five years. Special attention was given to housing, irrigation, and agriculture and fisheries. One main problem in delivering the assistance was that the initial plans to provide aid within a three-year period were too optimistic. Project experience suggests that a three-year time frame for such substantive support is too short.

The project supported the wide range of response measures taken by the government. In April 2005, the government established a new Rehabilitation and Reconstruction Agency (BRR) to coordinate assistance activities. The bank's program over the next few years was tailored to support the work of the BRR.

Responses to natural disasters remained a main focus of the bank in 2006. The international community was giving much attention to the major rehabilitation and reconstruction effort in Aceh. ADB, too, was implementing dozens of activities in different sectors across the province. The task of managing all of this work took up much time, as did participation in meetings of the Multi Donor Fund, an umbrella fund established on the request of the government to help coordinate the $7 billion response to the disaster.

And then, as if to emphasize the risks of natural disasters in Indonesia, in May 2006 an earthquake hit the Bantul area to the south of the city of Yogyakarta. Over 4,000 of the total of around 5,700 people who perished in the earthquake were estimated to have died in Bantul alone.

Looking ahead, as the first decade of the 2000s came to a close, the challenge for economic policymakers in Indonesia was to lift the growth rate toward the 7% level that President Yudhoyono had set as a target. For ADB, the question was how best to provide well-designed assistance in a country undergoing rapid change.

Middle-Income Country Issues (2007–2019)

In 2007 there was an optimistic mood with hopes of economic change across Indonesia. President Yudhoyono had been in office for two years and was promoting economic reform. It seemed that a sustained recovery was finally getting underway.

The international community, including ADB, needed to adjust to changing circumstances. Indonesia had been moving toward establishing a new set of relations with donors. The changes became clearer during the early years of the Yudhoyono administration. Increasingly, Bappenas and other key parts of government would take ownership of managing Indonesia's dealings with the donor community.

Strengthening Recovery

During 2007 and into 2008, macroeconomic performance in Indonesia steadily improved. Economic growth rose toward 7% per annum. Investment, too, was expanding quickly. Nevertheless, Indonesian policymakers were concerned about several issues. One was what many in Indonesia regarded as a major structural imbalance in the economy: the lack of strong growth in the manufacturing sector.

A second issue of concern was the need to promote investment in infrastructure. Investment in infrastructure had fallen away sharply after the Asian financial crisis. Responding to the problem, the Yudhoyono administration arranged several infrastructure summits in Jakarta. Nevertheless, it did not prove easy to build a pipeline of projects. Efforts to promote infrastructure, which ADB supported, remained a priority throughout the Yudhoyono administration and were taken up by the subsequent president, Joko Widodo (widely known as Jokowi), when he took office in October 2014. The strength of the economic recovery was a third concern. Although economic conditions had clearly been improving, the overall rate of growth was still noticeably below that of the precrisis years in the 1990s.

Beginning in late 2007, the global financial crisis in major industrial countries brought a marked slowing of global economic activity. As things turned out, the impact of the global financial crisis in developing Asia, including in Indonesia, was relatively mild. Growth in Indonesia was sustained, albeit at a somewhat reduced rate of around 4% per annum into 2009. President Yudhoyono was reelected in 2009. Promoting investment in infrastructure and designing programs to tackle climate change were nominated as key policy priorities for the Yudhoyono administration. Growth remained strong, at around 5% per annum, throughout the second term of the Yudhoyono presidency.

The government's Medium-Term Development Plan for 2010–2014 was released in 2010. The broad priorities of the plan were reflected in a wide range of supporting documents, one of the most important of which was the Masterplan for the Acceleration and Expansion of Indonesian Economic Development (MP3EI). The MP3EI, launched in May 2011, was the most comprehensive plan for the expansion of infrastructure ever prepared in Indonesia. The aim of the program was to raise the rate of growth in Indonesia toward the 7–9% range.

Further changes in international markets provided new challenges. Capital outflows began to take place during 2013 and a "taper tantrum" occurred following changes in monetary policy in the US (a "tapering" of monetary policy, reflected in a reduction of interest rates), which led to a marked depreciation of the rupiah. Overall economic growth slowed as well.

Measures to stimulate demand and promote economic growth were introduced by the new President Widodo. One area in which the government, and the new president himself, gave increased priority to was infrastructure. A range of new projects was announced, a number of which had been set out earlier in 2011 in the MP3EI. Thus in promoting investment in infrastructure, there was a considerable degree of continuity between the outgoing and incoming administrations.

New Era for Donors

In January 2007, President Yudhoyono announced that the CGI would be dissolved and that Indonesia would coordinate relations with the donor community directly rather than through the auspices of the CGI. The president's announcement marked the end of a four-decade relationship with the international donor community, arranged first through the IGGI (1967–1992) and then the CGI (1992–2007).

Following the dissolution of the CGI, the donor community continued to implement the agreed programs in Indonesia. Nevertheless, it soon became apparent that in the absence of the CGI, a clearer set of development policies was needed when Indonesia participated in international conferences and negotiations. With this goal in mind, in January 2009 donors and the government signed the Jakarta Commitment, a declaration that signatories would work together to apply the principles of development set out in recent international agreements. The Jakarta Commitment aimed to move the international aid program more in line with national priorities.

Measures were taken to strengthen the institutional capacity of Bappenas following approval of the Jakarta Commitment. In carrying on their agreed programs, donor agencies often needed to liaise with many different Indonesian agencies. However, Bappenas took the lead in coordinating overall relations between Indonesia and the donor community.

A comprehensive history of Bappenas and of planning in Indonesia since 1945 was also prepared. The study, *Bappenas dalam Sejarah Perencanaan Pembangunan Indonesia, 1945–2025* (Bappenas and the History of Development Planning in Indonesia, 1945–2025) was launched in 2012. The range of senior policymakers who contributed introductory comments to the history included Boediono, Jusuf Kalla, Armida Alisjahbana, J.B. Sumarlin, and Ginandjar Kartasasmita.

In 2014, when Widodo took office as the seventh president of Indonesia, the status of Bappenas as an agency within the government was upgraded. Under the new arrangements, Bappenas reported directly to the president. In July 2016, Professor Bambang Brodjonegoro from the University of Indonesia was appointed as planning minister. As minister, Brodjonegoro quickly moved to further strengthen the role of Bappenas within the government and with the donor community.

Place of ADB

The bank's activities in Indonesia at the beginning of the fifth ADB decade in 2007 reflected the key priorities of the time—support for the large post-tsunami reconstruction program in Aceh, and for efforts to promote decentralization across Indonesia. The broader outlines of the bank's work were guided by the priorities set out in the two CSPs for 2006–2009 and for 2012–2014.

In Aceh, ADB remained closely involved in the reconstruction and rehabilitation effort. The post-tsunami Aceh and Nias support program was one of the largest aid-supported reconstruction efforts ever seen in the developing world. Total reconstruction support from the government and international donors was estimated at $7.2 billion.

A second focus of ADB's work was continued support for Indonesia's ambitious decentralization program. The bank, along with numerous other partners agencies, had been providing assistance for the program since the first main laws had been approved in May 1999 and elaborated in

2004. ADB continued to support these activities in 2007–2009 and beyond. Nevertheless, despite the efforts of both the government and of donor partners, there was growing concern about the problems that had arisen in management in the public sector following decentralization.

The concerns of the donor community were reflected in a major stocktaking report on *Decentralization 2009* prepared by the United States Agency for International Development (USAID) Democratic Reform Support Program with the support of Bappenas. The report described the situation as follows: "a policy and legal tangle is being created in [decentralization/ local government] that is characterized by conflicting regulations; relations that are sometimes overly idealistic; or unworkable, or mired in old paradigms."

Against this background, in 2010 the Independent Evaluation Department of ADB released *Asian Development Bank Support for Decentralization in Indonesia*. The study noted that since 1998, the bank had provided four core decentralization support loans for $1.04 billion, $1.27 billion for sector-based decentralization support loans, and a further $2.93 billion for public sector management support loans with decentralization components. The conclusions of the study reflected the concerns of both the government and the donor community at the time. In terms of relevance, it was judged that ADB's work had been "variable." It was suggested that more attention was needed on the steps required to implement good policies. However the study recommended that the bank continue support for decentralization because "the government is increasingly assertive in policy development and has welcomed support that is facilitative."

ADB Activities

The bank's strategic approach during this period reflected the priorities set down in the CSP for 2006–2009. When that CSP was prepared, the investment climate in Indonesia was still seen as somewhat discouraging. The country also seemed to be losing competitiveness. The CSP had therefore been framed with the aim of supporting the government's hopeful goal of moving toward a growth rate of 7% by 2009, of reducing poverty and unemployment, and of promoting good governance through combating corruption.

The 2006–2009 CSP set out five areas of engagement for ADB:

(i) improved infrastructure and infrastructure services;

(ii) deepened financial sector;

(iii) improved decentralization;

(iv) accelerated achievement of the Millennium Development Goals (MDGs); and

(v) strengthened environment and natural resource management.

To implement this program, the CSP suggested that a pipeline of loans was needed, consisting of a balance of some program lending and increased amounts of project lending.

As things turned out, the balance of ADB's lending during the next few years shifted markedly toward program rather than project lending. Partly, the change reflected evolving preferences on the Indonesian side for program rather than project loans. But partly, too, the shift toward program loans took place because as the unexpected global financial crisis unfolded in 2007–2008, it became urgent for Indonesia to have access to international sources of funds to draw upon if needed.

In late 2008, the international community, joined by ADB, moved quickly to prepare a large multidonor assistance package with the aim of bolstering economic stability in Indonesia. A package of $5 billion designed as a contingent loan—to be drawn on only if needed—was agreed upon. The objective was to send a strong signal to markets of confidence in Indonesia's economic management from major partners—the World Bank, ADB, Japan, and Australia. ADB made a commitment to provide $1 billion for a Public Expenditure Support Facility (PESF). In the event, the ADB funds were not drawn upon. The loan was canceled in December 2010 without disbursement. Nevertheless, the package was judged to have contributed significantly to rebuilding confidence at a difficult time for Indonesia.

In the midst of these uncertain conditions, Indonesia hosted the 42nd Annual Meeting of ADB in May 2009. The event, held in Bali, was a significant one for Indonesia. It was a measure of the convening power of Indonesia in regional economic affairs. The statements at the bank meeting reflected international concerns. In his opening address, President Yudhoyono summarized the global outlook by noting that "the world economy is facing the worst downturn since the great depression of the 1930s…We have no clear indication of whether the worst is already behind us or whether there is more bad news around the corner."

For several years following the global financial crisis of 2007–2008, policymakers in Jakarta were concerned about events in the global economy. In 2012, following the earlier 2008 PESF loan, a second major $5 billion support agreement was agreed to by international partners. ADB provided a $500 million Precautionary Financing Facility loan as part of the overall package. The aim of the large package, as was the case with the earlier $5 billion agreement, was to bolster international confidence in international markets in Indonesia's ability to service government debt.

In the meantime, ADB had prepared a strategy for its work over the 2012–2014 period. As had been the case with the earlier strategic plan for 2006–2009, the bank's CSP for 2012–2014 anticipated a shift from program to project lending. At the time, the approach seemed appropriate. However, Indonesia's budget financing needs widened during 2012 and 2013. Continuing weaknesses in eurozone countries left Indonesia vulnerable to risks of international contagion because of its relatively open capital market. The government decided that it was best to continue to borrow for fast-disbursing program loans rather than project loans.

During the next few years, the bank's work in Indonesia shifted markedly toward the provision of large program loans, especially to support activities in the public financial management sector. In September 2014, ADB approved the first phase of a series of program loans to support the Stepping Up Investments for Growth Acceleration Program (SIGAP). In 2015 there were two more large program loans, and in 2016—the final year of ADB's fifth decade of operations in Indonesia—the bank continued this approach. In shifting in this way toward a phase-based and programmatic approach after five decades of work in Indonesia, ADB had moved away from project-based activities in the 1970s and 1980s toward a much broader approach relying on program and results-based lending in the two decades after the Asian financial crisis.

Beyond 50 Years: 2017–2018

In early 2017, around midway through President Widodo's first term in office, Indonesian policymakers took stock of the economic prospects and concluded that the outlook was mixed. On the positive side, economic growth had been sustained at about 5% per year for a considerable period and the range of reform measures that had been introduced appeared to be supportive of sustained growth. On the other hand, international economic conditions remained quite uncertain.

One central concern for policymakers was the rate of economic growth. Official policy was to aim for a growth rate of perhaps 6% or 7% per year. It seemed that there were various barriers holding back an increase in the growth rate. The Widodo administration had introduced 16 reform packages since taking office in late 2014 and had boosted spending on infrastructure. Nevertheless, it seemed that further steps to stimulate domestic demand were necessary.

Political considerations increasingly affected policymaking during 2018. Nationwide elections were held in April. As the year drew to a close, both external and internal economic conditions remained challenging. In the US, the Donald Trump administration was calling into question some of the main principles of long-established international economic relations. At the same time, global trade was slowing. Internally, policymakers remained concerned with the need to support economic growth.

Bappenas continued to work to strengthen Indonesia's systems for aid coordination, both with domestic stakeholders and international agencies. Major international development forums were held in 2018 and in 2019 which involved some thousands of participants from across Indonesia in discussions about development policy. The government aimed to encourage international partners to ensure that their programs were consistent with Indonesia's own policies for the delivery of aid. In coordinating the response to the Palu earthquake and tsunami disaster in September 2018, for example, the government set out guidelines for the delivery of international assistance. Foreign partner agencies were asked to observe a range of conditions—such as closely regulating the number of staff actively working in the field—in planning to deliver aid following the disaster.

Lessons and Challenges

Looking back, the long-term international assistance effort that ADB was part of was a remarkable program. During the 50 years from the late 1960s when ADB first joined with the broader international program to support Indonesia's development effort, there has been strong cooperation between leading Indonesian policymakers and international development partners.

There were ups and downs along the way, both in the progress of Indonesia's own overall development programs and in the success of activities supported by the international community. Nevertheless, the overall program of cooperation between Indonesia and the international community must surely be judged an outstanding success, both in terms of its support at an overall level for good development policy in Indonesia and in terms of the delivery of many thousands of individual projects and activities.

At the overall level, the international community worked closely with Indonesian policymakers to support good development policy. Perhaps the single most important reason that the international aid program in Indonesia since the late 1960s has been a success is that the partnership between Indonesia and the international community has been an effective one. The lead has always been taken by Indonesian policymakers. Even during the difficult negotiations with international agencies amidst the Asian financial crisis, the key decisions were taken by Indonesian ministers. On the donor side too, there has been a well-judged relationship with Indonesian partners. The collective approach of the international community, acting through the assistance program, has been to adjust activities to respond to the priorities of the government.

Asian Development Bank

ADB has been a reliable partner in Indonesia's development effort during the past 50 years. The bank's role has evolved over the decades. As Indonesia needed to respond to changes in the international environment, so ADB adjusted the forms of assistance provided (Table ES 2).

The three key characteristics of the institution as a multilateral development bank have been attention to multilateralism, a focus on development, and its role as a bank. Each of these aspects of the bank's activities has been reflected in the programs in Indonesia. As a multilateral institution that gives special emphasis to regional programs, ADB has supported Indonesia's regional role in a variety of ways. Second, in its efforts to fulfil the ADB Charter requirement "to contribute to the acceleration of the process of economic development of the developing member countries in the region,"

Table ES 2: Main Phases in ADB Assistance to Indonesia

Period	Stages in Indonesian development	ADB response
1969–1972	Recovery period; beginning of First Five-Year Development Plan	ADB provided ADF (concessional) funding offering support for individual projects
1973–1974	First oil boom	ADB shifted toward blend of concessional and market-based (OCR) loans
1975–1984	High oil flows occurred	ADF lending ceased; OCR loans for individual projects were provided
1985–1989	Sharp falls in oil price	ADB softened terms of assistance with a greater emphasis on support for local cost finance and for program loans
1990–1996	Successful economic liberalization	ADB shifted assistance toward OCR loans provided through project and program loans
1997–1999	Asian financial crisis	Emergency assistance provided in cooperation with other main multilateral and bilateral partners
2000–2007	Concerns about need to reduce level of national debt	Lending to Indonesia from ADB and other agencies was constrained
2008–2010	Global financial crisis, leading to uncertainties about Indonesia's access to international financial markets	ADB provided emergency liquidity support, mainly by support for program loans
2010–2016	Continuing uncertainties in global markets.	ADB assistance continued to be provided through program lending
2017–2019	Moving toward upper income status	Increasing focus on economic competitiveness in Indonesia and economic reform

ADB = Asian Development Bank, ADF = Asian Development Fund, OCR = ordinary capital resources.

the bank's program in Indonesia since the late 1960s has been designed to be supportive of the priorities set out by the government.

The third role of ADB in Indonesia was as a financial institution. It was the original goal of the founders of ADB that the new organization would mobilize resources to help finance the growing development needs of Asia. In its work as a bank, in the period to December 2018 the bank provided over $37 billion of loans, grants, and other forms of assistance to Indonesia. It was also active in playing a wider role in promoting the development of financial markets in Indonesia.

Four Efforts

Another way of gaining an overall view of ADB's work in Indonesia is to consider the bank's contribution to Indonesian development in four main areas: support for capital accumulation through the provision of project and program loans; assistance to strengthen economic management; involvement in cross-cutting issues; and involvement in the preparation of knowledge products.

(i)   The bank's support for capital accumulation has been one of its main priorities in Indonesia, especially during the first two decades of operations and into the 1990s. During the first decade of operations, ADB was a project bank. In 1980, loans began to be approved for activities across specific sectors. During the succeeding decades, the bank provided many project and program loans which promoted both public and private investment in Indonesia.

(ii)   A second contribution to Indonesia's development effort has been the way in which ADB's lending was designed to help strengthen economic management, especially in times of pressure and crisis. During the 1980s, the government began to give increased attention to the need to promote structural adjustment. In response, ADB, along with other international partners, began to provide program loans for policy reform to bolster stability and to attract international investment flows to Indonesia. The government again found it useful to access program lending from ADB during the Asian financial crisis and beyond, especially after 2007 and when the global economic crisis led to uncertainties in financial markets. Many of these program loans were accompanied by policy dialogue designed to help promote structural adjustments.

(iii) Support for cross-cutting issues has been a third major part of ADB's work in Indonesia. Activities of this kind have included attention to disaster response efforts; measures to improve governance; decentralization; and to numerous social issues such as poverty alleviation, the needs of women and children, and health and education reform programs. To help address these issues, the bank has drawn on all of the main forms of assistance that it offers including project and program lending, grant funding, and numerous TA activities.

(iv) The bank's involvement in the preparation of many knowledge products is a fourth way in which ADB has contributed to Indonesia's development effort. The first TA project that the bank sponsored for any borrowing country was the grant-financed activity in Indonesia in 1967 for a study of ways to improve food supplies. Since 1967, ADB has approved TA loans and grants to support a very large number of policy-oriented studies in Indonesia. The bank has also sponsored many other economic, sectoral and social studies about regional changes in Asia which have encouraged discussion about development policy in Indonesia.

Looking Ahead

Indonesia faces numerous development challenges. The priorities set out by President Widodo in July 2019 for his second administration point to several of the most pressing issues. The president emphasized the need for expanded investment in three main areas—infrastructure, human capital, and job-creating activities. He also urged reform of the bureaucracy. The fifth priority mentioned by the president was effective fiscal management. ADB will be expected to help promote these and other national goals in Indonesia in the decade ahead.

ADB will need to strengthen its own work as well. The bank's approach for the next 10 years was set out in *Strategy 2030* issued in July 2018. The emphasis on the goal of supporting infrastructure development listed in *Strategy 2030* is consistent with the focus on infrastructure which President Widodo has frequently referred to. In addition,

ADB President Takehiko Nakao—prior to stepping down from his presidency on 16 January 2020—pointed to three areas where the bank needs to strengthen its work: providing a combination of finance and knowledge for developing countries, promoting good policies, and expanding programs of regional cooperation.

Indonesia's needs can be expected to continue to change. ADB should be ready to be flexible in responding to Indonesia's development priorities; in this way, the bank can look forward to being an effective development partner for Indonesia in the decades to come.

CHAPTER 1

Introduction

On 24 November 1966, Indonesia's Finance Minister Fransiscus Xaverius Seda, known as Frans Seda, was in Tokyo. Seda, who had been appointed minister of finance by Acting President Soeharto less than four months earlier, had arrived in Japan to attend an international conference. Along with a range of other key economic advisers and officials, he would play a central role in guiding Indonesia's economic recovery from the difficult years of the early and mid-1960s.

Seda's immediate task in Tokyo was to represent Indonesia at the inaugural meeting of the Asian Development Bank (ADB). Indonesia hoped it would be possible to arrange for the country to be accepted as one of the founding members of the bank. As it turned out, Seda's visit to Japan was entirely successful. Indonesia was not only welcomed by international delegates to the ADB inaugural meeting as a founding member of the bank but would, during the next three decades, become one of the most important partners of the institution in the Asian region.

The story set out here is about the work of ADB in Indonesia during the past 50 years. The narrative is part of the broader context of ADB's partnership with Indonesia and the bank's role as a member of the international community. This book will describe how ADB, as an Asian regional institution, has worked in Indonesia to provide financial resources, technical assistance, and knowledge to support development and regional cooperation in Southeast Asia.

ADB was established in 1966 at the meeting that Seda and his delegation attended in Tokyo. The bank is, by nature, an Asian institution. It was established with the support of Asian leaders who believed that regional cooperation supplemented with international financial resources would help promote development in Asia.

Several key ideas underpinned the establishment of ADB. One was that Asian countries needed to join together to promote development in Asia. A second was the realistic recognition that additional resources "both from within and outside the region" (as the ADB Charter put it) were needed to promote development. A third idea was that the establishment of a strong and credible regional bank would be an effective organization to achieve these goals.

The story will outline ADB's work with Indonesian partners and with the international community. But there is also an emphasis on ADB's characteristics as a multilateral development bank. Each of these features— multilateralism, development, and its role as a bank—is essential to the work of the organization. And as the activities of the institution are discussed in the chapters below, it will become clear that in its work in Indonesia, ADB has steadily widened the range of programs carried out under each of these three features of its operations. As Indonesia's own development program has evolved during the past 50 years, so ADB's activities have expanded to support Indonesian goals.

A Multilateral Agency

ADB is multilateral in the sense that its members are both governments from across the Asia and Pacific region and from nonregional countries. When the bank was established in 1966 it had 31 members: 19 from the Asia and Pacific region and 12 from elsewhere. By 2019, it had 68 members: 49 in the Asia and Pacific region and 19 elsewhere. ADB is also multilateral in the sense that it has numerous international partners. Although the ADB Charter sets out that the bank is "Asian in its basic character"—which means that most of its activities are in the Asia and Pacific region, it cooperates closely with developing member countries in the region, and many of its staff are from Asia and Pacific countries—its outreach goes beyond Asia.

ADB cooperates with a wide array of partners at local, regional, and global levels. The main groups that the bank must constantly work with are the official representatives of member governments. In Indonesia, as in most countries, it has been the custom to appoint the minister of finance as the governor for the bank (Appendix Table A2.2). In Indonesia, this has generally meant that the Ministry of Finance has been the first point of contact for ADB. One of Indonesia's most well-known ministers of finance, Ali Wardhana, was the bank's governor for Indonesia for 15 years from 1968 to 1982. For nearly all of the time that Indonesia has been a member of ADB, one of the 12 members of the ADB Board of Directors in Manila has been from Indonesia (Appendix Table A2.3). Most recently, in practice, there have been many other links between ADB and Indonesian institutions as well—with the Indonesian National Development Planning Agency (Bappenas), numerous sectoral departments (such as the Ministry of Public Works and Public Housing) and state-owned enterprises (such as the State Electricity Company [PLN]), with many community-based and education institutions, and with numerous private sector firms and groups. ADB's activities with these institutions in Indonesia have varied widely over the years. In many cases, ADB has joined with partners—both Indonesian agencies and other international development organizations—to consider strategy, to implement activities, and to conduct policy dialogue.

ADB's work in Indonesia has also been designed to support Indonesia's international role. At the regional level, as will be seen below, ADB and Indonesia have worked together on a range of activities across Southeast Asia. And at the wider international level, ADB has joined in numerous arrangements to strengthen support for Indonesia's development efforts.

Development Activities

One of the main purposes of ADB, set out in the Charter, is "to foster economic growth" in Asia and the Pacific. Implicit in this goal is the expectation that the bank will both *promote* change in developing countries and (which in practice is often a rather different thing) design its programs to *support* the development goals of member countries. ADB has aimed to do both of these things in Indonesia.

Beginning in the late 1960s, the bank responded to the urgent priorities of the Government of Indonesia to boost rice and agriculture production. Later, throughout the 1970s and 1980s, rapid structural adjustments were needed in Indonesia when large realignments in international markets took place.

During this period, ADB introduced important changes in the types of loans and other services it offered to Indonesia. During the Asian financial crisis in 1997–1998, the bank again quickly adjusted to changing circumstances. Since then, ADB's program has reflected Indonesia's changing needs in the post-Asian financial crisis period. The bank joined with the rest of the international community to provide special assistance following the Asian tsunami in 2004; several loans were agreed to in 2009 and 2012 to strengthen financial support facilities for Indonesia when there was heightened uncertainly in international markets following the global financial crisis; and, more recently, ADB loans in such sectors as power have been tailored to respond to the increased priority that the government has been giving to infrastructure across the nation.

Three broad themes reflecting trends in Indonesia emerge in the chapters below. The first theme is that of transformation. The transformation in Indonesia since the late 1960s, when ADB first began operations in the country and the outlook for the Indonesian economy was very difficult indeed, has been astonishing. In 1968, the eminent Indonesian economist and newly appointed minister for trade, Sumitro Djojohadikusumo, said that it would take "something like a generation" (interpreted to mean around 25 years) to overcome the earlier mismanagement of the Indonesian economy.[1] In the event, despite various periods of difficulties, especially during the Asian financial crisis, the overall performance of the Indonesian economy exceeded all expectations (Figure 1.1).

A second theme relates to resilience. Many shocks of various kinds have affected economies across developing Asia in recent decades. Nevertheless, the region has proved remarkably resilient. Indonesia, too, has been buffeted by numerous shocks—domestic and international, economic and political—and on the whole has weathered them well. In the 1970s and into the 1980s, international oil prices moved through several boom-and-bust scenarios, bringing much uncertainty to the Indonesian economy. Yet Indonesian policymakers coped well with the changes, adjusting national programs quite quickly. More recently, the Asian financial crisis imposed enormous strains on the Indonesian political and economic systems, and had lasting effects that took Indonesia some time to recover from. Nevertheless, by around 2005 Indonesian institutions had largely adjusted to the extraordinary range of reforms adopted in the post-Soeharto era, which soon became known as the *Reformasi* (Reform Era) period.

The third theme relates to stability. One element of stability, both across much of developing Asia and in Indonesia, has been attention to the need for careful fiscal and monetary policies. Indonesia, for example, has maintained disciplined fiscal and monetary policies for the past five decades. The several generations of economic "technocrats" who have been influential since the late 1960s have succeeded, on the whole, in holding firm to cautious macroeconomic policies. Another element of stability has been attention to the need to preserve peace and regional cooperation. During the last five decades, the policies of successive Indonesian administrations have been directed to the promotion of peace

---

[1]   Arndt, 1968, Survey, 2.

**Figure 1.1: Per Capita Gross Domestic Product in the People's
Republic of China, India, Indonesia, and Japan, 1900–2010**
(in 1990 international Geary–Khamis dollars)

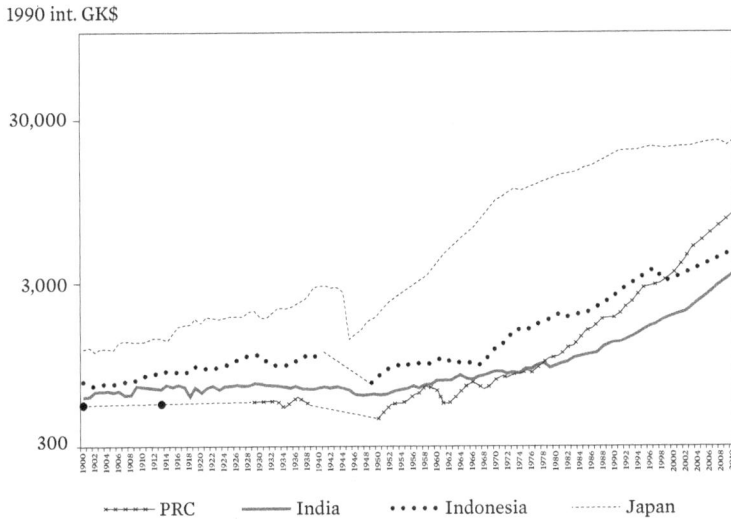

GDP = gross domestic product, int. GK$ = international Geary–Khamis dollars, PRC =
People's Republic of China.

Notes:
1. GDP in long-term constant prices (1990 int. GK$).
2. Data for Indonesia are unavailable from 1942 to 1948.
3. Data for the PRC are unavailable from 1901 to 1912, from 1914 to 1928, and from 1939
   to 1949. Single-year estimates for 1900 and 1913 are from the Maddison Project.

Source: The Maddison Project. 2013. New Maddison Project database. http://www.
ggdc.net.maddison/maddison-project/home.htm (accessed 14 February 2017).

and stability both at home and in the Southeast Asian region. Indonesia's
strong support for the Association of Southeast Asian Nations (ASEAN)
reflects this approach.

Finance

One role of ADB as a development bank is to act as a financial intermediary,
raising funds to support development activities in member countries that
are eligible for funding, or borrowing countries, such as Indonesia. When
ADB was established, Asia was poor and had a desperate shortage of

capital. Fifty years later, the need to promote investment in Asia is still one of the key development priorities in the region.

But ADB's role as a financial institution has been broader than its activities as a bank. The institution has aimed to encourage attention to the need for high-quality investments in borrowing countries, and has also worked to support the strengthening of financial markets across the region. The bank has always emphasized prudence as well, and the importance of maintaining sound economic and financial principles when selecting projects in borrowing countries.

To help improve the quality of investment programs the bank aims first to set high standards in its own operations. Bank investments are subject to close scrutiny before being presented to the ADB Board of Directors for approval. Once agreed, activities are then monitored during implementation, and after completion are regularly evaluated to judge the success of the investment programs. In addition, the bank also supports numerous programs designed to improve the overall quality of investment in borrowing countries. Many seminars, workshops, and training sessions are held, and books and briefing notes prepared, in support of these activities.

Financial markets in developing countries in Asia need strengthening as well. For one thing, it will be barely possible to mobilize the very large amounts of funds needed to support expanded investment programs unless there are deeper and wider financial markets across the region. In Indonesia, for example, the domestic bond market is still relatively small. The lack of a well-developed bond market is a key constraint limiting the ability of both public sector agencies and private firms to raise funds to support investment in the infrastructure sector. For another thing, stronger markets along with more effective regulatory institutions are needed to help reduce the risks of financial crisis occurring in Asia. The Asian financial crisis which began in Thailand in mid-1997 imposed huge economic and social costs, especially in Indonesia. For these reasons, in recent decades ADB has supported many activities designed to help improve the operations of financial markets in Indonesia and in other borrowing countries in Asia.

ADB in Indonesia

The narrative below tells the story of ADB's work in Indonesia. Organized chronologically by decade, the chapters trace major developments in Indonesia and show how the bank responded. But the ADB story needs to be set in context. The bank is, quite consciously, an institution which is "Asian in its basic character." It has always aimed to be a good development partner, both in working with other international agencies and, especially, in responding to the priorities set out by the government. The narrative below combines these themes.

Development challenges in Indonesia became increasingly clear during the 1950s. The leaders of the new republic were grappling with both internal and external challenges. Internally, political conflicts occupied much of the attention of Indonesia's policymakers.[2] Externally, Indonesia's leaders aimed to establish Indonesia's place as one of the major nations of the developing world (Chapter 2).

The first decade of ADB's work in Indonesia between 1967 and 1976 was a period of stabilization and recovery (Chapter 3). The first oil boom in 1973–1974 opened up welcome opportunities for the government to increase spending on *pembangunan* (development) programs. During the next decade (1977–1986) of the bank's operations, the second oil boom provided further revenues to support expanding levels of investment in Indonesia (Chapter 4). But when the international price of oil began to fall rapidly in the early 1980s, the need to reform policies quickly became clear.

In the third decade (1987–1996), structural adjustment proceeded apace in Indonesia as numerous adjustment packages (as they were called) were adopted to promote a range of market-oriented policies (Chapter 5). In 1997, in the first year of ADB's fourth decade (1997–2006), the Asian financial crisis brought economic turmoil to various countries in Asia, especially Indonesia (Chapter 6). It took almost 10 years for Indonesia to recover from the effects of the crisis. While the country was recovering, the devastating Asian tsunami on 26 December 2004 struck Indonesia, hitting hard Aceh province and Nias island, claiming over 167,000 lives in Indonesia alone—and spreading across the Indian Ocean to Thailand, Sri Lanka, India, and beyond (Chapter 7). During the fifth decade (2007–2016), economic recovery strengthened in Indonesia (Chapter 8). The Indonesian

---

[2]   The classic study is Feith, 1962, *Decline*.

economy weathered the effects of the global financial crisis (2007–2008) well; although, following the crisis, the overall annual economic growth rate settled at around 5% rather than the 7% policymakers had hoped for.

Both lessons and challenges can be identified from Indonesia's remarkable development experience (Chapter 9). Looking back, pragmatic policymaking and a willingness to adjust national programs quickly when necessary have been key characteristics of economic management in Indonesia in the last 50 years. Looking forward, a wide range of challenges exists. Flexible policymaking will continue to be needed. Effective cooperation between Indonesia and the international community will also continue to be helpful in underpinning good policy in the decades ahead.

Figure 1.2: ADB Approvals for Indonesia as % of GDP, 1969–2016

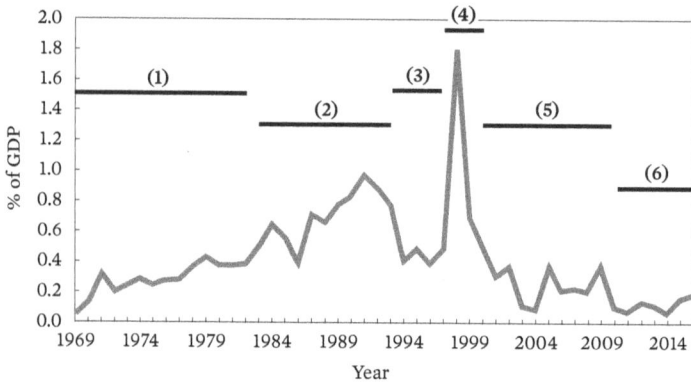

GDP = gross domestic product.
Note: The stages shown in the figure are as follows.
(1) ADB steadily expanded lending during the 1970s.
(2) Structural adjustment in Indonesia: ADB supported the reforms.
(3) Post Berlin Wall: ADB approvals fell reflecting Indonesia's high growth and apparent need for less reliance on official international finance.
(4) Asian financial crisis; sharp jump in ADB approvals.
(5) Reduced ADB lending reflecting a period of lower borrowing by Indonesia because of priority given to reducing public debt after the Asian financial crisis. Indonesia took over aid coordination from the Consultative Group on Indonesia in 2007.
(6) Move toward graduation.
Source: ADB.

During this 50-year period, ADB's program expanded steadily until the early 1990s and then fluctuated somewhat in response to circumstances in Indonesia. The bank's loan approvals rose from around 0.2% of Indonesian gross domestic product (GDP) during the 1970s (Appendix Table A2.1) and averaged around 0.4% of GDP during the five decades to 2016 (Figure 1.2). After the Asian financial crisis, for various reasons (see Chapter 7 and Chapter 8 below) Indonesia reduced the level of borrowings entered into from international agencies such as ADB.

Overall Assistance to Indonesia

As background for the discussion below, it is helpful to consider the outline of the overall international assistance effort in Indonesia since the late 1960s. Various foreign aid activities had been carried out in Indonesia in the 1950s and during the early 1960s, but the programs were mostly small and were not part of any large-scale coordinated international effort to promote development.[3] The program of international assistance, including ADB's activities discussed in the chapters below, began in the late 1960s and expanded quickly during the 1970s (Chapter 3).

The international program that began in Indonesia in the late 1960s has been one of the largest sustained aid efforts in post-war history (Table 1.1). International assistance flows can be measured in various ways but as a guide to the total size of flows over the 50-year period to 2016, the lower limit of total assistance in constant (2016) prices is $150 billion (net flows) and an upper estimate is approximately $340 billion (gross flows). These flows amounted, respectively, to around 1% and 2.4% of Indonesian GDP over the period.[4]

Overall flows of assistance were relatively high (as a share of Indonesian GDP) in the early 1970s when donors supported major development

---

[3] See Shakow, 1964, *Foreign Economic Assistance*, and van der Eng, 2015, International Food Aid. See also the discussion in chapters 3 and 4, Mustopadidjaja, 2012, *Bappenas*.

[4] Official development assistance (ODA) and other official flows (OOF) are measures of official flows agreed to for development purposes recorded by the Development Assistance Committee (DAC) of the Organisation for Economic Co-operation and Development (OECD). ODA mainly refers to official flows provided on concessional terms, often as grants. OOF are official flows that do not meet the conditions for eligibility as ODA, either because they are not primarily provided for development purposes or because they have a grant element of less than 25%. See OECD, DAC Glossary of Key Terms and Concepts, for definitions of the different types of assistance flows.

Table 1.1: Total International Official Flows to Indonesia, 1967–2016
($ million)

	1967–1976	1977–1986	1987–1996	1997–2006	2007–2016	Total 1967–2016
Current Prices						
Gross flows						
Total official flows	8,283	25,332	67,167	65,821	77,491	244,095
Of which: ODA gross	5,409	9,300	23,098	21,434	27,343	86,584
OOF gross	2,873	16,033	44,069	44,387	50,148	157,510
Net flows						
Total official flows	6,934	15,920	32,045	21,801	11,832	88,532
Of which: ODA net	5,061	7,374	16,073	14,414	4,480	47,402
OOF net	1,873	8,546	15,972	7,387	7,352	41,130
Constant 2016 Prices						
Gross flows						
Total official flows	36,695	58,926	90,216	80,428	73,182	339,447
Of which: ODA gross	25,537	21,738	31,501	26,105	25,523	130,404
OOF gross	11,157	37,188	58,715	54,323	47,659	209,042
Net flows						
Total official flows	30,395	37,231	44,258	27,061	11,517	150,463
Of which: ODA net	23,865	17,325	22,143	17,804	4,184	85,322
OOF net	6,530	19,906	22,115	9,257	7,333	65,141

ODA = official development assistance OOF = other official flows.

Note: Deflator is Organisation for Economic Co-operation and Development (OECD) Development Assistance Committee overall deflation index.

Source: OECD, *GeoBook: Geographical Flows to Developing Countries*.

programs (Figure 1.3). The level of assistance declined over time as Indonesia moved toward middle-income status. In recent years, the gross flow of total official assistance has been around 1% of GDP while the net flow (which subtracts repayments that Indonesia makes to international creditors from gross flows) has been close to zero.

There were marked fluctuations in assistance flows because, as will be seen in the chapters below, the international community responded to changing needs in Indonesia. Seven stages can be identified (Figure 1.3):

(i)   Initially, as the Indonesian economy was recovering in the early and mid-1970s, donor support was strong.

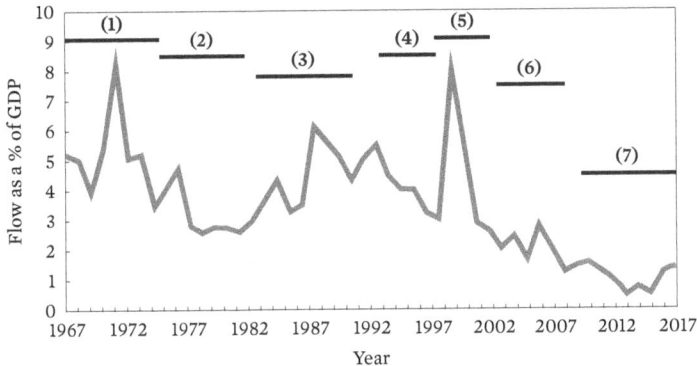

Figure 1.3: Total Official Gross Flows as % of GDP, 1967–2016

GDP = gross domestic product.

Note: The stages shown in the figure are as follows.

(1) High assistance flows in the early 1970s.

(2) Lower flows following two oil price increases in the early and late 1970s.

(3) Support for structural adjustment in Indonesia during the 1980s.

(4) Post Berlin wall: international flows fell reflecting Indonesia's high growth and apparent need for less reliance on official international finance.

(5) Asian financial crisis; sharp increase in international support.

(6) Reduced borrowing by Indonesia reflecting the priority given to reducing public debt after the Asian financial crisis. There was a surge in international flows around 2005 following the tsunami in Aceh in 2004. Indonesia took over aid coordination from the Consultative Group on Indonesia in 2007.

(7) Move toward graduation.

Source: Organisation for Economic Co-operation and Development, *GeoBook: Geographical Flows to Developing Countries.*

(ii) In the later 1970s when revenues to Indonesia from the first (1973–1974) and second (1979) oil booms allowed the government to implement large increases in development spending, partners began to cut back on the level of assistance.

(iii) When international oil prices weakened in the early 1980s and Indonesian policymakers responded with programs of structural adjustment, the international community supported the reform efforts; total gross flows rose to over 5% of GDP in the late 1980s.

(iv) During the 1990s, the Indonesian economy began to grow rapidly and it seemed that there was less need for foreign assistance. Further, following the fall of the Berlin Wall in 1989 and the end of the Cold War, some donors became increasingly critical of the style of the New Order government established by President Soeharto in the late 1960s. Foreign aid flows fell during the 1990s reaching a low point in 1997 just as the Asian financial crisis began to unfold.

(v)   The international community provided emergency financial support to Indonesia during the Asian financial crisis. Total gross flows rose sharply to over 8% of GDP in 1998. A good deal of the financial support was provided on a short-term basis so the level of assistance fell back once the immediate crisis had passed.

(vi) Following the Asian financial crisis, Indonesia's debt-service ratio rose sharply so Indonesian policymakers gave high priority to reducing the level of foreign debt. Total flows declined as Indonesia cut back on international borrowings with the aim of reducing the debt-service ratio as quickly as possible. The foreign assistance program following the Asian tsunami in December 2004, however, boosted flows for several years.

(vii) From around 2007, international flows settled at a relatively low level as Indonesia moved toward middle-income status and began to graduate from a number of international programs.

The most important partners for Indonesia in this sustained program of international support (measured in terms of gross flows) were Japan, the World Bank, and ADB (Table 1.2). Japan was by far the largest bilateral donor providing around one-third of total gross flows over the five decades to 2016. Multilateral agencies—mainly the World Bank and ADB—provided another 30% of total flows. Germany and the US also contributed significant amounts of assistance.

The role of ADB, working with other international partners and the Government of Indonesia in this major assistance program, was a significant one. The bank's overall efforts (loans, grants, and TA activities) provided around 10% of the total international gross flows to Indonesia over the five decades to 2016. ADB's participation also reflected the commitment of an Asian regional institution to supporting development in

Table 1.2: Total Official Gross Flows to Indonesia, 1967–2016
($US million, current prices)

	1967–1976	1977–1986	1987–1996	1997–2006	2007–2016	Total 1967–2016	%
DAC Countries[a]							
Japan	2,238	6,602	28,130	23,583	20,590	81,142	33.2
Germany	653	2,243	6,142	3,779	2,506	15,323	6.3
United States	2,037	2,153	2,753	5,518	2,577	15,039	6.2
Netherlands	495	1,035	1,470	8,788	890	12,677	5.2
Australia	264	546	1,637	1,294	4,220	7,960	3.3
France	501	2,158	786	364	1,987	5,796	2.4
Other DAC Countries[b]	1,168	3,605	6,341	3,556	14,604	29,274	12.0
DAC Countries, total	7,356	18,342	47,259	46,881	47,374	167,212	68.5
Multilaterals, total	926	6,709	19,682	18,778	30,074	76,170	31.2
Other[c]	1	282	226	162	42	713	0.3
Official flows, total	8,283	25,332	67,167	65,821	77,491	244,095	100.0
Memo items:							
Asian Development Bank	87	1,082	6,464	8,613	9,607	25,853	10.6
World Bank Group, total	679	5,078	12,503	8,940	17,497	44,698	18.3

DAC = Development Assistance Committee of the Organisation for Economic Co-operation and Development (OECD).

Notes:

[a] Countries which are members of DAC.

[b] Includes Austria, Belgium, Canada, the Czech Republic, Denmark, Greece, Finland, Hungary, Ireland, Italy, the Republic of Korea, Luxembourg, New Zealand, Norway, Poland, Portugal, Spain, Sweden, Switzerland, and the United Kingdom.

[c] Non-DAC countries and private donors.

Source: OECD, *Geographical Flows to Developing Countries.*

Indonesia. The international community has often looked for reassurance that Asian partners are ready to support regional development efforts in Asia, so the bank's sustained involvement in Indonesia has bolstered the sense of international burden sharing throughout the five decades.

CHAPTER 2

Indonesia in the Region

Many of the development challenges that Indonesia faced in the 1960s and 1970s were already evident in the 1950s. One of the key issues was regionalism—whether regional institutions could be strengthened in a way that would support development across Asia and, if so, how best to promote Asian regionalism.

In the mid-1950s, Indonesia's first president, Sukarno, had bold plans both for Asian regionalism and to build ties of postcolonial solidarity across the developing world. There was talk of Afro-Asian solidarity, "the awakening of Asia," and strengthening "the voice of Asia" at the international level. These aspirations were reflected in the ambitious goals set out at the Bandung Conference in Indonesia of 1955. The Bandung Conference was chaired by President Sukarno and attended by world figures such as Premier Zhou Enlai from the People's Republic of China, Prime Minister Jawaharlal Nehru of India, and President Gamal Abdel Nasser of Egypt.[1]

The aspirations reflected in the declarations from Bandung were important ones. Both then and later, commitment to Asian regionalism was strong. What was less clear during the 1950s was how to convert the political declarations into practical programs. One overriding constraint was the shortage of finance. It was this constraint that later, in the 1960s, helped build early support for the establishment of the Asian Development Bank (ADB). And it was, moreover, one of Asia's first major regional institutions, the United Nations (UN) Economic Commission for Asia and the Far East, based in Bangkok, which sponsored the series of major international meetings between 1963 and 1966 that led to the formation of the bank.

For a time after the Bandung Conference, and into the 1960s, there were few determined efforts to initiate new programs to promote regionalism. Rather, in Southeast Asia the attention of many policymakers was taken up by growing concerns about instability. In Indonesia, political and economic circumstances became more uncertain and more inward-looking in the late 1950s. Indonesia's support for regionalism came under strain.

---

[1] J. Mackie, 2005, *Bandung*.

There were several years of sharp friction in Southeast Asia after 1963 during the period known as *Konfrontasi* (Confrontation) when President Sukarno opposed the formation of a new Federation of Malaysia. At the beginning of January 1965, President Sukarno announced that Indonesia would withdraw from the UN in protest at the proposal to give Malaysia a seat on the UN Security Council. Then, later in the year in August, arrangements for the establishment of the Federation of Malaysia failed when marked disagreements led to Singapore's painful exit. Nearby, conflict in Viet Nam was beginning to widen in an ominous way as the United States (US) and other Western countries responded to the perceived threat of communism and of the risk of a domino effect across the Mekong countries.

Domestic developments within Indonesia were marked by turbulence and uncertainty. During the early 1960s, both Western observers and many Indonesians had become alarmed by the growing influence of the large Indonesian Communist Party. A showdown came in September 1965 in a terrible period of conflict when perhaps half a million Indonesians died.[2]

The events of 1965, and the changes that followed during 1966, marked a turning point. The senior economic figures in the new administration in Jakarta quickly began to consider steps that might be introduced to stabilize the domestic economy. They also recognized that expanded regional and international cooperation would help promote economic recovery. Indonesia's official notification of plans to leave the UN was withdrawn and in June 1966 an International Monetary Fund (IMF) mission visited Indonesia to discuss membership arrangements in the fund under the new administration. At the same time, IMF staff began to review the economic situation in Indonesia and, by August, its personnel were assisting in the preparation of a stabilization program.[3] By late 1966 a series of economic measures had been announced, including steps to encourage a more outward-oriented approach to national development. As will be seen below, the new policies included steps toward addressing the difficult foreign debt commitments that had built up during the early 1960s.

Indonesia's own efforts at economic diplomacy expanded during 1966 and 1967. High-level diplomatic missions including Foreign Minister Adam Malik and other senior figures such as Sri Sultan Hamengku Buwono IX were sent abroad to strengthen Indonesia's credentials. Measures were

2   Wanandi, 2012, *Shades.*
3   Sutton, 1982, *Indonesia 1966–70*, 17.

taken to restore Indonesia's place in international organizations such as the United Nations Conference on Trade and Development (UNCTAD) in Geneva and the Food and Agriculture Organization of the United Nations (FAO) in Rome.

Indonesia's plans to become a founding member of ADB were part of the new administration's steps to reengage with the international community. One of the attractions of membership of ADB was that in joining the bank, Indonesia was indicating a firm commitment to regionalism. Another was the opportunity to join with other countries in Southeast Asia to discuss common development challenges and possible approaches to promoting regional economic growth.

In August 1967, another major step toward stronger regional cooperation was taken when five nations came together to establish the Association of Southeast Asian Nations (ASEAN).[4] Although one main objective underpinning the formation of ASEAN was to bolster regional security in the face of growing conflict in Viet Nam, another main objective was to strengthen economic cooperation. The ASEAN Declaration signed in Bangkok on 8 August 1976 noted the need for "a firm foundation for common action to promote regional cooperation in South-East Asia" and went on to declare that the countries of the region shared "a primary responsibility for strengthening the economic and social stability of the region."

These early efforts in the 1950s and 1960s to build regional institutions led to the expansion of many other programs during the following decades (Table 2.1).[5] Indonesia's role in supporting regional financial cooperation and integration in Southeast Asia has expanded in recent years. Speaking at an East Asia Summit workshop in Jakarta in 2007, Finance Minister Sri Mulyani Indrawati outlined some of the reforms that Indonesia hoped to see from economic cooperation in the region:[6]

> There has been significant work in promoting greater regional financial cooperation and integration. However, there remains scope to do more. In particular, the nations of East Asia must continue to develop local capital markets, and to integrate with other regional markets, and with global markets. Strengthening domestic financial markets and promoting further financial integration can assist

---

[4]   The five nations were Indonesia, Malaysia, the Philippines, Singapore, and Thailand.
[5]   ADB, 2008, *Emerging Asian Regionalism.*
[6]   Indrawati, 2007, Developing Broader Regional Financial Integration.

Table 2.1: Selected Regional Institutions and Indonesia

1947	ECAFE	UN Economic Commission for Asia and the Far East (later became Economic and Social Commission for Asia and the Pacific) was established
1955		Bandung Conference held in Indonesia
1966	ADB	Asian Development Bank established
1967	ASEAN	Association of Southeast Asian Nations formed
1982	SEACEN Centre	South East Asian Central Banks Research and Training Centre created
1989	APEC	Asia-Pacific Economic Cooperation agreed to
1991	EMEAP	Executives' Meeting of East Asia-Pacific Central Banks
1992	GMS	Greater Mekong Subregion: Cambodia, two provinces of the People's Republic of China, the Lao People's Democratic Republic, Myanmar, Thailand, and Viet Nam formed
1997	ASEAN+3	ASEAN, Japan, the People's Republic of China, and the Republic of Korea
1993	IMT-GT	Indonesia–Malaysia–Thailand Growth Triangle formed
1994	BIMP-EAGA	Brunei Darussalam–Indonesia–Malaysia–Philippines East ASEAN Growth Area created
2000	CMI	Chiang Mai Initiative agreed to
2003	AEC	ASEAN Economic Community established
2005	EAS	East Asia Summit agreed to
2009	CMIM	Chiang Mai Initiative Multilateralization created
2016	AMRO	ASEAN+3 Macroeconomic Research Office established

East Asia achieve higher and more sustainable rates of economic growth. ... Financial integration can reduce the cost of capital, support the transfer of technology, promote further development of domestic financial markets, improve macroeconomic policymaking, and strengthen institutions.

More broadly, Indonesian foreign policy emphasizes the centrality of ASEAN in the Southeast Asian region. In her annual foreign policy speech in January 2018, for example, Foreign Minister Retno L.P. Marsudi emphasized that "collective leadership and concerted action" were needed to preserve ASEAN's place as the prominent player in the region.[7] The ASEAN Secretariat was first established in Jakarta by the foreign ministers of the association in 1976. It was initially housed in the Indonesian Department of Foreign Affairs before moving to its own headquarters at the existing location in South Jakarta in 1981. More recently, a new ASEAN Secretariat building was opened next to the original headquarters at a ceremony attended by President Joko Widodo in August 2019.

In ADB's own work across Asia, the bank has given priority to activities designed to strengthen regional cooperation, including ASEAN.[8] The bank has joined with other multilateral agencies and member governments to support many types of regional and subregional programs that Sri Mulyani referred to in her 2007 speech. Indonesia, as an important partner for ADB, has participated in a large number of these activities during the past 50 years.

---

[7] Marsudi, R., 2018, Indonesia: Partner for peace. For a discussion of ASEAN's place in Southeast Asia, see Chia, S.Y., 2013, The ASEAN Economic Community.

[8] ADB has produced numerous publications about ASEAN activities in cooperation with ASEAN partners. See, for example, Menon and Lee, 2019, *An Evolving ASEAN Vision*.

CHAPTER 3

Early Years
(1967–1976)

When the Asian Development Bank (ADB) began operations in Manila in late 1966, economic policymakers in the Soeharto government in Indonesia were beginning to tackle the daunting task of promoting rehabilitation and growth across the nation. The new Soeharto government and Western countries had a strong shared interest in bolstering economic stability in Indonesia. Reforms were urgently needed. The economic management of the nation had been chaotic during the early years of the 1960s. By 1965, inflation had turned into hyperinflation and the monetized economy was close to collapse. The first priority for the incoming team of economic policymakers was thus to restore some semblance of macroeconomic stability.

One of the most urgent issues needing immediate attention was a looming debt crisis—"a mountain of debt," as one of the main economic policymakers of the time, Radius Prawiro, put it. He described the problem as follows:[1]

> The country was not only poor and essentially bankrupt; it was carrying a debt burden that threatened to keep it impoverished for decades to come. In 1966, the initial instalment on twenty years of past borrowing was coming due. The country could not pay. This, in turn, disqualified Indonesia from new loans. New investment was cut off and the country was steadily growing poorer. Indonesia had fallen into the debt trap that has ensnared so many poor and disadvantaged countries.

This stark description of the situation reflected the views of the new government. Throughout most of 1966, senior economic ministers in Indonesia devoted much of their time to economic diplomacy, meeting with international financiers and representatives of aid donor organizations, both in Indonesia and abroad.

---

[1] Prawiro, 1998, *Indonesia's Struggle for Economic Development*, 58.

In mid-1966, soon after his appointment as governor of Bank Indonesia, Prawiro visited Tokyo to lay the groundwork for a planned meeting of Indonesia's creditors in September. The reception on the Japanese side, in discussions with Finance Minister Takeo Fukuda, was very helpful:[2]

> Minister Fukuda gave his personal support to ensure that Japan would help Indonesia in this time of duress. Without Minister Fukuda's initiative and determined effort, it is unlikely that Japan would have been able to support Indonesia in that moment of crisis.

In September an Indonesian delegation met with the Paris Club countries in Tokyo to discuss Indonesia's national debt problems.[3] This meeting ended without firm commitments to provide Indonesia with aid. Participants agreed, however, to hold another meeting to discuss debt problems in Paris before the end of the year.

It was against this background that in late November, Finance Minister Frans Seda and the Indonesian delegation arrived to attend the inaugural meeting of ADB. The first session began at 10 a.m. when Fukuda was elected as chair of the conference. Shortly after, the meeting formally approved Indonesia as an inaugural member of the bank. Takeshi Watanabe, the first president of ADB, recorded in his memoirs that, "As soon as this decision was taken, Dr. Frans Seda, Finance Minister of Indonesia, who was seated among the observers, proceeded to the members' section amidst applause."[4] These few small steps by Seda in the ADB meeting reflected, more broadly, the overall approach of the government at the time of taking every opportunity available to reengage with the international community.

The following month, in December, the conference of the Paris Club countries was reconvened as planned. By this time, further stabilization measures had been introduced in Indonesia and signs of economic improvement were becoming clearer. At the Paris Club meeting, Indonesia's creditors agreed to reschedule loans coming due in the next few years and proposed that outstanding debts should be repaid over a longer period. The group also agreed to meet again in Amsterdam in February 1967.

---

[2]   Prawiro, 1998, *Indonesia's Struggle for Economic Development*, 78.
[3]   Details are in Prawiro, 1998, *Indonesia's Struggle for Economic Development*, 63.
[4]   Watanabe, 1977, *Towards a New Asia*.

The Inter-Governmental Group on Indonesia

Further discussions about Indonesia's debt levels were held at the Amsterdam meeting. But by far the most significant event—the importance of which was not appreciated at the time—was that a new aid group, soon to become known as the Inter-Governmental Group on Indonesia (IGGI), was born (Appendix Table A2.5). Prawiro explained the process:[5]

> The IGGI was not the first example of an organization founded to resolve serious problems in sovereign debt. The World Bank chaired an aid consortium when India faced a financial crisis in 1958. ... Very quickly, however, the IGGI distinguished itself as a remarkable forum for dealing with Indonesia's complex debt problems. One of the organization's greatest strengths was its relative informality. The IGGI had no official charter. It was not established through any binding legal agreements. It had no permanent secretariat or any of the institutional trappings to confer it the status of an 'official organization'. Nor was it designed to be an international 'collection agency' for outstanding foreign debt. It was an international body which imposed nothing on its members. The purpose of the IGGI was simply to serve as a forum to facilitate coordinated action among its members and the exchange of views.

Originally, the IGGI was created only for the purpose of finding a solution to Indonesia's debt crisis. The group was not expected to have a long life span. Nevertheless, some sort of loose institutional organization of donor countries was needed. It would clearly be helpful if some country or organization served as the chair of the group. What arrangements, then, might be made to establish a new IGGI aid club?

As is often the situation with such international arrangements, the institutional procedures for the IGGI needed to be negotiated. Developing countries such as Indonesia tended to be more comfortable having multilateral organizations coordinate international arrangements. Indonesia would have preferred that the World Bank chair the IGGI. But at the time, Indonesia was in arrears in payments on World Bank loans so the World Bank could not take on the role of chair of the group. Another possible organization which might have chaired the IGGI was ADB. But ADB had only recently been established and was not yet ready to take on

---

[5]   Prawiro, 1998, *Indonesia's Struggle*, 64.

new tasks such as convening an international aid group. Other candidates were Japan and the Netherlands. In the event, it was agreed that the Netherlands would accept the role as chair. Prawiro[6] explained that:

> Indonesia believed that the Dutch would be an earnest and sympathetic leader. For these reasons, Indonesia supported having the Dutch chair the IGGI. Holland accepted this responsibility and, until the disbanding of the IGGI in 1992, it played a highly valued role.

The February 1967 meeting of donor countries in Amsterdam discussed, among other things, Indonesia's need for assistance during the coming year, estimated to be around $200 million. This was, in effect, the first meeting of the IGGI. The new group soon became established as the main forum for discussions about international aid coordination for Indonesia.[7]

Next Steps for Indonesia

The early years of economic recovery—through to 1968 and 1969—were difficult ones for Indonesian policymakers. The immediate priorities in the stabilization and rehabilitation period in 1966–1968 were to introduce measures to overcome the urgent economic and financial difficulties facing the nation and to consider what longer-term steps were needed to promote growth. Recalling the events of the period, one of Indonesia's most well-known economists and policymakers, Professor Widjojo Nitisastro, observed that "two big events" took place at the University of Indonesia (UI) in Jakarta in 1966.[8] The first was a "Seminar on Economics and Finance" in January organized by the Indonesian Students Action Front of the Faculty of Economics of UI (KAMI-FEUI). The second was a "Symposium on the Awakening Spirit of '66: Exploring a New Path" convened by UI and the Indonesian Scholars Action Front (KASI) in May.

The events were significant for several reasons. First, a number of the participants in these seminars soon became leading economic policymakers in the New Order government established by President Soeharto. These included Widjojo himself as well as others such as Mohammad Sadli, Emil Salim, Seda, Sri Sultan Hamengku Buwono IX, Subroto, Soemantri

---

[6]   Prawiro, 67.
[7]   Posthumus, 1972, The Inter-Governmental Group, 55–66.
[8]   Widjojo, 2011, *The Indonesian Development Experience*, 25.

Brodjonegoro, and Ali Wardhana.[9] Second, many of the ideas discussed at these conferences were adopted as the basis of the main economic policies approved at a major meeting of the national Provisional People's Consultative Assembly (MPRS) in July 1966.[10]

The broad outlines of the new policies approved by the MPRS in 1966 emphasized a pragmatic rather than an ideological approach to economic management. A rehabilitation program focusing on food production, infrastructure, export promotion, and clothing was announced. General Soeharto, chairman of the Cabinet Presidium at the time, set out the approach to be implemented as follows:[11]

(i)   by rendering a more proper role to market forces, create a wider and equal opportunity for participation in the development of our economy by all creative efforts, state and private, domestic and foreign alike;

(ii) the achievement of a balanced state budget;

(iii) pursuance of a rigid yet well-directed credit policy of the banking system; and

(iv) establishment of a proper link between the domestic and the international economy through a realistic exchange rate, and thus creating stimuli to reverse the downward trend of the balance of payments.

As it turned out, these and other measures announced during the stabilization and rehabilitation period came to underpin some of the main approaches to economic policy in Indonesia for the next 50 years. The adoption of a balanced budget principle, for example, served to introduce much stricter controls over government spending. Although in practice some leeway was allowed in the precise way that the balance was estimated, the arrangement was a key step toward establishing fiscal discipline. The new approach made it possible for Indonesian economic policymakers to maintain cautious fiscal policies for decades to come.

---

[9] The list is provided in Widjojo, *The Indonesian Development Experience*, 18.
[10] A detailed comparison between the main decree adopted by the Provisional People's Consultative Assembly and the ideas discussed in the two University of Indonesia conferences is provided in Widjojo, *The Indonesian Development Experience*, Chapter 5, 47–74.
[11] Arndt, 1966, Survey, October, 4.

The introduction of a new Foreign Investment Law in January 1967 was also seen as an important step. It signaled a willingness to revise earlier anti-foreign investment sentiments and to welcome international investors. Initially foreign investors were cautious but confidence grew throughout 1967 and 1968. The first major contract under the new law was signed in Jakarta in April 1967 with the American company Freeport Sulphur Inc. Under the new agreement, Freeport would have the right to explore and exploit copper deposits in the Papua (formerly Irian Jaya) region. In return for these rights, the company undertook to invest $75 million in development in Papua, including the construction of a port, airstrip, township, dam, and roads.

The Freeport mine soon became one of the largest foreign investment projects in Indonesia and provided sizeable revenues to the national budget for many years. Five decades later, in 2018, after extensive negotiations with Freeport, it was agreed that Indonesian local interests backed by the Government of Indonesia would assume majority ownership of the mining project.

Growing International Support

It took some time during these early years of Indonesia's recovery for the international community to reach agreements about the provision of long-term assistance. At first, some European countries and the United Kingdom held back, waiting to see what approach other countries would take. At the IGGI meeting in February 1967, donor countries had agreed that Indonesia would need $200 million in external assistance during the year but no firm pledges were announced. But there was a useful start toward establishing a coordinated aid program when the United States (US) offered to provide one-third of the funds needed, provided other countries contributed the rest. Subsequently, in an announcement that foreshadowed Japan's willingness to become a major contributor to Indonesia's long-term development effort, Tokyo agreed to match the American offer. By the time that the next meeting of donor countries was held in Scheveningen in the Netherlands in June, Germany and the Netherlands along with several other countries had promised support and a total of $187.5 million was in sight. Possible assistance from Australia seemed likely to bring the total to over $190 million.

These were still only preliminary steps toward the establishment of an effective aid program. It was not until early 1968 that a firmer consensus emerged across IGGI donor countries about the coordinated arrangements needed to provide substantial long-term support. On the Indonesian side, the new team of economic technocrats had indicated that they were keen to work constructively with the international community. On the donor side, the US had decided to take a lead and to actively encourage international support for the recovery efforts in Indonesia.

Several factors led the US to adopt the new approach. One was that US diplomats and senior USAID staff had maintained regular contact with Widjojo Nitisastro and other economic technocrats who had joined the new government and had confidence in them.[12] The American links with some of these economists went back to the 1950s. Young Indonesians such as Mohammad Sadli had studied in the US with scholarships funded by the official US International Cooperation Administration.[13] Later, during the difficult years of the early 1960s, the Ford Foundation had provided support for a number of young economists from UI to undertake graduate studies in the US. The program had been arranged with the support of Professor Sumitro Djojohadikusumo, Indonesia's most senior academic economist, who was dean of the Faculty of Economics at UI at the time.

But just as important for American policymakers were the growing difficulties in Viet Nam. American policy toward Southeast Asia at the time was focused on the goal of supporting pro-American leaders in South Viet Nam. When the political balance in Indonesia shifted decisively toward a pro-Western stance in 1966 and 1967, key military and strategic policymakers in Washington welcomed the change. Support in Washington quickly grew for the provision of substantial aid to the new administration in Jakarta.

Encouraged by the lead from America and Japan, other donor countries soon began to prepare expanded aid programs for Indonesia. Other events were serving to encourage the international community to provide increasing support to Indonesia as well. In 1968, the incoming president of the World Bank, former US Secretary of Defense Robert McNamara, announced that his first overseas visit after taking office would be to Indonesia. Commenting on these events, H.W. Arndt, head of the Australian National University's (ANU) Indonesia Project, noted:[14]

---

[12] Hollinger, 1996, *Economic Policy Under President Soeharto*, 21.
[13] Arsjad Anwar *et al.*, 1992, *Pemikiran, Pelaksanaan, dan Perintisan Pembangunan Ekonomi*, xiv.
[14] Arndt, 1968, Survey, June, 14.

The aid picture was also improved by a decision by the World Bank (IBRD) announced in May during a visit to Jakarta by its new president, Mr. Robert McNamara. The Bank would grant Indonesia a $4 million credit (through its affiliate, the International Development Association) and would take the unprecedented step of establishing in Jakarta a resident Bank Mission to advise the Indonesian Government on economic policy in general and on specific rehabilitation and development projects in particular. Apart from the direct benefits of this assistance, the Bank's strong expression of confidence in the Suharto government and its economic policies could hardly fail to make an impression on the members of the Inter-Governmental Group as well as on private investors.

IGGI meetings provided a convenient mechanism for aid coordination so donors agreed to continue to meet regularly in the Netherlands. During the next two decades, and into the 1990s, the IGGI served as the main forum for international discussions about development policy in Indonesia.

The meetings of IGGI were well organized. They were attended by a team of key officials from Jakarta led by senior economic ministers and by delegations from donor countries. Main multilateral organizations such as the International Monetary Fund (IMF), World Bank, and ADB presented reports at the meetings and numerous other international organizations sent observers to follow the discussions.

The papers prepared for IGGI meetings made aid coordination easier as well. It became the practice for the World Bank to prepare an annual "grey cover" report providing a survey of economic developments in Indonesia and recommending annual aid targets. These reports, summaries of which usually found their way into the international media, helped bolster confidence across the donor community and in international financial markets in the economic policies being adopted by Indonesia.[15] From the Indonesian point of view, IGGI meetings provided a useful platform for the government to liaise with the donor community. Prawiro, governor of the central bank, Bank Indonesia, (1966–1973) described the IGGI as "perhaps the world's most effective organization in bilateral and multilateral economic relations."

---

[15] Throughout the 1970s and 1980s, *Far Eastern Economic Review*, the leading international weekly magazine on Asian affairs at the time, regularly carried stories summarizing the World Bank's annual grey cover publications presented at annual IGGI meetings.

Nevertheless, despite these encouraging steps, for some time a cloud of uncertainty continued to hang over Indonesia's economic prospects. The country's debt problems seemed almost unsurmountable. To find a solution, Indonesia and the IGGI asked a senior German banker, Hermann Abs, to prepare a report. In mid-1969 Abs presented the results of a careful study of the situation. The Abs report became the basis for a settlement that most donor countries agreed to in April 1970. Although some further negotiations over outstanding debt issues were still needed with the Soviet Union and several other socialist countries, the process set out in the Abs report served to reestablish Indonesia's creditworthiness.[16]

ADB Begins Work

Stabilization of domestic food markets—and especially guaranteeing the supply of rice at reasonable prices—was one of the government's top priorities in the late 1960s. The problem of ensuring adequate food supplies was a major concern in other parts of developing Asia as well, so one of the first policy-oriented activities that the newly established ADB announced was to support a major survey of agriculture—the *Asian Agricultural Survey*.[17] The survey team began work in July 1967, visiting 15 developing countries in Asia and the Pacific, including Indonesia. In early 1968, the team presented a report that dramatically highlighted the potential for new agricultural technology to boost food production.

The *Asian Agricultural Survey* was prepared just as new high-yielding varieties of rice were beginning to be more widely adopted in Asia. It reflected the optimism of the time that substantial improvements in food security appeared to be within reach. The broad approach recommended by the survey was welcomed within ADB and provided impetus to the bank's early focus on agriculture.[18] Within a few years, large-scale programs to promote the new high-yielding varieties of rice had been introduced in Indonesia and ADB tailored its projects in the country to support the new programs.

---

[16] Prawiro, pp. 67–69.
[17] One of the members of the consultative committee advising on the activities of the study was Soesilo Prakoso, deputy regional representative in the FAO regional office in Bangkok.
[18] For a detailed survey of ADB's approach to working in the agriculture sector and the promotion of rural development, see Wihtol, 1988, *The Asian Development Bank*.

From the beginning of ADB's first activities in 1967, Indonesia was an important partner. Indeed, as will be seen below, for almost three decades into the 1990s, Indonesia was the single largest borrower from the bank. This was because Asia's two giant developing countries, India and the People's Republic of China (PRC), did not begin to borrow from ADB until the mid-1980s. It took some time for the total level of loans to India and the PRC to surpass the size of the bank's portfolio in Indonesia.

Reflecting the priority that the bank gave to establishing a strong program in Indonesia, several of ADB's earliest operational activities were carried out in the country. The bank's first technical assistance (TA) project grant approved for an individual member country was for a study of ways to improve food supplies in Indonesia. The TA specialist team began work in October 1967 and completed a report with recommendations for the government in early 1968 (Box 3.1). The following year, 1968, the government asked for more technical assistance in the agriculture sector. A second TA was approved to provide various experts to deliver advice on food policy, technical aspects of food production, and Indonesia's rural credit system.[19]

ADB aimed to expand its investment activities as well so a pipeline of project lending was built up. The bank's first loan from the concessional low-interest special fund facility was for an agriculture infrastructure project in Indonesia—the Tajum Irrigation Project, approved in 1969 (Box 3.2). Other projects soon followed. A second loan in 1969 was for an oil palm estate project in Sumatra. ADB lending for this project, as for the Tajum project, covered only the foreign exchange costs of the activity. It was agreed that the government itself would cover local costs.

The approach in the First Five-Year Development Plan (Repelita I) emphasized the need to expand the supply of *sandang-pangan* (basic goods) in Indonesia. Food production, especially, and the expanded output of essential commodities such as clothing, were seen as important. The goals of the plan were generally regarded as realistic. Nevertheless, many observers were cautious. After all, the development challenges at the time seemed immense and it was hard to see how resources could be mobilized in Indonesia to support new development programs. The country still needed to depend largely on the support of the international donor community to fund development activities.

---

[19]　ADB, 2016, *ADB Through the Decades*, Vol. 1, 21.

Box 3.1: ADB's First Technical Assistance Grant: Food Supply Issues in Indonesia

After discussions with the Government of Indonesia, it was agreed that the TA mission approved to start work in late 1967 would focus on the following issues:

(a) review the current situation at the time relating to the production and marketing of food crops, and, if relevant, other agriculture crops;

(b) identify bottlenecks and constraints having an adverse effect on maximizing the contribution of agriculture, especially food crops, to the economic stabilization and rehabilitation program at the time;

(c) provide recommendations on, first, ways in which bottlenecks and constraints on food production could be tackled by the government immediately during the stabilization and rehabilitation period, and second, preliminary actions that might be taken immediately to ease constraints in later periods; and

(d) assess the resources and budget needed to implement the recommendations of the mission.

ADB = Asian Development Bank, TA = technical assistance.
Source: Summarized from ADB, *Annual Report 1967*, 21.

Box 3.2: Tajum Irrigation Project

The Tajum Irrigation Project loan, approved in June 1969, was a key step for the bank. It was the first ADB loan for agriculture infrastructure, the first loan to Indonesia, and the first loan financed from the bank's concessional low-interest special funds (which later became the Asian Development Fund). The project was in a relatively less developed area in Central Java and aimed to help the Government of Indonesia strengthen irrigation systems. The project supported the introduction of improved agriculture methods and encouraged an efficient water management system. At that time, irrigation systems in Central Java were rather simple and crops in paddy fields were often reliant on rain-fed farming methods.

ADB = Asian Development Bank.
Source: ADB. 2016. *ADB through the Decades. Volume 1*, 18–20.

One encouraging aspect of the situation was that the confidence of the international community in the commitment of the new leadership in Indonesia was growing. At a meeting of the IGGI in Scheveningen in the Netherlands in mid-June 1967, bilateral donor countries agreed to try to find the relatively large amount of $500 million of assistance requested by Indonesia. America and Japan were the two largest donors. America offered to provide nearly half of the total amount (some of it as food aid), and Japan committed to help with another one-quarter. The multilateral development banks were still in the early stages of expanding their pipelines in Indonesia but the World Bank had concessional commitments—through the International Development Association (IDA)—of over $50 million, while ADB offered $10 million during 1969 with further loans being planned for the next few years.

ADB's programs during the first few years of Repelita I reflected the priorities of the new Indonesian plan. In 1970, ADB approved two projects with concessional soft-loan funds supporting a focus on the agriculture sector and rice production. At the time, according to Leon Mears, a leading international agricultural adviser in Indonesia, "food policy was rice policy."[20] The first project was a $10 million loan for an expansion of the state-owned Pusri fertilizer plant in Palembang in Sumatra. The second was for a smaller $2.7 million investment in the Gambarsari-Pesanggahan irrigation project in Central Java. The loan for the large Pusri plant was designed to help boost the production of fertilizer, urgently needed because of the plans set out in Repelita I to expand the *Bimbingan Massal* (mass guidance) national rice program known as Bimas, which had been initiated in the early 1960s. The loan for Pusri was a significant commitment because it was, at that stage, the largest concessional loan that had been approved by ADB and was also the first bank loan supported with cofinancing from other lenders.

During the next few years, the international assistance program to Indonesia expanded. ADB, too, broadened the range of activities it supported (Table 3.2). In 1971, several more loans for agriculture were approved—for rubber and oil plantations in North Sumatra; for improvements within Bank Rakyat Indonesia which specialized in the provision of credit for rural areas; and for a third irrigation project, the Sempor Dam in Kebumen regency in Central Java.

---

[20] Mears and Sidik Moeljono, 1981, Food Policy, 23.

Table 3.1: Notable Events, 1966–1976

Item	Comment
1966	
Indonesia joins ADB	As a founding member in Tokyo
1967	
Agricultural mission	First ADB TA to any member country
IGGI established	Donor group for aid coordination
1968	
Agricultural development study	Second TA provided to Indonesia for agriculture
1969	
Tajum Irrigation	First ADB loan to Indonesia
1970	
Pusri Fertilizer Plant Expansion	First cofinancing project for ADB
1971	
Bank Rakyat Indonesia modernization	First ADB loan in the financial sector in Indonesia
West Sumatra Power Supply	ADB's first power loan in Indonesia
1972	
Tanjung Priok Port	ADB's first loan for ports in Indonesia
1973	
Irian Jaya Power	First ADB involvement in Papua
1974	
East Java Agricultural Credit	ADB's first rural credit loan in Indonesia
1975	
Surabaya Institute of Technology	First ADB loan in Indonesia for technical education
1976	
Road improvement	First ADB loan in Indonesia for the road sector

ADB = Asian Development Bank, IGGI = Inter-Governmental Group on Indonesia, TA = technical assistance.

Table 3.2: ADB Early Lending to Indonesia, 1969–1973

Loan	Sector	$ million	Terms of loan
1969			
Tajum Irrigation	Irrigation	1.0	Concessional
Sawit Sebarang Oil Palm Estate	Plantation	2.4	Concessional
1970			
Pusri Fertilizer Plant Expansion	Fertilizer	10.0	Concessional
Gambarsari-Pesanggrahan Irrigation Rehabilitation	Irrigation	2.7	Concessional
1971			
North Sumatra Rubber and Oil Palm	Plantation	7.4	Concessional
Bank Rakyat Indonesia modernization	Banking	3.4	Concessional
Pontianak Power	Power	4.6	Concessional
Sempor Dam and Irrigation	Irrigation	9.2	Concessional
West Sumatra Power Supply	Power	7.1	Concessional
1972			
Wampu River Flood Control and Development	Flood control	5.9	Concessional
Tanjung Priok Port Development	Ports	5.3	Concessional
Riau Fisheries Development	Fisheries	2.5	Concessional
Surabaya Port Development	Ports	5.5	Concessional
Pekanbaru Power	Power	2.6	Concessional
1973			
Ujung Panjang Power	Power	6.3	Concessional
Irian Jaya Power	Power	2.6	Concessional
East Java Sugar	Plantation	17.5	Concessional and OCR
Irian Jaya Fisheries Development	Fisheries	7.9	Concessional and OCR
Minahasa Power	Power	7.9	Concessional and OCR

ADB = Asian Development Bank, OCR = ordinary capital resources.

Source: ADB annual reports, various years.

Power shortages across Indonesia were a severe constraint on development in the early 1970s. There had been very little investment in the power sector in Indonesia throughout the 1950s and 1960s. At the end of the 1960s, total installed capacity in the public electricity sector in Indonesia was less than 700 megawatts, an extremely low level for a country with a population of around 110 million people. Annual electricity output in the public sector in Indonesia was less than 20 kilowatt-hours per person (compared with around 7,000 kilowatt-hours per person in the US in the 1970s).[21] In reality, more than 70 years after public supplies of electricity were first introduced in Indonesia by the Dutch colonial government in the 1890s, only a small proportion of the Indonesian population had any significant access to electricity. At the time that Repelita I was launched, most Indonesians had no access to even a few bulbs for lighting in their homes at night or to enough power to use simple electrical items like fans, irons, or small refrigerators.

In response to what was regarded as an unacceptable situation, the Government of Indonesia looked to both the World Bank and ADB to provide finance to make a start in expanding power supplies across the nation. A widely accepted method of delivering much international aid at the time was to provide assistance through the design of specific projects rather than through program aid. This approach—reliance on project aid—was adopted in Indonesia in the electricity sector in the 1970s.[22] The World Bank posted electrical engineers as experts from its headquarters in Washington to Jakarta to work with the State Electricity Company (PLN) and the Indonesian Ministry of Public Works to prepare projects.

Consistent with this approach, ADB also prepared a pipeline of power projects for different parts of the country. Over the next several decades, both ADB and the World Bank would provide large amounts of finance to support many electric power projects in the generation, transmission, and distribution sectors of the industry in Indonesia. Indeed, there are few sectors in any developing country in the world which have received as much combined support from the World Bank and ADB as the electric power sector in Indonesia.

---

[21] McCawley, 2015, Infrastructure Policy, 273.

[22] The process of preparing a substantial list of activities for an assistance program containing much project aid is discussed in Posthumus, 1972, The Inter-Governmental Group on Indonesia.

In 1971, ADB began what was to become a large bank program in the power sector in Indonesia. Loans were approved for projects in Pontianak in Kalimantan (Borneo) and in West Sumatra. In Pontianak, as the provincial capital of West Kalimantan, export-oriented industries such as rubber, coconut, and forest projects were important. Power shortages were holding back the expansion of commercial activities in the capital. ADB agreed to provide a loan of $4.6 million to support the overall cost of the project of $6 million. As was the practice at the time, the ADB loan provided finance for the foreign exchange components of the project. It was agreed that the local rupiah costs would be financed by the government.

The second power loan approved in 1971 was for the foreign exchange costs of a project near Padang, the capital of the province of West Sumatra. Like many of the activities supported by the international community in Indonesia, the project was a complex activity. The project involved the completion of a hydropower plant at Batang Agam near the town of Bukittinggi as well as the purchase of urgently needed diesel-generator plants and the rehabilitation of local electricity systems. The ADB concessional loan financed $7.1 million of the costs of the activity on the understanding that the local costs of the rest of the $9.9 million project would be financed by Indonesia.

During the next few years ADB provided more loans in the power sector. In 1972, support for a project in Riau province in Sumatra was approved to help improve local power supplies which had been unreliable. In 1973, three more loans were approved. Two of the projects were in Sulawesi— one in the main capital of Makassar (known as Ujung Pandang at the time) and another in the Minahasa area of North Sulawesi. The third was in the eastern area of Indonesia in Jayapura in Papua.

ADB was providing support for other infrastructure sectors as well. Finance was agreed to for improvements at Indonesia's main ports, such as Tanjung Priok in Jakarta and Tanjung Perak in Surabaya. Maritime activities—both interisland shipping and international linkages—had always been a vital part of national life in Indonesia. But in the early 1970s, even Indonesia's main ports were in a parlous state. The facilities at ports and harbors had been neglected for several decades. Quays, lighthouses, and other navigational aids were badly run down and in many ports there had been little dredging for many years. The result was that in 1969, it had been reported that the "efficiency of shipping use is now only about a third of what it was in 1955."[23]

---

[23] Penny and Thalib, 1969, Survey, 26.

Significant loans were also approved for other sectors. In 1973, a relatively large loan of $17.5 million was approved to support increased production in the Jatiroto and Semboro sugar factories in East Java. The sugar industry had been a major industry in Java for many years before World War II so there were hopes that the output of the sector could be rehabilitated. In the outer islands in Papua, ADB provided $7.9 million for a project to strengthen the fisheries sector. The aim was to promote exports and create jobs by improving cold storage facilities and providing diesel engines for fishing vessels.

During the first four years of ADB's operations in Indonesia, until 1972, all of the bank's loans were approved on soft-loan concessional terms. These loans were, in effect, provided on near-grant terms. Typical repayment periods set down for the loans were between 25–30 years, with a grace period of perhaps 10 years before any repayments were required, and a concessional interest rate of around 2.5% per annum.

ADB could only support loan terms of this kind by drawing on the resources of the special funds established within the bank with contributions from donor countries. However the special fund resources were limited so they needed to be disbursed mainly for priority projects in countries coping with difficult economic circumstances. By 1973, when economic conditions in Indonesia had begun to improve, it was thought that the time had come to begin the process of graduating the borrowing program for Indonesia to draw on the more market-oriented ordinary capital resources (OCR) provided by ADB.

Changes in Indonesia

As ADB was strengthening its pipeline in Indonesia during this period, a number of events occurred that would influence the aid program that the international community, working through the IGGI, would deliver during the next few years. First, concerns about food policy—and especially about rice supplies—became an urgent issue for senior policymakers during 1972. The dry season in Java in 1972 proved to be especially dry. It is now known, over four decades later, that an El Niño weather event was occurring. But less was understood about El Niño weather patterns at the time. When it became clear, toward the end of 1972, that national rice stocks were lower than forecast, speculation in rice markets exacerbated uncertainty about the government's ability to manage national food supplies, and rice prices rose sharply. By early 1973, emergency imports of rice had helped stabilize prices. Nevertheless, the arrival of the emergency imports, partly dependent on donor grants of food aid, had underlined the pressing need to continue to support policies bolstering food security in Indonesia.

No sooner had rice prices been stabilized than other inflationary pressures emerged. In 1972, inflation in Indonesia had been mainly triggered by domestic factors arising from the shortages in food markets. But during the next few years, external factors fueled price increases. Indeed, although it was not clear at the time, the global economy was moving into a very difficult period of "stagflation" during which high rates of inflation were accompanied by low rates of economic growth and rising unemployment.

These uncertain times in global markets, however, brought a huge windfall gain to Indonesia. In late 1973, political tensions in the Middle East led to sharp increases in the world price of oil. The resulting oil shock served to divide developing countries in Asia into two groups. Oil importing countries (such as India and the Philippines) were hard hit, while oil-exporting countries (such as Indonesia) benefited. In a survey of the economic situation in early 1974, Grenville observed:[24]

> The oil price increase represents a great opportunity and challenge for Indonesia. Budget revenues in 1974/75 will…be two-and-a-half times the level of 1972/73 and, as a percentage of GDP, may rise from about 16 per cent in 1972/73 to 25 per cent or more. This opens the opportunity for greatly increased social welfare expenditure and for a much larger government role in investment.

Delivery of Aid

In the midst of this period of fast-moving economic change, several dramatic political events occurred which complicated the delivery of development assistance in Indonesia during the next few years. The first event occurred in November 1973 when the chair of the IGGI, Dutch Minister for Development Cooperation Jan Pronk, arrived for a visit in Jakarta. Pronk's arrival sparked small demonstrations and considerable debate about the role of foreign aid and investment in Indonesia's development strategy.

It was into that uncertain environment that Japanese Prime Minister Kakuei Tanaka arrived in Jakarta in early January 1974 for an official visit

---

[24]   Grenville, 1974, Survey, 4.

to Indonesia. Tanaka's visit was the trigger for large-scale demonstrations in Jakarta and elsewhere across Indonesia. The demonstrations quickly posed a major challenge to the authority of the government. It was clear, too, that the extensive unrest reflected widespread concern about the perceived influence of foreign investors and international agencies in Indonesia. The anti-foreign demonstrations in Jakarta in mid-1974 quickly became known as *Malapetaka Limabelas Januari* (Fifteenth of January Disturbances), shortened to the Malari disturbances. Within a short period of time, the government introduced a range of new policies to limit foreign influences in the country. The new policies were designed to emphasize the importance of the national commitment of the government.

At the time, it was not easy for either Indonesian policymakers or international observers to respond to the events. Too many things were changing too quickly. Within Indonesia, the reliance on foreign aid to help fund domestic development spending suddenly came under sustained attack. President Soeharto, in his new year message in 1974, defended the use of foreign aid. "Not a single cent [of aid money]," he said, "was used for non-developmental purposes."[25] The role that the highly respected team of economic technocrats had played since the late 1960s was also strongly criticized. One criticism of their role was that they had "exercised an economic dictatorship and were themselves, in turn, influenced by foreign economic interests, and called for closer cooperation with Japan and the replacement of aid loans, with their political ties, by commercial borrowing guaranteed by [state-owned oil company] Pertamina's wealth."[26]

However the suggestion that the ministerial team of economic technocrats was overly dependent on foreign advice was firmly discounted by staffers and other who worked with them. Bruce Glassburner, a US economist with much experience in Indonesia during the 1970s, noted that the national orientation, as he put it, of the technocrats was:[27]

> evident in their carefully guarded independence of judgement in policy matters. The assertion that they have allowed themselves to be dictated to by foreign advisers, most notably the IMF, AID, IBRD, and Harvard Advisory Group is quite at variance with the facts. Such advice has been sought, but more frequently than not, ignored. The

---

[25] Grenville, *ibid.*, 10.
[26] Published in the *Ekspres* newspaper; quoted in Grenville, *ibid.*, 10.
[27] Glassburner, 1978, Survey, 28.

most common experience of the foreign advisor is one of frustration, because his advisory efforts appear to be largely fruitless. The Indonesian economists choose the advisers they wish to listen to, and are very selective in the process.

Mari Pangestu observed that foreign advisers were "well utilized" by Ali Wardhana but that it was the Indonesian ministers who took the final decisions:[28]

> Pak Ali was instrumental in the use of technical assistance...the [Indonesian economic] technocrats would use inputs from many sources, but at the end they would design the policy that was appropriate for Indonesia, since they understood what could or could not be done given the political economic considerations. So they were in no way "steered" by foreign advice, but rather the foreign advisers were well utilized by the technocrats to meet Indonesia's needs. On the role of foreign support at the beginning of the new order when the economy was in bad shape, Pak Ali confidently related to us that the foreign agencies basically followed and agreed to the economic policies adopted by Indonesia because of the seriousness that the team showed in handling the economic problems and issues.

Against this background, with loud voices calling on the government to demonstrate clearer independence from foreign influence, the official response to the changing situation was complicated by the fact that the Second Five-Year Development Plan (Repelita II) was launched in March 1974. The plan had been prepared before the political mood had changed and before implications of the sharp increases in oil prices had been considered. Indonesian policymakers, therefore, were still uncertain as to how to respond to the new situation.

The international donor community, too, was considering what the implications of the new situation were for the provision of aid to Indonesia. On one hand, Indonesia suddenly had generous amounts of resources available to support development. Just 12 months earlier, it had seemed that the country's development efforts would be severely constrained by a shortage of resources. The resource constraints on Indonesia's development program therefore seemed less urgent. On the other hand, it was clear that Indonesia's long-term economic recovery was still less than

---

[28]   Pangestu, 2015, *A Tribute*, 6.

robust. Further, large-scale investment programs were still clearly needed to promote development.

In the midst of this uncertain environment in Indonesia and across the global community, the community continued to provide strong support to Indonesia. Writing in mid-1974, Arndt noted that:[29]

> Neither talk about excessive 'dependence' nor abundance of oil revenue deterred the Indonesian authorities from putting to the IGGI consortium the usual request for aid, nor did the aid donors show any public hesitation in acceding to the request. The amount asked for was $850 million for 1974/75. Since not all donor countries at the Amsterdam meeting of IGGI early in May announced their pledges, the precise amount was not yet clear, but the aggregate, including credit by the international banks, seemed likely to exceed $900 million.

The international community decided that there was still an important role for donors to play in providing both resources and technical assistance to Indonesia. As a result, international organizations such as ADB welcomed the new resources available to Indonesia from the oil boom of 1973–1974 while, at the same time, continuing to plan to expand their own programs.

However the willingness of donors to maintain providing substantial amounts of assistance was tested during the next two years when the debt-fueled Pertamina crisis came to dominate headlines in Indonesia and abroad. Although rumors had been circulating for months about high levels of debt that the major state-owned oil company Pertamina had been entering into, it was not until June 1975 that Planning Minister Widjojo Nitisastro provided a detailed report to the Indonesian Parliament.[30] It turned out that Pertamina had entered into several billions of dollars of unauthorized borrowings and had been reluctantly forced to turn to the government for support when short-term borrowings had fallen due. The revelations of large-scale excessive borrowings and mismanagement in Pertamina dealt a serious blow to Indonesia's credibility in international circles as an effective development partner. Nevertheless, once an official explanation had been provided to the Indonesian Parliament and it became clear that the government was moving to tackle the crisis,

---

[29] Arndt, 1974, Survey, 20.
[30] The official government explanation to the parliament is contained in Chapter 16, Pertamina Crisis 1975, in Widjojo, 2011, *Indonesian Development Experience*, 179.

international donors agreed to help Indonesia implement reforms which included much closer supervision of Pertamina's operations.

Next Steps for the Bank

During these years ADB broadened its program in Indonesia in various ways. Partly, the changes reflected new priorities of the government set out in Repelita II and in official decisions announced by ministers from time to time. But partly the changes reflected new approaches adopted by ADB as well.

In the mid-1970s, there was increasing discussion across the international development community about the need to look beyond economic growth as a main policy objective and to widen the approach to development challenges. ADB was being urged by donor nations and Asian member countries alike to pay more attention to socioeconomic development projects and programs. At the same time, borrowing member countries were calling on ADB to reform various aspects of the way it managed its operations—to expand the use of local currency financing, to improve procedures for the procurement of goods and consultants, and to introduce program loans.

The ADB pipeline of projects in Indonesia broadened out over a wider range of sectors during the mid and late 1970s (Table 3.3). Loans were approved in 1974 to double the capacity of a spinning mill in Cipadang near Bandung in West Java and to construct a cement plant at Baturaja in South Sumatra to help strengthen domestic supplies of key commodities. The expansion of the Cipadang spinning mill was expected to reduce reliance on yarn imports, while the construction of the cement plant at Baturaja was planned to contribute toward national and regional self-sufficiency in cement production. The request for ADB financing for these projects reflected the long-standing objective of strengthening self-sufficiency in the industrial sector in Indonesia.

The next two years—1975 and 1976—marked the final two years of ADB's first decade of work in Indonesia. From one point of view, the activities of the bank were still largely responsive to requests from Indonesia and still lacked firm strategic directions. But already, and less noticeably, ADB was beginning to expand a long-term program focused on the provision of basic infrastructure in Indonesia.

Table 3.3: ADB Lending to Indonesia, 1974–1976

Loan	Sector	$ million	Loan Terms
1974			
Fiber production and processing	Agriculture	13.2	OCR
Bandung Water Supply	Water	11.5	Concessional
Baturaja Cement	Industry	37.0	OCR
Cipadang spinning mill	Industry	13.7	OCR
1975			
Java Fisheries Development	Fisheries	13.2	Concessional
Gohor Lama Palm Oil Processing	Plantation	11.3	OCR
Garang hydroelectric	Power	2.7	OCR
Teluk Lada Area Development (Phase I)	Development	12.2	OCR
Surabaya Institute of Technology	Education	14.5	OCR
1976			
Maninjau Hydropower	Power	39.7	OCR
Road improvement	Roads	20.0	OCR
Bandung Urban Development and Sanitation	Urban	1.1	OCR
Second Road	Roads	48.2	OCR

ADB = Asian Development Bank, OCR = ordinary capital resources.
Source: ADB Annual Reports, various years.

In 1976, a large bank loan for $39.7 million was approved to support a project to supply power in West Sumatra, including in the area near the provincial capital of Padang. At the same time, without fanfare, ADB was beginning a roads program that would become a major part of the bank's work in Indonesia over the next several decades. In 1976, two road projects were approved, both for investments in Java. The first was to support the improvement of roads in Central Java and East Java. The second was to provide finance for an upgraded highway between the major towns of Surabaya and Malang in East Java. ADB's programs to attract financing from the Middle East following the oil price increases of 1973–1974 were reflected in the financing for the project: The Saudi Fund for Development provided cofinancing amounting to $50 million.

Annual Meeting in Indonesia

In 1976 Indonesia hosted in Jakarta the Ninth Annual Meeting of the bank. The event had symbolic importance for Indonesia. It signaled growing national confidence as a member of the international community and was held in the newly opened and impressive Borobudur Hotel, not far from the *Istana Negara* (National Palace) in central Jakarta. Since being confirmed as president of Indonesia in 1967, President Soeharto had generally made a practice of avoiding the international limelight. However he presided over the opening of the ADB meeting. In his presidential speech he outlined Indonesia's view on a range of key aspects of international economic relations at the time.[31]

After welcoming delegates to Jakarta, the president delivered a clear statement of the importance of development to Indonesia:

> We, in Indonesia…put our development efforts at the highest level in the national scale of priorities. We bolster our development with the spirit of struggle as strong as that which made us successful in gaining our national independence thirty years ago. Nation-building is the continuation of our independence struggle.

The strong focus on development reflected the emphasis that Soeharto himself had, since becoming president almost a decade earlier, in elevating the goal of *pembangunan* (development) to become the central theme of long-term economic policy in Indonesia. And pressing home the theme, the president linked the priority for development in Indonesia with the dramatic changes taking place in other parts of Asia. He said that:

> …the prevailing motivation and diligence of the Indonesian nation are part of a general pattern growing nowadays in Asia. In this region, progressive changes are now taking place. If, twenty-five years ago, this region was engulfed by endless struggles and transformation from colonial order to independence, today the most predominant aspect is the effort to give substance to independence through development.

Soeharto also referred to the gap between industrialized countries and developing nations. He said that world tensions reflected "the economic inequality and the low standard of living of the majority of mankind." And turning to the role of ADB in the region, and of the need for finance, he observed that:

---

[31]   Soeharto, 1976, Address.

...the Asian Development Bank must contribute its share, joining in action with developing Asian nations in order to accelerate the development endeavour they are busily engaged in. ... One of the questions faced by developing Asian countries...is the lack of funds to generate development. Providing a greater amount of financial assistance should actually become the principal attention of the Asian Development Bank.

A final theme was that industrialized nations had an obligation to help developing nations. Advanced nations, the president said, should provide increased contributions to ADB to support development in Asia.

The central messages that President Soeharto emphasized reflected the views that other leaders across developing Asia had supported for many years. Not all of the priorities that the president pointed to were likely to be universally agreed by delegates from industrial country members of ADB. But in pointing to these issues, Soeharto was taking up some of the central themes set down in the Bandung Conference 20 years earlier. The president was reminding international delegates that developing countries in Asia had views about development and international relations that had been frequently outlined since the end of the colonial period in Asia at the end of World War II.

Ten Years Old

In 1976, ADB was approaching its teenage years of operations in Indonesia. The bank had begun work in Indonesia in 1967 with strong support delivered through a TA program to bolster food security. During the next few years, bank activities had first focused on work in the agriculture and irrigation sectors before broadening out into other infrastructure sectors such as power, water, and education.

In 1977, addressing his first ADB annual meeting as bank president, Taroichi Yoshida discussed these trends. He noted that lending for agriculture remained a key part of ADB's work and that in 1975 and 1976, loans for agriculture and agro-industry had made up over 30% of bank lending. Nevertheless, drawing on the results of ADB's research about challenges in the agriculture sector, Yoshida emphasized that the main constraints on agricultural production in developing countries in Asia at the time were environmental and institutional.

The work of ADB and other international agencies had supported strong growth in Indonesia since the late 1960s. In 1967, very few households in Indonesia had any access to electricity at all. Electricity consumption per capita, at 15 kilowatt-hours per year, reflected this situation. During the next few years, production began to expand markedly as international agencies including ADB provided funds for projects in the electric power sector. By 1976, electricity consumption per capita had doubled to 30 kilowatt-hours per year; to be sure, electricity was still in very short supply but at least output was beginning to increase rapidly. Food production had begun to expand in an encouraging way as well: By 1976, rice production was almost 16 million tons, over 60% higher than the output of 9.3 million tons recorded in 1967.

When President Soeharto had said, at the annual meeting of ADB in Jakarta in 1976, that "We, in Indonesia . . . put our development efforts at the highest level in the national scale of priorities," he was defining the broad outlines of the work that ADB needed to address in its second decade in Indonesia. Looking ahead, the program of ADB activities needed to continue to focus on development. In the next decade, the bank would widen both the scope of its sectoral activities, and the types of loans and other support it would provide in Indonesia.

The Asian Development Bank has made its first operational commitment by offering technical assistance to Indonesia in the field of food production.

ADB President Takeshi Watanabe said yesterday the first operational effort of the bank was in response to Indonesia's request.

A rapid expansion of food production in 1967 and 1968 is generally considered to be of crucial importance to the success of the stabilization and rehabilitation program recently launched by the Indonesian government.

The ADB's technical assistance mission to Indonesia will concern itself with an identification of the problems of the transitional period, with particular reference to the current production and marketing situation relating to food crops, Watanabe said.

It is hoped, he added, that the mission's work would result in a framework of recommendations that would enable the Indonesian government to overcome identified bottlenecks and step up food production.

The ADB's technical offer to Indonesia is a followup of the study made by the bank's reconnaissance team, headed by Dr. Bong H. Kay, which visited that country in June-July.

An article from *The Philippines Herald* on 1 September 1967 discusses the first technical assistance (TA) activity in Indonesia, which supported efforts to increase food production. It was also the first ADB TA in any of the bank's member countries.

The first ADB loan to Indonesia was to support the Tajum Irrigation Project in Central Java in 1969.

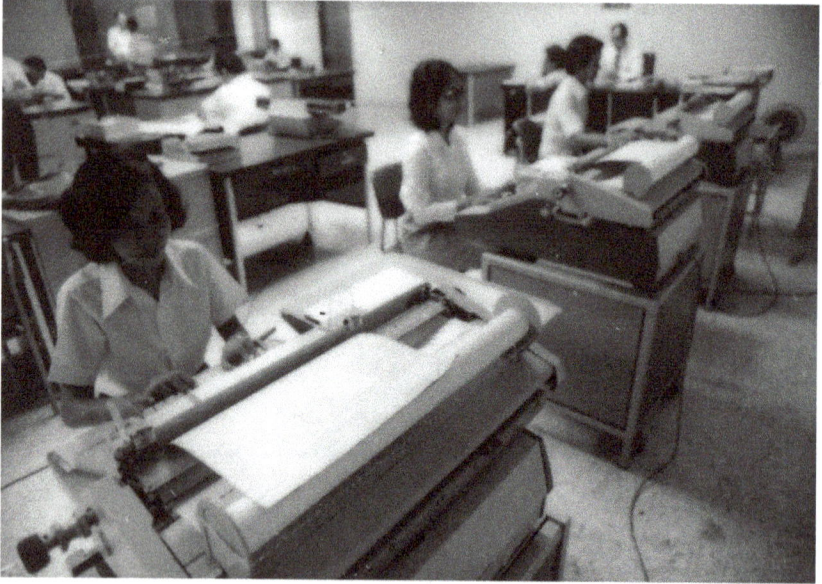

An ADB loan to modernize Bank Rakyat Indonesia in 1971 was the first ADB project in the financial sector in the country.

The Institute of Technology Surabaya was the recipient of the first ADB loan in Indonesia for technical education (1975).

The Road Improvement Project, approved in 1976, was the first ADB loan for the road sector in Indonesia.

Indonesian President Soeharto (*left*) presides over the opening of the Ninth Annual Meeting of ADB in Jakarta in 1976. Vice President Sri Sultan Hamengkubuwono IX (*second left*) and ADB President Shiro Inoue (*second right*) were also in attendance.

CHAPTER 4

A Widening Role
(1977–1986)

As the second decade of the Asian Development Bank (ADB) story in Indonesia began, the immediate prospects for the Indonesian economy were somewhat uncertain. On one hand, the worst of the difficulties posed by the Pertamina crisis had largely been overcome, improvements in the international economy were encouraging, and the major investment surge made possible by the 1973–1974 boom was fueling growth. On the other hand, it was unclear how long the revenues from the oil windfall would continue to hold up. Senior Indonesian policymakers were already considering what adjustments would be needed when the revenues began to fall away.

The oil-fueled investment boom had taken a strong hold by 1976 following large increases in government spending during the previous several years. Indeed, in the face of rapid increases in development expenditures, there were concerns that many of the plans for new projects had not been properly scrutinized. There were also worries that the unexpected push to get new projects underway had meant that high-technology but relatively capital-intensive schemes had been adopted. The ambitious list of national projects mentioned included a new domestic satellite and associated telecommunications systems, color TV, fertilizer plants, oil refineries, an expansion of the Krakatau steel plant in Banten, substantial increased spending on electricity projects, additions to the Garuda Indonesia jet fleet, and an expansion of a proposed aluminum plant at Asahan in North Sumatra.

Not everybody in Indonesia agreed with these spending plans. There were concerns about the capital-intensive nature of the projects and critics pointed to the need to create jobs. The international donor community, for its part, needed to consider the implications of the public sector investment boom. For one thing, in some cases the rapid expansion in project activities funded out of the Indonesian development budget made it difficult for Indonesian agencies to devote enough attention to working with international partners. For another, the oil boom and its consequences had led to rising resentment in Organisation for Economic Co-operation and Development (OECD) industrial nations toward oil-producing countries such as Indonesia. The question arose of whether foreign aid was still needed if countries such as Indonesia could afford to finance large investment programs and, at the same time, build up foreign exchange reserves.

New Challenges

However by early 1977, there were already signs that the main economic stimulus in Indonesia from the 1973–1974 oil boom was beginning to wane. And new problems were emerging. In the agriculture sector, worrying issues had come to the fore. The Bimas rice intensification program which had been accorded high priority for over a decade was running into difficulties. Indeed, it was not yet clear that the Green Revolution would succeed in Indonesia. Difficulties in the agriculture sector included insect pests, lagging fertilizer use, and mounting arrears in credit repayments. These issues were serious because they posed a threat to the tenuous state of food security in Indonesia.

These and other challenges meant that by 1978, it appeared that the period of the oil boom had ended. It seemed that, thanks to the oil bonanza, Indonesia had been able to maintain a high rate of growth of consumption and capital formation but that a difficult period of structural adjustment to lower rates of growth lay ahead.

Discussions about long-term development strategy during 1978 were influenced by official thinking about the Third Five-Year Development Plan (Repelita III), due to come into operation in April 1979. It was accepted that the rate of economic growth would slow from the annual rate of 7.6% during the Second Five-Year Development Plan (Repelita II) period (1974–1979) to perhaps 6.5%. There was also considerable emphasis in public discussion about the need "to make development more equitable."[1] And then, in an entirely unexpected move, the Government of Indonesia announced a large devaluation of the rupiah in mid-November 1978. The size of the devaluation—50% or 33.3% depending on the method of calculation chosen—underlined the fact that the intention of the move was to encourage substantial structural adjustment across the Indonesian

[1] These issues of development strategy were outlined in detail by Soedjatmoko, a well-known Indonesian intellectual, in Soedjatmoko, 1978, National Policy Implications.

economy. It was generally assumed that the prime objective was to develop a more export-oriented economy so that Indonesia was less dependent on oil revenues and to deliver a boost to both the primary sector and manufacturing with a consequent gain in employment.

External Shocks

But no sooner than policy measures had been introduced to encourage economic adjustment to the end of the oil boom, further events disrupted international markets. In early 1979, a second oil shock was triggered by the revolution in Iran and other events in the Middle East. Oil prices rose sharply, from around $13 per barrel in 1978 to over $30 by the end of 1979. The jump in the price of oil quickly led to concerns, especially in industrialized countries, about the likely recessionary impact of higher energy costs.

Despite these concerns, the new chair of the United States (US) Federal Reserve, Paul Volcker, decided to give priority to fighting inflation rather than stimulating the economy. Although the US economy was beginning to slow sharply, on 6 October 1979 Volcker announced that US monetary policy would be tightened—a decision which was immediately dubbed the "Volcker Shock." The federal funds rate, a key tool of monetary policy, rose quickly from around 11% in 1979 to over 20% in 1981. The abrupt tightening of monetary policy in the US quickly spilled over to the global economy. Interest rates soon began to rise across the world.

These events brought mixed blessings for Indonesia. On one hand, Indonesian policymakers were concerned about the implications of a deterioration of economic conditions in industrialized countries. Addressing the annual meeting of the International Monetary Fund (IMF) and World Bank in September 1980, Minister for Finance Ali Wardhana said:[2]

> On the whole, the situation of the world economy, whether examined for the short run or the long run, remains bleak. Growth, inflation and balance of payments developments continue to be precarious...Most disturbing of all is the widening gap between the countries of the North and South...the increasing resource gap faced by developing countries, especially the poorer among them, not only dooms them to

---

[2] Ali Wardhana, 1980 Indonesia: Ali Wardhana Governor of the Fund, Chapter 13 in Pangestu, 2015, *A Tribute*, 85.

live at often subhuman levels but it also threatens to become a serious impediment as far as the world economy is concerned.

Ali Wardhana noted that greater flows of international resources to developing countries were needed. Some sources of additional flows that had been suggested, he said, included increased official development assistance, improved access to capital markets, increased levels of investments, and expanded flows from new financial entities.

On the other hand, the second oil boom dramatically eased the constraints on development programs in Indonesia, at least in the short-term. In summarizing the effects of the oil price increases, in mid-1980 Boediono observed:[3]

> …recently issued 1979/80 provisional figures show that during the year, the country's foreign exchange reserves increased by over $1.6 billion, or 58 per cent of the level of reserves at the beginning of the year. In nominal terms, the increase is the largest ever experienced. In terms of real purchasing power, the increase is greater than that during the 1973/74 oil boom…Another notable feature is the emergence of a current account surplus of almost $2.4 billion. This phenomenon of surplus in the current account is the first in the history of independent-Indonesia.

But looking further ahead, Boediono, like many other Indonesian policymakers at the time, remained cautious:[4]

> Behind this reasonably bright short run picture, the country's longer term development problems remain as pressing as ever. An extra $2–3 billion of foreign exchange reserves is just a scratch over the surface of these formidable long-term problems. The key issue is how to sustain the country's capacity to finance (preferably out of her own strength and resources) her development in the coming years.

Among other things, Boediono said that a longer-term view regarding the management of the nation's natural resources was needed. As things turned out, this thoughtful view of the potential benefits of the second oil boom for Indonesia would soon turn out to be justified.

---

[3]   Boediono, 1980, Survey, 2
[4]   Ibid., 2.

Donor Programs 1977–1980

Against this background, donors continued to provide strong support to Indonesia (Appendix Table 3.1). At the Inter-Governmental Group on Indonesia (IGGI) meeting in mid-1976, donors committed to bilateral programs of aid of $1.1 billion, an increase of 22% over the level announced the previous year. In addition, the World Bank and ADB announced tentative plans for another $670 million in loans. The following year, contrary to reports that some member countries might scale down their aid levels, at the 20th IGGI meeting in Amsterdam donor governments again increased their aid commitments.

By this stage, for several years donors had been adjusting their aid programs to reflect the priorities that had been outlined in Repelita II in 1974. Greater attention to regional development, along with a focus on social objectives, had been emphasized in the plan. Nevertheless, infrastructure projects in the road, irrigation, and power sectors were also still important in donor programs, reflecting a belief that the provision of infrastructure, including in rural areas, was one of the best ways of raising productive capacity and reducing poverty. A significant part of the infrastructure effort was directed toward supporting development in the outer islands. New transmigration and land settlement schemes were also being undertaken with the support of international agencies, especially the World Bank.

The approach at IGGI meetings was to, first, spend time discussing policy issues and, then, for donors to announce their plans for assistance during the coming year. In 1977, for example, the IGGI meeting was presented, as usual, with a detailed World Bank "grey cover" report on economic developments in Indonesia which also included estimates of Indonesia's expected external resource requirements in the year ahead. The report was, as most official reports on the Indonesian economy at the time tended to be, cautiously optimistic in pointing encouragingly toward recent gains while, at the same time, noting challenges ahead. Recent gains mentioned in the 1977 report included progress in resolving the Pertamina crisis, a reduction in the rate of inflation, and hopeful signs of a decline in birth rates reflecting the impact of family planning programs during the previous decade. In response, during the IGGI meeting, delegates from some partner countries expressed concern about challenges such as continuing problems in the administration of aid and inequalities in the distribution of gains from development.

The following year, IGGI donors met in May 1978 in Amsterdam. Broadly, the level of assistance that the international community agreed to provide to Indonesia remained constant in real terms. Among bilateral partners, Japan maintained an established commitment of one-third of the total of bilateral assistance while the US pledged roughly one-quarter. Commitments from the multilateral development banks had been rising so that the amount offered from multilateral sources in 1978 had grown to surpass the total flows from bilateral donors.

The tone of the official press communique following the meeting was one of general satisfaction with the performance of the Indonesian economy. But as usual, some concerns were mentioned by donors. In fact, the concerns reflected those expressed by Indonesian policymakers at the time—maintenance of overall economic growth in the face of expected stagnation in the oil sector and the related problem of finding alternative foreign exchange earnings; job creation; improvement in the pattern of income distribution; and reduced dependence on food imports.

In 1979, the donor group met again to discuss the broad approach toward development set out in Repelita III for the period 1979–1984. The following year, at the 23rd IGGI meeting in May, donors agreed to an aid program of around $2.1 billion for 1980–1981. As was often the case at IGGI meetings, the estimates of the precise level of pledges were not entirely clear because not all donors offered firm details of what they planned to provide. Nevertheless, in broad terms, the total level of donor assistance remained constant in real terms. All countries except Canada, the United Kingdom and the US raised their aid commitments.

ADB Programs

At the beginning of ADB's second decade in Indonesia, there was still much concern on the part of Indonesian policymakers about the performance of the agriculture sector, especially about food security. Reflecting these concerns, the bank's work continued to include a range of activities in the agriculture sector.

The doubts about food security arose because the expected increases in rice production resulting from the Green Revolution had not materialized. The disquiet about these trends was reflected in the Second Asian Agricultural Survey, a major study sponsored by ADB in 1977. The survey suggested that the benefits of the Green Revolution had not been as effective as hoped in lifting living standards in rural areas across Asia:[5]

> For the region as a whole, food production growth has barely kept pace with population growth, and in some countries, despite the introduction of the new foodgrain technology, per capita cereal production actually fell during the past decade. ... Overall, the most optimistic view which can be taken of the food situation is that the region is not much worse off now than at the time of the first Asian Agricultural Survey [in 1967/68] ... Rural poverty is thus particularly widespread [in the Developing Member Countries of ADB] and there is a general consensus that the problem has worsened considerably in the past decade.

In broad terms, the trends in Indonesia were similar to those in other countries in the region. In 1980, a leading expert on the rice sector in Indonesia, Leon Mears, said that "the goal of self-sufficiency in rice by 1985 (or any reasonable time thereafter) will be very hard to achieve."[6]

This focus on the need to pay more attention to the distribution of the benefits flowing from the Green Revolution reflected growing concern about the issue of poverty in Indonesia. Until the mid-1970s there had been a reluctance in official policy circles in Indonesia to openly discuss poverty. However, following both growing interest in international circles and an influential report by Professor Sayogyo of Bogor Agricultural University in 1975, the measurement of poverty and policies needed to address the issues began to be more widely discussed.[7]

The main emphasis of the Asian Agricultural Survey was on challenges and opportunities within the agriculture sector across developing Asia. But to assist policymakers in designing programs to provide foreign aid in agriculture, the survey included a thoughtful discussion of the role of international assistance. The views set out reflected international thinking about foreign aid at the time. The recommendations were intended to encourage ADB and other development agencies to introduce reforms to improve aid delivery.

---

[5] ADB, 1978. *Rural Asia*. 2–3.
[6] Mears, 1981, Food Policy, in Booth and McCawley, 1981, *The Indonesian Economy*, 49.
[7] Sayogyo. 1975. *Usaha Perbaikan Gizi Keluarga*. Booth, 2016, *Economic Change*, 179, discusses Sayogyo's approach and provides a brief history of the measurement of poverty in Indonesia.

In broad terms, the survey suggested that both donors and aid-recipient agencies should look for ways to encourage increased aid flows and to find ways of streamlining the delivery and the monitoring of assistance (Box 4.1). During the next few years, ADB adopted the main suggestions. In ADB's program in Indonesia, the recommendations from the survey provided a road map for changes in the bank's work program into the 1980s.

Box 4.1: Summary of Recommendations from the Second Asian Agricultural Survey, 1978

Changes suggested for donors

1. Increase aid flows. More food aid may be necessary.

2. Decrease the costs of aid.

3. Increase the proportion of program lending, where justified.

4. Increase the amount of foreign exchange aid in local currency expenditures.

5. For program lending, revise loan appraisal procedures to accommodate the particular requirements of a program lending approach.

6. Relax procurement and disbursement procedures and promote regional procurement.

7. Avoid tying aid to procurement in the donor country.

8. Introduce better statistical support for operations in rural areas.

Changes suggested for aid-recipient countries

1. Implement more self-help efforts in parallel with aid approvals to improve the additive effect of aid.

2. Avoid Exim bank credits from donor countries for the agricultural sector, and for employment-oriented and rural development programs, unless thoroughly justified.

3. Prepare a longer portfolio of better-prepared proposals for foreign aid. Proposals should reflect an employment-oriented approach.

4. Improve the rural data base to facilitate aid flows that contain substantial amounts for local currency expenditure.

Source: ADB, 1978, *Rural Asia*.

As well as supporting projects in agriculture, during the next few years ADB continued to expand its activities in the infrastructure sectors where it had a comparative advantage. Projects in power, roads, and ports were approved, and the earlier support for education was extended to a number of new activities. In the power sector, there was some investment in the generation sector but the most significant support was for transmission projects: in 1977, $45 million was approved for power distribution networks in Central Java and North Sumatra; in 1978 a second power distribution loan supported expansions in transmission and distribution lines in West Java; and in 1979 a large loan for $83.6 million was arranged to finance an extra high-voltage transmission line in Java as well as other facilities (Table 4.1).

One new area of activity for ADB was support, agreed to in 1978, for a transmigration and area development project in Sulawesi. During the 1970s, the government had begun to give increasing attention to various aspects of population policy across the nation.[8] The family planning programs adopted in the late 1960s and expanded during the early 1970s had generally been regarded as successful. In the mid-1970s, the government decided to supplement these efforts by promoting transmigration out of Java with the aim of resettling large numbers of people in Sumatra and Kalimantan.[9] The World Bank provided considerable support for these transmigration schemes while ADB generally focused on activities in other sectors.

To support the government's population programs, ADB approved financing for the Southeast Sulawesi Transmigration and Area Development project. The scheme involved the establishment of new transmigrant irrigated settlements, improvements to infrastructure such as roads in existing settlements and villages, and strengthening agriculture services. The bank's project was undertaken with over $5 million of cofinancing from the European Economic Community (EEC) and $10 million from the Islamic Development Bank, based in Jeddah in Saudi Arabia, which was looking to expand its pipeline of activities in Indonesia.

---

[8]   A survey of population policies during the 1970s is in Hull, T.H., and Ida Bagus Mantra, 'Indonesia's Changing Population,' Chapter 7 in Booth and McCawley, 1981, *The Indonesian Economy*.

[9]   A summary of World Bank work in transmigration in Indonesia is at World Bank, Independent Evaluation Group, 2012, Transmigration in Indonesia.

Table 4.1: ADB Lending to Indonesia, 1977–1981

Loan	Sector	$ million	Loan Terms
1977			
Lodoyo Irrigation	Irrigation	20.5	OCR
Power Distribution	Power	45.0	OCR
Fourth Port	Ports	17.5	OCR
Bank Pembangunan Indonesia (Bapindo)	Finance	30.0	OCR
Baturaja Cement (supplementary)	Industry	23.0	OCR
1978			
Second Power Distribution	Power	31.4	OCR
Third Road	Roads	34.0	OCR
Bali Irrigation	Irrigation	18.0	OCR
Ujung Pandang II	Power	26.0	OCR
Senior Technical Schools	Education	24.0	Concessional
Teluk Lada Area Development (Phase II)	Development	3.4	OCR
Fifth Port	Ports	26.3	OCR
Southeast Sulawesi transmigration and development	Rural	34.3	OCR
1979			
Bandung urban development	Urban	32.3	OCR
University of Hasanuddin (Sulawesi)	Education	25.0	Concessional
Java extra high-voltage transmission	Power	83.6	OCR
Fourth Road	Roads	27.0	OCR
Tulungagung Drainage	Irrigation	39.0	OCR
South Kalimantan Livestock Development	Livestock	20.5	OCR
1980			
Second Java extra high-voltage transmission	Power	60.7	OCR
Sumatra Fisheries Development	Fisheries	14.0	OCR
Cibaliung Irrigation	Irrigation	35.0	OCR
Lower Citanduy Irrigation	Irrigation	55.2	OCR
Fifth Road	Roads	28.0	OCR
Second Senior Technical Schools	Education	26.0	OCR
Small Towns Water Supply Sector	Water	32.0	OCR
Palm oil processing and smallholder	Plantation	28.0	OCR

continued on next page

Table 4.1   *continued*

Loan	Sector	$ million	Loan Terms
1981			
Nucleus Estate and Smallholder Cotton	Plantation	23.0	OCR
Wadaslintang Multipurpose	Multipurpose	87.7	OCR
Bali Irrigation	Irrigation	33.6	OCR
University of North Sumatra	Education	26.0	OCR
Sumatra Livestock Development	Livestock	16.7	OCR
Surabaya Distribution and Sulawesi Power	Power	76.0	OCR
Semarang Water Supply	Water	35.5	OCR
Medan urban development	Urban	39.3	OCR

ADB = Asian Development Bank, OCR = ordinary capital resources.
Source: ADB annual reports, various years.

During ADB's second decade of operations in Indonesia, bank projects were increasingly designed to combine ADB's own funds with cofinancing from partner financial institutions. By expanding cofinancing arrangements, the bank was aiming to strengthen its role as a financial intermediary and to promote expanded flows of external capital into Indonesia. ADB's international financial partners found it useful to join with the bank in supporting projects in Indonesia because cofinancing procedures reduced their investment risks and transactions costs. No borrowing country in Asia had ever defaulted on an ADB loan. From the point of view of cofinancing partners, the administrative procedures required by international agencies such as ADB and the World Bank were relatively straightforward. The result was that in 1978, for example, ADB was able to attract cofinancing of over $40 million for the Fifth Port Project at Belawan, the major harbor for Medan in North Sumatra. In 1980, cofinancing was arranged for the two largest bank activities approved during the year, the second Java extra high-voltage transmission project and the Lower Citanduy Irrigation scheme in Central Java.

As well as working with international partners to encourage increased international flows to developing countries in Asia, during the 1970s the bank had been exploring ways to improve operations in domestic financial markets in borrowing countries. For a time, it seemed that a program of strengthening local development finance institutions (DFIs) such as domestic development banks might be effective. The aim was to work with these local institutions to channel long-term capital to the private sector and to help develop domestic security markets. It was also hoped that that local DFIs would prove to be an effective vehicle to provide increased financing, through on-lending, to small and medium-sized enterprises.

In Jakarta, the Indonesian Development Bank (Bapindo) appeared to be a promising local partner. Bapindo needed to access foreign currency resources to meet the foreign exchange needs of both private and public sector agencies within Indonesia to finance development projects. With this goal in mind, in 1977 ADB approved a $30 million loan to Bapindo. The World Bank, too, had approved support for Bapindo several years earlier in 1972, and later agreed to continuing assistance during the 1980s.

As things turned out, Bapindo's operations ran into various problems. Economic conditions in Indonesia became difficult during the deep economic recession of 1983–1984 and Bapindo's financial situation deteriorated. Later, in the 1990s, Bapindo's reputation was damaged when a domestic borrower embezzled a large amount of money from the institution. Bapindo was finally closed during the 1997–1998 financial crisis in Indonesia when it was merged with three other banks to form a new institution, Bank Mandiri.

The experience that ADB had with Bapindo reflected problems that emerged over time in working with DFIs in other countries in the region. For a range of reasons, DFIs in Asia during the 1970s and 1980s often failed to achieve their goals. Too many institutions were held back by organizational weaknesses, mismanagement, political pressures, and a difficult economic environment. Over time, ADB decided to scale back its involvement with DFIs.[10]

Changes in Approach

Other changes in ADB's operations were taking place as the bank implemented reforms with the aim of broadening its approach to operations in the region. The international development agenda had widened during the 1970s and would continue to expand in the 1980s and 1990s. The ADB program in Indonesia reflected these changes (Table 4.2).

---

[10] A survey of ADB's experience in supporting financial intermediation for private sector development and small and medium enterprises is in ADB, 2008, *Support for Financial Intermediation*.

Table 4.2: Notable Events, 1977–1986

Item	Comment
1977	
Bank Pembangunan Indonesia	First development finance institution (DFI) loan by ADB in Indonesia
1978	
Sulawesi Transmigration and Area Development	First involvement by ADB in transmigration in Indonesia
1979	
Hasanuddin University	First ADB loan for a university project in Indonesia
1980	
First ADB sector loan	Small Towns Water Supply Sector project approved for Indonesia was ADB's first sector loan
1981	
Wadaslintang Multipurpose	Major irrigation, flood controls and power project in Central Java, and largest ADB loan in Indonesia so far
1982	
Brackish Water Aquaculture	First ADB loan in Indonesia for small-scale *tambak* (brackish water) low-income farmers
1983	
Major structural adjustments introduced	Devaluation of the rupiah and major tax changes marked significant moves toward deregulation of the economy
1984	
TA program loan for multi-sectoral feasibility studies	First ADB loan of this kind in any country
1985	
Health and Population Project	First ADB loan for health in Indonesia
1986	
Special project implementation loan	To assist with the need to implement structural adjustment measures following the fall in oil prices

New forms of lending began to be introduced in the late 1970s. During the first decade of operations ADB had been a project bank; loans had been provided for individual projects. But it had become clear that developing countries in Asia needed to borrow for other purposes as well—for multiproject loans, for example, which financed a group of small activities each of which was too small to justify a separate loan, or for sector lending to finance a group of subprojects in a specific sector.

In June 1980, ADB introduced sector lending.[11] This new form of lending was one of the steps being progressively implemented to broaden the range of services and loans that the bank offered. Sector loans were designed to include modest amounts of program support and local cost financing for borrowing countries. The aim was to help finance the investment needs in specific sectors or subsectors and to help borrowing countries strengthen sector policies and institutions. Sector lending had been introduced in response to requests from borrowing countries to ADB to provide more flexible types of loans.

Sector lending was perceived to have several advantages including the promotion of larger loan sizes, greater institution-building impact, and faster disbursements. This form of lending was expected to be particularly useful in agriculture and rural development activities, water supply and sanitation, education, and the health sector, as well as small industry. In 1980, ADB approved its first sector loans, one of which was for water and other urban infrastructure in Indonesia.

The relationship between Indonesia and ADB broadened throughout this period. During the 1970s, Indonesia's borrowing portfolio with ADB had continued to expand. By 1980, Indonesia had surpassed the Republic of Korea to become the largest borrowing country from the bank. Over the years 1967–1980, Indonesia's borrowings amounted to over 15% of total bank lending, ahead of lending to the Republic of Korea (14.6% of the total) and the Philippines (14%).

Economic Changes

At the beginning of 1981, economic conditions in Indonesia appeared promising. A boom in 1980, supported by high levels of spending in an oil-financed public expenditure program and a record rice harvest,

---

[11] ADB, 1980, *Sector Lending*. Manila.

encouraged confidence. But the optimism was largely dependent on international oil prices. When global oil prices began to fall in late 1981, the mood changed quickly. The difficulties caused by the sharp reversal in international oil prices came at a time, paradoxically, when the gains from the Green Revolution in rice were finally bringing important benefits to Indonesia. Nevertheless, by early 1982 it was clear that major adjustments in economic policy were needed.

During the next few years, Indonesian policymakers introduced a bold range of economic reforms. The main immediate concern was to respond to the twin resource gaps caused by the fall in the oil price in access to foreign resources, and in the impact on the domestic budget. But soon, after policy measures had been introduced to respond to the initial shock, it became clear that longer-term economic strategy in Indonesia would need to promote widespread reform. Radius Prawiro characterized changes announced in 1983 following further falls in the price of oil as having a long-term effect on the approach to development strategy in Indonesia:[12]

> This was one instance when it was no exaggeration to say that a national hardship was a 'blessing in disguise'. The initial steps the government took to cope with the problems involved monetary, fiscal, and exchange rate policies. However, at the same time, the government had begun a long-term process of reorienting the country's basic model of development. The significance of these changes would not be apparent for several years. However, had the government not begun the reform process in 1983, the crises ahead could have been thoroughly devastating.

During the rest of the 1980s, and into the 1990s, numerous structural adjustment packages of policy were announced by the government with the aim of encouraging new sources of growth in the country.

The broad aims of the numerous policy changes introduced during this key period of economic change were later summarized by Ali Wardhana as follows:[13]

> The reforms that the Government of Indonesia has implemented over the past decade [1983–1993] have reflected, on the whole, a consistent desire to achieve three basic objectives:

---

[12] Prawiro, 1998, *Indonesia's Struggle for Economic Development*, 222.
[13] Ali Wardhana, 1994, Financial Reform, 102.

1.   To move toward a predominantly market-based financial system;

2.   To provide effective protection as needed for the general public so that they could benefit from the services offered by the financial system; and

3.   To build a financial system that would support stable and healthy growth of the national economy.

An early step toward promoting structural adjustment was a 28% devaluation of the rupiah in March 1983. Supporting this change, several months later in June, significant reforms were announced for the financial sector. Arndt described these changes as "the first major move towards deregulation of a major sector of the economy since the late 1960s."[14] Ali Wardhana also saw the changes as a major step toward deregulation:

> It is probably correct to characterize the very first steps taken by the Indonesian Government in 1983 as deregulation. These initial steps consisted of the removal of direct central bank control over the state banks' interest rates, and over credit allocation by all banks. Subsequent measures affecting the financial system involved a two-pronged change: measures were introduced that further reduced direct control, while steps were also taken to introduce a reliance on indirect rule or action, either by strengthening prudential regulations or by improving the system of indirect monetary management. This later stage is best characterized as regulatory reform.

Later in 1983, as part of the overall approach to promoting economic adjustment, wide-ranging changes to the tax system were introduced. Malcolm Gillis, a senior advisor with many years of experience working in Indonesia, described the changes as "ambitious and far-reaching, perhaps more so than any previous tax reform anywhere... The tax reform, allowing as it did for a much more diversified and simplified revenue structure, proved immensely helpful in maintaining economic growth and stability throughout the eighties."[15]

In 1984, Indonesia's Fourth Five-Year Development Plan (Repelita IV) for the period 1984–1989 was released. The draft plan document reflected the sluggish economic performance of the previous few years. The expected

[14]   Arndt, 1983, Survey, 25.
[15]   Gillies, Dr. Ali Wardhana, 235.

growth rate for the five years to 1989 was put at a modest 5% per annum. For the donor community, two features of the outlook set out in Repelita IV were of special interest: the contribution to levels of investment and government revenues expected from foreign aid; and the planned approach to structural reform of the economy in response to the difficult international economic conditions at the time.

The forecasts set out in Repelita IV indicated that the government hoped the level of investment would grow throughout the plan period and that aid flows would increase as well. Total investment was forecast to expand from around 23% of GDP in 1983–84 to almost 30% at the end of the decade (Table 4.3). Aid inflows were also predicted to grow from around 3.8% of GDP in 1983–1984 to 5.5% five years later, so it was clear that the government would welcome continuing support from the international community.

The details of the planned strategy for structural change across the economy were less clear. The key issue was whether to implement measures to promote an export-oriented strategy or, rather, to favor import

Table 4.3: Planned Investment and Government Receipts and Spending as a Share of GDP, Various Years

	1978/1979[a]	1983/1984[a]	1988/1989[b]
Planned investment			
Domestic savings	17.6	16.1	25.1
Foreign inflow	3.6	6.9	4.4
Total investment	21.2	23.0	29.5
Government			
Total domestic revenues	17.1	19.1	24.7
Aid inflows	3.6	3.8	5.5
Routine expenditures	10.2	10.0	15.1
Development expenditures	10.6	12.7	15.1

GDP = gross domestic product.

Notes:

[a] Budget figures.

[b] Target for last year of Fourth Five-Year Development Plan.

Source: Rosendale, 1984. Survey, 25.

substitution policies. As things turned out, during the next few years a range of policy decisions were taken to open the Indonesian economy to international markets and to promote Indonesian manufactured exports. One of Indonesia's leading economists, Thee Kian Wie, described the changes during this period as follows:[16]

> The deregulation measures also included a series of trade reforms which were taken in 1985 and early 1986 aimed at reducing the "anti-export bias" of its trade regime. These trade reforms included:
>
> (a)   An across-the-board reduction in tariff rates in March 1985, and
>
> (b)   Measures to provide internationally-priced inputs to export-oriented companies.
>
> In addition to these trade reforms, the government pursued a supportive exchange rate policy to improve the international competitiveness of non-oil exports, including manufactured exports. … The stabilization measure and structural reforms soon bore fruit, as domestic and foreign investment in export-oriented projects rose steadily after 1986. As a result, non-oil exports, particularly manufactured exports, rose rapidly. … The rapid growth of manufactured exports fuelled the rapid growth of the manufacturing sector which, in turn, fuelled the growth of the whole economy. Hence, within a relatively short time, the manufacturing sector had replaced the oil sector as a major engine of growth and as a major source of export revenues.

The series of reforms, which were underpinned by a devaluation of the rupiah in 1986, quickly bore fruit. There was a marked surge in growth in the manufacturing sector. Between 1985 and 1992, non-oil manufacturing grew at an average rate of more than 11% per annum. For the first time in Indonesia's history, the pattern of economic growth began to resemble that in other rapidly growing neighboring Asian countries.[17]

Donor Activities in the Early 1980s

By the early 1980s, there was again some questioning in the donor community about the role of foreign aid in Indonesia. In 1980, as revenues

---

[16]   Thee, 2012, *Indonesia's Economy*, 102.
[17]   Hill, 1996, *The Indonesian Economy*, 155.

from the second oil boom flowed into Indonesia, the country's foreign exchange reserves rose quickly. Some observers wondered whether Indonesia really needed continuing support from donors when the national balance of payments appeared so healthy.

Others, however, argued that a temporary oil boom did not weaken the case for a sustained aid program to Indonesia. Indonesian policymakers, for example, were aware that the oil boom might not last and that, in any case, the development tasks that needed to be tackled were still daunting. At the 24th meeting of the IGGI in May 1981, for example, the leader of the Indonesian delegation, Widjojo Nitisastro, noted that assistance was still needed from the international community, not least because of the skill transfers often included in aid programs.[18] Although it was acknowledged during the meeting that "bridging the resources gap" was no longer the main factor underpinning the provision of foreign aid, partner countries still agreed to a level of assistance of $2.1 billion for the 1981–1982 period, about the same level as for the previous year (Table 4.4).

Table 4.4: IGGI Commitments and Disbursements, 1974–1981
($ million)

	Commitments		Disbursements	
	Annual	**Cumulative**	**Annual**	**Cumulative**
1974	1,485		633	
1975	2,031	3,516	1,550	2,183
1976	1,194	4,710	1,316	3,499
1977	436	5,146	1,086	4,585
1978	962	6,108	659	5,244
1979	1,313	7,421	1,162	6,406
1980	2,100	9,521	n.a.	n.a.
1980	2,100	11,621	n.a.	n.a.

IGGI = Inter-Governmental Group on Indonesia.
Source: Daroesman, 1981, Survey, 9.

---

[18] Daroesman, 1981, Survey, 9.

The case for continued significant aid flows was strengthened by the World Bank report presented to the IGGI meeting in 1981.[19] The World Bank pointed to the possibility of a reemergence during the 1980s of resource gaps, both in terms of foreign exchange and domestic savings. If resource gaps of this sort reappeared, Indonesian policymakers would find themselves facing a situation similar to that which had greatly limited their options in the pre-oil boom period before 1973–1974.

The World Bank canvassed a package of policy reforms along three main lines to underline the implications of this scenario. The first was the adoption of new trade policies aimed at promoting the growth of non-oil export industries, such as labor-intensive manufacturing, in which Indonesia could expect to be competitive over the longer term. The second was the expansion of measures to increase the efficiency with which capital was used. Steps in this direction might include discouraging excessive capital intensity in the public sector and freeing private investment from onerous regulatory controls. Third, it was suggested that much greater efforts at domestic resource mobilization might be considered. Measures to improve domestic resource mobilization had been somewhat neglected during the oil boom period but, looking ahead, it seemed likely that renewed efforts would be needed.

During the next few years, donors continued to provide support for Indonesia. Multilateral agencies such as the World Bank, IMF, and ADB urged the international community to do so, pointing to the challenges facing Indonesia in a low oil price environment. Indonesian policy advisers, for their part, helped bolster confidence in the international community by speaking frankly about the reforms needed. Well-known senior ministers Widjojo and Ali Wardhana played key personal roles in explaining the challenges that Indonesia was facing to the international community.

Numerous other Indonesian policymakers did so as well. In September 1982, for example, the doyen of Indonesian policymakers and one of the nation's most well-known economists, Professor Sumitro Djojohadikusumo, outlined some of the economic adjustments needed after a meeting with President Soeharto. He said had recommended three ways of easing the impact on Indonesia of the world recession occurring at the time: quickly finishing the execution of projects already underway and postponing all others; accelerating the training of labor; and accelerating the training of teachers.[20]

---

[19]   World Bank, 1981, *Indonesia*.
[20]   Gray, 1982, Survey, 50.

Donor support for Indonesia continued as a series of policy changes were introduced in 1984 and 1985 to promote structural reform. However, it became more difficult for Indonesia to implement aid projects in an effective way during this period. Firm controls over government spending in Indonesia sometimes meant that the agreed rupiah funding required to match foreign currency spending for aid projects was not available.

Donors became increasingly concerned about delays which were occurring in project implementation. Recognizing the need to overcome the constraints caused by the shortages of rupiah funds, in 1986 at the IGGI meeting in June, several delegations—including those from Japan, Australia, and the Netherlands—indicated that they were ready to provide more funding in local costs. On the Indonesian side, to examine the problems holding back the implementation of projects, at the end of July a high-level group was formed, with the deputy head of Bappenas, Saleh Afiff, as chair of the team.[21]

ADB in the Early 1980s

During the first half of the 1980s, ADB maintained support for mainstream projects in such areas as agriculture, energy, and roads. But at the same time, in response to requests from the Government of Indonesia to venture into new areas, loans were approved for some innovative activities (Table 4.5). The brackish water loan project agreed to in 1982, for example, launched ADB into the aquaculture sector in Java, Sulawesi, and Aceh. The aim was to help small-scale *tambak* (brackish water) fishpond farmers to increase production of shrimp and milkfish. *Tambak* farmers tended to be in lower-income groups so support for these activities helped strengthen the focus of ADB work on the poorer sections of the community.

Attention to the fisheries sector was supported by another 1982 loan for fish production in Papua. The aim of the project, in contrast to the *tambak* activities, was mainly directed toward the promotion of exports rather than domestic production. The hope was that the development of offshore and coastal skipjack and tuna fisheries in Papua would strengthen the prospects for exports from the eastern part of Indonesia.

Other loans approved in 1982 provided support for the agricultural sector as well. An agricultural credit loan was approved for rural village cooperatives (KUDs) in Java, Bali, and other parts of Indonesia. There was

---

21 Booth, 1986, Survey, 7.

Table 4.5: ADB Lending to Indonesia, 1982–1986

Loan	Sector	$ million	Terms of Loan
1982			
Second Irian Jaya Fisheries Development	Fisheries	34.0	OCR
Second Sulawesi Power	Power	41.3	OCR
Sixth Road	Roads	60.0	OCR
Vocational education	Education	40.0	OCR
Second Agricultural Credit	Agriculture	27.6	OCR
Irrigation Package	Irrigation	77.0	OCR
Sixth Port	Ports	5.4	OCR
Brackish Water Aquaculture Development	Aquaculture	23.0	OCR
Transmission and distribution system	Power	58.4	OCR
1983			
Second Irrigation Package	Irrigation	52.0	OCR
Small Towns Urban Development Sector	Urban	36.7	OCR
Second Irrigation Sector	Irrigation	85.0	OCR
Geological and Mineral Survey	Minerals	46.0	OCR
Power XVIII Project	Power	135.0	OCR
Agricultural Education Project	Education	68.0	OCR
1984			
National Estate Crop Protection	Plantation	63.0	OCR
Arakundo-Jambu Aye Irrigation and Flood Control	Irrigation	68.0	OCR
Nucleus Estate and Smallholder Oil Palm	Plantation	57.0	OCR
Seventh Port	Ports	86.0	OCR
Seventh Road (Sector) Project	Roads	95.0	OCR
Fisheries Infrastructure Sector Project	Fisheries	50.0	OCR
Second Kalimantan Livestock Development	Livestock	60.0	OCR
Third Senior Technical Schools Project	Education	83.0	OCR
Multisector Program	Multisector	25.0	OCR

continued on next page

Table 4.5   *continued*

Loan	Sector	$ million	Terms of Loan
1985			
Land Resource Evaluation and Planning	Land	23.4	OCR
IKK Water Supply Sector	Water	42.2	OCR
University of Sriwijaya Project	Education	37.9	OCR
Eighth Road	Roads	120.0	OCR
Fisheries Industries Credit Project	Fisheries	65.0	OCR
Health and Population	Health	41.6	OCR
Forestry Development	Forestry	28.0	OCR
Central Java groundwater irrigation	Irrigation	12.2	OCR
Second Bandung Urban Development	Urban	132.4	OCR
1986			
Second Nucleus Estate and Smallholder Oil Palm	Plantations	70.0	OCR
Eighth Port	Ports	40.0	OCR
Third Irrigation Package Project	Irrigation	120.7	OCR
Ministry of Public Works Manpower Training	Training	29.0	OCR
Irrigated Command Area Development	Irrigation	28.8	OCR
Special Project Implementation Assistance	Education	30.6	OCR

ADB = Asian Development Bank, OCR = ordinary capital resources.
Source: ADB annual reports, various years.

strong political and community support for the KUD sector in Indonesia. The provision of a bank loan reflected the hope that these organizations could be strengthened in village areas. Nevertheless, throughout the 1980s and into the 1990s, it often proved difficult to support the KUD sector. Legal and administrative difficulties often hampered the activities of the KUDs so their operations were frequently disappointing.

Activities in the energy sector were a priority in ADB's work in Indonesia in 1983. Both ADB and the World Bank had provided much support to the State Electricity Company (PLN) during the 1970s. The Power XVIII project approved in 1983, the largest ADB loan provided to Indonesia that year, was part of an established program of international support for the energy sector in Indonesia. The loan, as had become quite often the case with projects for electricity, was designed to include a diverse range of activities: hydropower schemes in East Java and South Sumatra; transmission and distribution networks in North Sumatra; a distribution system in Bali; and several other subprojects such as a feasibility study for a possible geothermal project in the Dieng Plateau in Central Java.

The support for the electricity sector during the 1970s and 1980s reflected, on one hand, the preferred approach of donors and, on the other hand, the concerns of Indonesian policymakers to strengthen energy security. Shortages of both basic fuels (kerosene, and diesel, and petrol supplies) and electricity were common across Indonesia at the time. It was not unusual for long queues of frustrated customers to form when kerosene or petrol was in short supply and prolonged electricity blackouts were common in almost all parts of the country. Both donors and the government saw investment in the energy sector as a priority.

The bank was also providing support for large infrastructure projects in other sectors. In 1982, a Sixth Road Project was approved for roads in Central and East Java and in Kalimantan. The project included technical assistance for the preparation of future activities in six more provinces in Indonesia. In 1984 a Seventh Road Project was approved, and the following year another road activity, the Eighth Road Project, was agreed to.

The emphasis on infrastructure projects in such sectors as electricity and roads was seen as desirable by the government because the basic infrastructure of the nation had deteriorated markedly during the 1950s and 1960s. There was a similar problem in the irrigation sector. New irrigation investments were urgently needed to support the increases in rice production encouraged by the Green Revolution. In 1982, an Irrigation Package loan was introduced which was designed to rehabilitate neglected irrigation systems in East Java and Central Java. The package included various activities: the construction of a barrage and feeder canal; improvement of weirs; clearing of heavily silted canals to improve water flow; and other works such as the development of flood control systems.

A Second Irrigation Sector loan was approved the following year to help increase food production in North Sumatra. Better management was seen as a key part of strengthening the local irrigation systems so the loan also provided finance for a Water Management Training Center and other administrative improvements. The International Fund for Agricultural

Development based in Rome joined with ADB as a cofinancing partner to support the project.

Three more irrigation loans were approved in the next few years. The Arakundo-Jambu Aye project in Indonesia's northernmost province of Aceh was added to the bank pipeline in 1984. The Arakundo River is one of Aceh's major rivers and the project was designed to provide an extensive package of works to support agricultural development in Lhokseumawe, a key area of the province. Activities included drainage and flood control, rehabilitation of canals and the construction of new canals, a new bridge, and the promotion of crop intensification along with training for famers. As was the case with many other bank projects, the activity attracted international cofinancing, in this case from the Saudi Fund for Development in Riyadh in Saudi Arabia. In 1986, a Third Irrigation Package was approved along with an Irrigated Command Area Development loan.

As well as the emphasis on agriculture and irrigation, there was a good deal of activity in urban areas. In addition to the small towns urban development project mentioned earlier, a large loan to support an urban development project in Bandung was approved in 1985. This loan was a follow-up to the earlier urban project in Bandung approved in 1976 and was designed to improve living conditions for low-income groups.

Nevertheless, although ADB had established a well-developed pipeline of activities in Indonesia, the increasingly difficult economic climate in the early 1980s made it harder for Indonesian agencies to work effectively with international partners. As the price of oil fell, curbs on government spending were introduced. Government departments were obliged to cut back on many activities. The pace of implementation of ADB-assisted projects began to slow and the delays became a matter of concern to both the government and the bank. Some of the problems reflected the administrative and regulatory requirements of the government, but others arose because ADB's procedures were not flexible enough to respond to the changed circumstances in Indonesia.

One reason for the delays was that the preparation of high-quality projects always took time. As a step toward ensuring that a pipeline of suitable activities was available, in 1984 the bank experimented by approving a TA loan for a Multisector Program. The aim of the loan was to support project implementation by funding the preparation of feasibility studies and detailed engineering designs for consideration by the bank or by other partners.

However, it continued to prove difficult to speed up the implementation of ADB projects. Indonesian agencies and the bank worked together to design better procedures. A range of improvements, such as clearer contracting arrangements and simplified guidelines for consultants, were introduced. But by 1986, it was clear that further steps needed to be taken to overcome the delays. In Manila, the ADB Board of Directors held several informal meetings to discuss difficulties being faced by the Philippines as well as Indonesia. For Indonesia, in recognition of the country's severe fiscal and budgetary constraints in the face of falling oil and commodity prices, the Board approved the use of loan savings to meet currency shortfalls of bank projects in several sectors.

Two further steps were taken in 1986 as well. Responding to a request from the Government of Indonesia, ADB posted staff in Jakarta on a full-time basis to assist in project implementation. In addition, a Special Project Implementation Assistance loan was approved to help finance the local currency requirements for six ongoing bank-assisted education activities to ensure project completion.

Into a Third Decade

Successful development across key sectors since the mid-1970s had brought marked improvements in living standards across Indonesia. Rapid expansion in the electricity sector continued. Electricity output grew at a sustained rate of around 16% per annum in the 10 years to 1986. The result was a dramatic increase in electricity consumption per person from around 30 kilowatt-hours in 1976 to over 100 kilowatt-hours per capita a decade later. Access to both private and public transport facilities also expanded quickly. Motorcycle registrations rose from around 1.4 million in 1976 to over 5 million in the mid-1980s as expanding access to consumer credit made it possible for many Indonesians to switch from using bicycles to motorized transport. And marked improvements in bus services for the public were reflected in a sixfold increase in the number of buses registered in Indonesia from around 40,000 in 1976 to nearly 260,000 at the end of the decade. Not surprisingly, Indonesian roads became more and more crowded.

During the second decade of ADB's operations in Indonesia the bank's program grew in size and widened into new areas of activity and into different forms of lending. As a borrower, Indonesia had become ADB's largest country partner, receiving approximately 21% of the bank's loans during the decade.

The scope of ADB's work had broadened as well. At the beginning of the decade in 1977, the bank was still mainly a project-oriented bank, largely focusing on the practical tasks of working on project loans. But as the bank's activities across Asia and in Indonesia became more diverse, there was a growing need to pay attention to the strategies underpinning ADB's work. By the end of the decade, the bank had adopted the practice of setting out an operational strategy which outlined the program in each borrowing country (Box 4.2). During the third decade, ADB would take on an even wider range of activities and the preparation of country strategies would become an increasingly important part of the bank's approach to working with developing member countries.

Box 4.2: ADB Operational Strategy in Indonesia, 1986

"The Bank's operational strategy in Indonesia takes note of the country's present need for labor-intensive development while focusing on the crucial objectives of supporting efficient economic development for the transformation of the oil-dependent economy into one that is more diversified and export oriented. This strategy broadly implies, at the macro level, continuing support of key subsectors and programs in agriculture, initiation of an increasingly direct role for the Bank in the industrial sector, selective involvement in physical and social infrastructure projects necessary for achieving efficiency improvements in the productive sectors and diversification of energy-resource development. On a sectoral basis, [the] Bank's strategy in agriculture is aimed at supporting the Government's efforts to diversify the agricultural base and optimize resource use. In the energy sector, the Bank's strategy supports the Government's plan to reduce dependence on oil as a source of energy by non-oil and renewable resources and improve energy demand management and conservation. Bank assistance to education and institutional development in Indonesia is of special significance in view of the severely limited availability of trained and skilled manpower. On a selective basis, Bank assistance is extended to support physical infrastructure, such as ports and roads, and social infrastructure projects in urban development, water supply, and health and population."

Source: ADB, *Annual Report 1986*, 48.

The Fifth Port project (1978) supported improvements at Belawan Harbor near Medan, North Sumatra.

The first ADB loan for a university project in Indonesia (1979) supported the expansion of Hasanuddin University in Makassar, South Sulawesi.

Housewives use new communal facilities built under the Small Towns Water Supply Sector project (1980), which was ADB's first sector loan.

ADB President Kimimasa Tarumizu (*second left*) in 1990 visits a reservoir built under the Wadaslintang Multipurpose project (1981) in Wonosobo, Central Java. At that time, the project was financed by the largest ADB loan in Indonesia. The President's Chief Advisor Masatsugu Asakawa (*third left*) also joined the mission.

CHAPTER 5

Adjustment in Indonesia
(1987–1996)

At the beginning of the third decade of the Asian Development Bank's
(ADB) work in Indonesia, economic prospects remained as uncertain
as they had been since the early 1970s. Certainly there had been strong
economic growth during the previous decade, but the two oil booms had
come and gone. The central economic challenge in the mid-1980s was
how to adjust to the new post-oil boom era which Indonesia appeared to
be facing.

During the third decade of ADB's activities, the bank needed to respond to
changing Indonesian priorities. In the latter part of the 1980s, Indonesian
authorities were concerned with the need to adjust to the end of the oil
boom. But by the early 1990s, priorities had begun to change. Seemingly, a
new period of post-oil boom growth had begun to take hold.

Adjustment

In 1987, the main economic challenge facing Indonesian policymakers was
the need to promote economic adjustment following the end of the oil
boom. Fortunately, senior policymakers had been considering the need for
adjustment for some years.[1] Describing the approach that policymakers
had in mind, one of Indonesia's most senior economic ministers, Ali
Wardhana, explained that after the slump in world oil prices in the mid-
1980s, there was a "a simple chain of economic reasoning" which outlined
the path of adjustment needed.[2] The path that Ali Wardhana outlined
emphasized economic growth, promotion of non-oil exports, deregulation,
and equitable distribution of the benefits of the reforms (Box 5.1).

Two important steps were taken in this direction in late 1986 and early
1987 when trade policy packages were announced. Both packages removed
non-tariff barriers, replacing the barriers with tariffs. The hope was that

---

[1] A summary of some of the main reforms during the 1980s is at ADB, 1989, *Asian
Development Outlook*, Policy reforms, 71.
[2] Wardhana, 1989, Structural Adjustment, 121.

Box 5.1: Reasons for and Path of Economic Reform in 1985

- Economic growth and development is a central goal of government policy.

- Economic growth requires export growth to pay for needed imports and to service debts.

- Given the level and uncertainty of oil prices, and Indonesia's level of proven oil reserves, the only reliable source of export growth for Indonesia is a wide range of non-oil exports both from agriculture and from manufacturing.

- Non-oil export growth requires an efficient, low-cost productive economy to enable firms to compete in world markets. This in turn requires a competitive domestic market.

- Protection and government controls, which had been the chosen policy instruments for many years, are inimical to this competitive domestic market; they have created the "high-cost" economy that the country is now trying to escape.

- To encourage exports and economic growth, therefore, Indonesia needs to dismantle its protective policies and government controls, and to deregulate its economy.

- A corollary is that non-oil government revenues must also be developed if the government is to play a constructive role in development.

- The benefits of deregulation and economic growth must be widely and evenly spread among the population. In particular, development of the rural areas should continue to be emphasized in any set of economic reforms.

Source: Wardhana, 1989, Structural Adjustment, 121.

tariffs would be easier to administer, easier to change, and would earn revenues for the budget. One of Indonesia's leading trade economists at the time (and later the minister for trade), Mari Pangestu, described the packages as "part of the long term, post-oil boom restructuring strategy which the Government has been following for some time."[3]

Several main issues were taking up much of the attention of policymakers. One was the level of foreign debt. The other was the need to promote structural adjustment. The level of foreign debt was, paradoxically, seen as a matter of policy concern and yet, in fact, was not really a problem. The

---

[3]   Pangestu, 1987, Survey, 1.

issue was regarded as a matter of concern partly because the international development debate at the time, largely reflecting the debt crisis in Latin America, was focused on debt issues. But another reason for the worries was a long-held concern in Indonesia about the implications of taking on foreign debt. The New Order government had come to office in the late 1960s faced with daunting debt problems; soon after, the Pertamina crisis in the mid-1970s had encouraged renewed concerns about debt burdens; and numerous commentators in the late 1970s and early 1980s had warned about the implications of taking on too much debt. Hobohm[4] summarized the views as follows: "The Government is clearly concerned about the foreign debt issue: government spokesmen have repeatedly stressed that foreign debts will not be permitted to become the 'nation's burden' and that further borrowing will only be undertaken if they are offered on very soft terms."

In fact, the level of national debt was comfortably contained within reasonable limits.[5] A significant proportion of the increase in the national debt since the early 1970s had been entered into on concessional terms. Much of the debt was long term (sometimes extending beyond 30 years) and carried low interest charges. This was useful debt for Indonesia to take on to support the national development efforts. The borrowings supported new investments in sectors such as infrastructure but imposed relatively low costs on the national budget.

The need to encourage structural adjustment was a second main concern for policymakers. Essentially, the debate was about the best way to promote the development of the Indonesian economy in the post-oil boom period. One view, held by "economic nationalists," was that the state needed to play a leading role to promote the growth of technologically advanced industries, such as aeronautics in Bandung. On the other hand, the "economic technocrats" were more cautious, arguing that all large national investment projects needed to be analyzed carefully to see whether the expenditures could be justified.

---

[4]   Hobohm, 1987, Survey, 5.
[5]   In the 1984 annual report prepared for the Inter-Governmental Group on Indonesia, for example, the World Bank reported that "Indonesia has been following a very prudent borrowing strategy despite substantial improvements in its creditworthiness…The rate of growth of debt has been moderate." See World Bank, 1984, *Indonesia Policies and Prospects*, 111.

Although much was made of the differences between these groups, in practice the divergences in views were perhaps not as large as suggested. In 1989, Mackie and Sjahrir described the different approaches:[6]

> A few years ago it was commonly said that there was a cleavage in the Cabinet between the 'technocrats' and the 'economic nationalists' or 'the engineers' (epitomised and led by Widjojo, Ali Wardhana and, currently, Sumarlin in the first category: by Habibie, Hartarto and Ginandjar in the second). Today, that polarisation appears to be much less sharp, while many of the key battles are fought out at the Director General level in interdepartmental committees. … There is a less clear-cut structural logic to the politics of deregulation than is sometimes suggested. Its advocates are themselves not doctrinaire about what it should entail, other than the elimination of market distortions, and have frequently pointed out that in some cases more government regulation is appropriate rather than less.

The October 1988 Package

The first of a series of key reforms in the financial sector was introduced in October 1988. These reforms, as it turned out, led to dramatic structural changes in the banking industry. They later had the unintended effect of contributing to the factors that led to the financial crisis in Indonesia in 1997–1998.

The October 1988 Package, dubbed Pakto 88, allowed for a sweeping liberalization of the banking sector.[7] Previously, the financial sector in general, and the banking sector in particular, had been closed to newcomers. Foreign banks in Indonesia had been required to confine their operations to Jakarta. Pakto 88 removed most of the restrictions on the banking sector. The changes allowed for new local banks to be established, including joint ventures with foreign banks. Conditions for setting up branches of banks were also simplified, and foreign banks were given new approvals to operate in six cities main outside of Jakarta including in Surabaya, Bandung and Medan. Nonbank financial institutions, as well, were permitted to open one branch in each of the six cities.

---

[6]   Mackie and Sjahrir, 1989, Survey, 32.
[7]   Details are in Simandjuntak, 1989, Survey, 21.

A series of other policy reforms were announced during this period (Table 5.1). Two more packages of changes were introduced in November and December 1988. And later, in 1990, several more sets of reforms extended the market-oriented approach to policy. In the event, Pakto 88 and the following regulatory changes opened the door to rapid changes in the financial sector. The number of banks, and the number of bank branches, expanded far more quickly than authorities had expected. In early 1990, Pangestu and Manggi Habir described the impact that the changes had brought:[8]

> Deregulation in capital markets and the banking sector has brought about tremendous growth in both sectors. ... Driving along Jakarta's main Thamrin-Sudirman freeway, one cannot miss the array of tall and impressive bank buildings—some finished, others partly completed—rising on either side of the road. But it is on the residential outskirts of the city that the impact of Pakto (the October 1988 bank regulation) is most noticeable. The density of bank branches in these areas is increasing dramatically, and many carry names which were quite unknown until recently. There is no doubt that Indonesia is experiencing a banking boom. New banks, branch networks, assets, loans and deposits are all on an upward trend.

Before Pakto 88, there were 111 banks and 1,728 bank offices in Indonesia. By the end of 1992, there were more than 203 banks and 4,407 offices. In addition, Indonesia's central bank, Bank Indonesia, was expected to monitor the performance of 12 nonbank financial intermediaries and more than 8,000 banks in villages across Indonesia.[9] Financial regulatory agencies, including Bank Indonesia, found it almost impossible to keep up with these changes.

By early 1991, the monetary authorities had become concerned about the rapid changes in the financial sector. In March 1991, a tightening of monetary policy dubbed the "Sumarlin shock" (named after the minister of finance, J.B. Sumarlin) was announced.[10] However the increased controls on domestic monetary policy, including higher rates of interest within Indonesia, encouraged firms in the Indonesian corporate sector to increase their overseas borrowings. During the 1990s, therefore, almost unnoticed,

---

[8]   Pangestu and Habir, 1990, Survey, 21 and 25.
[9]   Nasution, 1991, Survey, 34.
[10] Policies during this period, and the role that Sumarlin played at the time, are discussed in Bondan, 2012, *J.B. Sumarlin, 269–275.*

Table 5.1: Chronology of Adjustment Programs in Indonesia, 1983–1990

Policy Instrument	
Exchange Rate	1. Rupiah devalued by 28% against the US dollar on 30 March 1983 from Rp703 to Rp907 per US dollar. Exchange rate has been made more flexible since then.
	2. Rupiah devalued by 31% against the US dollar on 12 September 1986 from Rp1,134 to Rp1,644 per US dollar.
Fiscal Policy	1. Tight fiscal policy since 1983 marked by:
	a. large capital and import-intensive project (particularly investment in manufacturing, petrochemicals and mining), rephased in May 1983;
	b. major cutback in public real capital spending;
	c. more resources for social programs; and
	d. restraints on civil service employment and salaries.
	2. Tax reform enacted in January 1983, involving simplification of both tax structure and tax administration of all tax sources, excluding taxes on foreign trade.
Monetary and Financial Policy	1. Financial reform initialed on 1 June 1983 involving removal of credit and rate ceilings for state bank operations, reduction in the scope of credit programs and introduction of new market-oriented instruments of monetary control.
	2. New set of deregulation measures introduced in December 1987, October and December 1988, and March 1989 aimed at enhancing financial sector prudency and efficiency, and developing capital market by, among others, opening barriers to entry.
	3. Improved monetary management to control inflation and curb exchange rate speculation.
	4. Removal of central bank's direct credits ("liquidity credits") and major reduction of economic sectors covered by subsidized "priority credits" in January 1990 to curb inflationary pressures and credit fungibility.
	5. New regulations introduced on 14 March 1991, aimed at strengthening the capital base of banks and tightening supervision of financial institutions. The new measures require that the banking system meets the Bank for International Settlements (BIS) guidelines on the capital adequacy ratio of 8% of bank assets by December 1993.
Trade Policy	1. An across-the-board reduction in nominal tariffs introduced in April 1985, October 1986, and 28 May 1990.

continued on next page

Table 5.1 *continued*

Policy Instrument	
	2. Measures to provide internationally priced inputs to exporters announced on 6 May 1986 and 28 May 1990. This scheme permits exporters and suppliers of inputs for exporters to bypass the import licensing system and import tariff or, if they cannot bypass the system, to reclaim import duties, although the cost imposed by the NTBs cannot be rebated. The import bias of the protective system had been lessened but not uniformly.
	3. Major deregulation of import licensing system announced on 25 December 1986, 15 January 1987, and 28 May 1990.
	4. Additional measures to reduce and export bias announced in December 1987 by reducing regulatory framework for exporters.
	5. Major removal of NTBs, switch from non-tariff to tariff burners, and general reduction of tariff rates on 28 May 1990. Also covering simplification of licensing procedures in trade, manufacturing, health, and agricultural business, the policy package is aimed at reducing high-cost economy.
	6. Further removal of NTBs, general reduction of import tariffs and reopening of several business areas to new domestic and foreign investors announced on 2 June 1991. Several major features of the reform include outright import bans on cold-rolled steel coils, abolition of export quota system for palm oil and copra, introduction of import quota system for built-up commercial vehicles, and reopening of car component manufacture to new investors.
Other Regulatory Framework	1. Reorganization of customs, shipping and port operations announced in April 1985 to reduce handling and transport cost for exports and to simplify the administrative procedures governing interisland and foreign trade. Further deregulation of maritime activities announced on 21 November 1988 to reduce cost and encourage private sector participation, including foreign capital and foreign shipping companies.
	2. Measures to reduce investment and capacity licensing requirements, relax foreign investment regulations, and reduce the local content program.

NTB = non-tariff barrier.

Source: Nasution, 1991, Survey, 6.

the Indonesian corporate sector accumulated significant international debts. The repayment of this debt caused major problems when the value of the rupiah collapsed during the 1997–1998 financial crisis.

Later, reviewing developments during this period, Anwar Nasution suggested that key mistakes had been made during the reform process following Pakto 88. The mistakes, he said, had led to a "double mismatch" in the financial arrangements that Indonesian borrowers entered into during the 1990s:[11]

> The sequence of reforms was wrong. Prudential rules and regulations, and banking supervision, were inadequate. The situation led to excessive overseas borrowings from both the banking system and the corporate sector. Much of the borrowings were in the form of short term capital in foreign exchange which led to a "double mismatch." The borrowings were often used to finance long term investment in non-traded sectors of the economy that only earned rupiah in the long run.

The result was that when short-term debts in foreign currency (such as US dollars) fell due, Indonesian borrowers found themselves unable to meet their international obligations.

Changes for Donors

The third ADB decade was eventful for the donor community in Indonesia. The period began with strong donor support for the program of structural adjustment adopted by the Government of Indonesia in the mid-1980s. However, the mood in the international community began to change in the late 1980s. First, the fall of the Berlin Wall occurred in late 1989 and, then, the formal dissolution of the Soviet Union took place in 1991. Although many policymakers did not fully realize it at the time, this was the end of an era. Both the United States (US) and European countries, in their different ways, began to reconsider their relations with developing countries, including Indonesia. In 1992, as will be seen below, Indonesia responded to this changing environment by requesting that aid coordination arrangements be changed from management through the Inter-Governmental Group on Indonesia (IGGI) to the new, World Bank-organized Consultative Group on Indonesia (CGI).

---

[11] Nasution, 2018, personal communication, 12 August 2018.

At the beginning of the decade, donor programs, coordinated through the IGGI, were designed to be supportive of the adjustment policies that the government was implementing. Fiscal policy, both in 1986 and in 1987, had been conservative and had restrained national development expenditures. The disciplined policies reflected a determined approach on the part of policymakers to ensure that budgetary expenditures were contained. However, the sharp spending cuts led to difficulties in project implementation in major sectors such as transport and energy. Reductions in the availability of the rupiah funding needed to match foreign expenditures led to marked delays in project implementation.

There was a good deal of concern about these problems, both among Indonesian policymakers and in the international community. There had long been reservations in some circles in Indonesia about the implications of using foreign aid. Almost 10 years earlier, in the late 1970s, Daoed Joesoef, a senior policymaker who became an influential minister for education and culture (1979–1983), had said that foreign aid was an "evil necessity" which he was not "not happy about but which was needed."[12] The problem, according to Joesoef, was that the recipient of aid was "always under the thumb of the donor and that various consequences and risks might arise." Nevertheless, since the oil boom was clearly over, the pragmatic decision was taken on the Indonesian side that it would be best to look to international partners for more support. Pangestu noted that this new approach represented, in effect, a significant change in international economic policy for Indonesia: "The Government, which in the last fifteen years had taken pride in the reduced budgetary role of foreign assistance, now has to admit to greater reliance, albeit with the qualification that increased foreign assistance and its consequent debt burden is being used productively to ensure long-term development."[13]

One strategy adopted during this structural adjustment period was to maximize concessional loans from creditors such as Japan, the World Bank, and ADB.[14] The World Bank, for example, extended two trade policy loans in 1987 and 1988 and a private sector development loan in 1989. Japan provided substantial assistance as well, providing four special assistance (program) loans to Indonesia during this period. The availability of new

---

[12] Joesoef, 1977. Extracts here are translated from the original.
[13] Pangestu, 1987, Survey, 13.
[14] Nasution, 1991, Survey, 40.

concessional loans during 1987–1991 along with the increase in non-oil exports significantly improved the overall maturity and term structure of Indonesia's external debt.[15]

A second strategy supported by partners was to increasingly provide loan funds for rupiah-denominated spending.[16] When ADB first began work in Indonesia in the 1960s and early 1970s, it was accepted international practice for multilateral banks such as the World Bank and ADB to provide finance for the international costs, mainly in US dollars, of their project activities. Borrowing countries such as Indonesia were expected to provide matching local expenditure funds. But over time it became clear that there were sound economic and financial reasons for the multilateral banks to provide some funding for local costs as well.

In Indonesia, when sharp restrictions on government spending were introduced in the mid-1980s, delays in the implementation of aid projects soon began to be reported. In early 1986, the aid pipeline (made up of the backlog of commitments waiting to be drawn on) was put at $14 billion, partly resulting from the shortage of rupiah funds needed to match international project expenditures.[17] There were concerns that the problem would soon worsen, so both local policymakers and international observers urged that more flexibility be introduced into funding arrangements. Glassburner, for example, suggested that "the Inter-Governmental Group for Indonesia…might be enlisted to expand soft term lending to provide 'rupiah counterpart' funding for delayed aid projects."[18]

At IGGI meetings in 1988 and 1989, donors endorsed these steps to ensure that the international aid program was supportive of Indonesia's continuing reform program. Untied fast-disbursing programs and local currency lending was seen as providing Indonesia with immediate balance of payments support as well as rupiah funding for development expenditures in the national budget.[19]

---

[15]   Nasution, ibid., 41.
[16]   McCawley, 2017, *Banking on the Future*, 141.
[17]   Glassburner, 1986, Survey, 7.
[18]   Glassburner, ibid., 20.
[19]   Nasution, ibid., 15.

ADB in the Third Decade

Three features marked ADB's activities at the beginning of the third decade of the bank's work in Indonesia (Table 5.2):

(i)   support for the government's structural adjustment program;

(ii)   an expanding capacity to deliver the bank's program in Indonesia; and

(iii)   greater attention to issues in the financial sector.

In support of these programs, over 40 loans and a wide variety of technical assistance (TA) activities were approved during the first five years of the decade.

First, in cooperation with the rest of the international community, the bank responded to Indonesian priorities by introducing measures to support structural adjustment programs. In 1987, in a significant move in recognition

Table 5.2: Notable Events, 1987–1996

Item	Comment
1987	
Indonesia Resident Mission	Opened in Jakarta
Two concessional loans approved	ADB reintroduced concessional lending to Indonesia to support structural adjustment programs
1988	
Financial Sector Program Loan	ADB began to give increasing attention to issues in the financial sector supporting policy reform
1989	
Report on ADB's role in the 1990s	The report outlined a wider role for ADB; this approach was reflected in bank work in Indonesia in the 1990s

continued on next page

Table 5.2 *continued*

Item	Comment
1990	
Two large loans approved for agriculture and irrigation	ADB was continuing to provide substantial support for food production and rural development
1991	
Japanese Foreign Minister Michio Watanabe visited Jakarta	Reflecting views in the international community, Watanabe spoke of reducing the level of concessional loan support for Indonesia
1992	
CGI launched	New CGI group replaced IGGI for aid coordination
Power XXII Loan ($350 million)	Largest ADB loan ever approved for any country
1993	
Flores Emergency Reconstruction	First major ADB loan for disaster recovery in Indonesia
1994	
ADB country strategy	The 1994 *Country Operational Strategy*, the first formal ADB strategy for Indonesia, set out a major review of the bank's work in Indonesia for the 1990s
1995	
BIMP-EAGA launched	ADB supported the BIMP-EAGA program
1996	
North Java Road Project	The project reflected ADB's continuing emphasis on road projects including in key parts of Java

ADB = Asian Development Bank, BIMP-EAGA = Brunei Darussalam–Indonesia– Malaysia– Philippines East ASEAN Growth Area, CGI = Consultative Group on Indonesia, IGGI = Inter-Governmental Group on Indonesia.

of Indonesia's emerging resource constraints, the bank provided soft-loan concessional financing for the first time since 1979 for two blended loans—one for irrigation and one in the industries sector (Table 5.3).

Table 5.3: ADB Lending to Indonesia, 1987–1991

Loan	Sector	$ million	Loan Terms
1987			
Second Bapindo Project	Banking	60	OCR
Power XIX (Sector) Project	Power	96	OCR
Third Irrigation Sector Project	Irrigation	120	OCR and ADF
Ninth Road (Maintenance) Sector Project	Roads	150	OCR
Non-Oil Export Promotion Program	Industries	150	OCR and ADF
1988			
Agro-Industries Credit Project	Agriculture	30	OCR
Marine Sciences Education Project	Education	73	OCR and ADF
Nucleus Estate and Smallholders Cocoa/Coconuts	Plantation	48	OCR
Second Medan Urban Development Project	Urban	175	OCR
Second Health and Population Project	Health	39	OCR
Financial Sector Program	Finance	200	OCR and ADF
1989			
Ninth Port Project	Ports	22	OCR
Nusa Tenggara Agricultural Development Project	Agriculture	119	OCR and ADF
Second Brackish Water Aquaculture Development Project	Aquaculture	38	OCR
Tenth Road (Sector) Project	Roads	120	OCR
Second Vocational Education Project	Education	100	OCR and ADF
Development Finance Loan Project	Finance	200	OCR
Secondary Cities Urban Development (Sector)	Urban	120	OCR and ADF
Timber Plantation Project	Timber	33	OCR

continued on next page

Table 5.3   *continued*

Loan	Sector	$ million	Loan Terms
1990			
Six Universities Development and Rehabilitation	Education	114	OCR
Food Crop Sector Program	Agriculture	250	OCR and ADF
Integrated Irrigation Sector Project	Irrigation	200	OCR and ADF
Power XX Project	Power	235	OCR
Agricultural Technology Schools Project	Agriculture	85	OCR
Second IKK Water Supply Sector Project	Water	39	OCR
1991			
Botabek Urban Development Project	Urban	80	OCR
Bandar Lampung Urban Development Project	Urban	33	OCR
Inland Project Waterways	Water	45	OCR
Power XXI Project	Power	300	OCR
Second Fisheries Industries Credit Project	Fisheries	100	OCR
Second Land Resource Evaluation and Planning	Land	57	OCR
Technical Education Development Project	Education	100	OCR
Bogor and Palembang Urban Development Project	Urban	140	OCR
Eleventh Road (Sector) Project	Roads	150	OCR
Tree Crop Smallholder Sector	Plantations	135	OCR
Central Java Groundwater Irrigation Development	Irrigation	51	OCR

ADB = Asian Development Bank, ADF = Asian Development Fund Bapindo = Indonesian Development Bank, OCR = ordinary capital resources.

Source: ADB annual reports, various years.

The industry sector loan for the Non-Oil Export Promotion Program was the first program loan agreed to by ADB for any borrowing country under a new program lending policy that had just been approved. In November 1987, the ADB Board of Directors in Manila had agreed to a revised lending policy for ADB program loans designed to meet medium-term sectoral needs in borrowing countries. The hope was that this approach would make it easier to provide fast-disbursing loans to countries introducing economic reforms.[20]

Program lending was not a new instrument for ADB. The bank had initially introduced program lending almost 10 years earlier in 1978. The earlier types of program loans were fast-disbursing loans designed to help borrowing countries increase productive capacity in high-priority areas. However one of the main advantages of the new program lending arrangements was that there was much more flexibility to meet the needs of borrowers. Loan proceeds were used, first, to finance economy-wide or sector-specific imports. And once the loan proceeds had been disbursed against imports, counterpart funds were generated in local currencies. These funds could then be used by borrowing governments for such things as development purposes or for activities in a specific sector.[21]

The Non-Oil Export Promotion Program loan was designed to support Indonesia's structural adjustment efforts to stimulate non-oil exports. Consistent with the broader approach allowed for under the sectoral approach, it was agreed that in the implementation of the loan, ADB would continue policy dialogue with the government to review the impact of the reform policies. Further, in support of a more flexible approach, during the next few years, seven more blended loans were approved to assist Indonesia to maintain investment programs despite the budget constraints on development expenditures.

The second feature of ADB's work in Indonesia during this period was the strengthening of the bank's capacity to deliver programs in a more effective way. One step in this direction was the opening of a permanent Indonesia Resident Mission (IRM) in 1987. Previously, ADB had managed the operational program in Indonesia from the bank's headquarters in the Philippines. This arrangement had meant that there were many visits by bank staff from Manila each year. Despite these frequent visits, in practice it had often been difficult for ADB staff to maintain effective personal links

---

[20]   ADB, 1988, *Annual Report 1987*, 43.
[21]   Counterpart funds were generated when an aid-recipient government (such as the Government of Indonesia) used US dollars (usually received as part of an international assistance program) to help finance the import of goods for local use. In the process of providing the US dollars for imports to local firms and citizens, the aid-recipient government would have received payment in local currency (such as rupiah in the case of Indonesia). The local currency, in turn, would have been kept in a "counterpart fund" account. These counterpart funds, therefore, became available to the recipient government to use for domestic programs.

with their counterparts in Indonesia or to monitor the implementation of bank activities in the field.

Partly as a result of these problems, the pace of implementation and loan disbursements of bank-assisted projects had been relatively slow in 1985 and 1986.[22] In an effort to overcome the delays, ADB and the government agreed to changes in their procedures. The government in 1986 had established a special team in its National Development Planning Agency (Bappenas) with Minister of Administrative Reform Saleh Afiff as chair to speed up project implementation. The opening of ADB's IRM also helped improve the management of bank programs. The IRM introduced a comprehensive project monitoring system with a regular report on the status of project implementation and was able to liaise more closely with Indonesian partner agencies on program and policy issues. The bank also continued to conduct semi-annual country project review missions involving colleagues from its headquarters in Manila.

Another measure that helped improve program delivery was the preparation of a country operational strategy for Indonesia. This was an important step in the evolution of ADB's program in the country. It reflected both a broadening approach in international thinking about the role of development assistance and new policies agreed to by the ADB Board.

Within ADB, at the headquarters in Manila, there had been discussion for some time about the need for the bank to prepare more rigorous country programs. A major study of the bank's long-term strategic operations completed in 1983, *Study of Operational Priorities and Plans of the Asian Development Bank for the 1980s*, had been critical of the practice in ADB of focusing on pipelines of projects and activities rather than having a country-centered approach. The study recommended that a country-centered approach should be adopted "in close consultation with the country concerned and should rest on an analysis that moves logically from a proper examination of the country's macroeconomic situation, thence to sectoral and other cross-cutting priorities issues, and only then on to project selection."[23]

---

[22] ADB, 1986, *Annual Report 1986*, 49.
[23] ADB, 1982, *Study of Operational Priorities*, 7.

The bank adopted this recommendation. During the next few years, steps were taken to begin the process of preparing country strategies for borrowing countries.

For Indonesia, the first phase of the operational strategy prepared in 1987—which was a modest extension of the strategy statement issued the previous year—was influenced by the impact of changes in the international economy. The strategy provided an analysis of Indonesia's vulnerability to external factors (such as the weakening oil market and declining prices for primary products) as well as the need to promote structural reform (Box 5.2). The overall approach of the strategy was to maintain a broad overview of all sectors so as to ensure "that all investments are balanced and that bottlenecks to growth do not arise."[24] This approach was criticized nearly two decades

Box 5.2: ADB's Operational Strategy for Indonesia, 1987

"The Bank's operational strategy, formulated in 1987, supports the efficient adjustments needed to transform an oil-dependent economy into one that is more diversified and export-oriented, while promoting more labor-intensive development. Broadly, this strategy included addressing policy issues on non-oil exports, continuing to support key agricultural subsectors and programs, forging an increasingly direct role of the Bank in the industrial sector and being selectively involved in the physical and social infrastructure projects needed to improve productivity and diversify energy-resource development.

On a sectoral basis, the Bank's strategy in *agriculture* supports the Government's efforts to diversify the agricultural base and optimize resource use. In the *energy* sector, the Bank supports the Government's plan to reduce the country's dependence on oil by developing non-oil and renewable resources and to improve the operating efficiency of the National Power Utility. In the *industrial* sector, the Bank strategy supports resource-based and labor-intensive industries with good export potential, particularly the small and medium industries subsectors. Bank assistance to *education and institutional development* in Indonesia is of special significance in view of the severely limited availability of trained and skilled manpower. On a selective basis, Bank assistance is extended to support physical infrastructure, such as ports and roads, social infrastructure projects in urban development, water supply and health and population."

Source: ADB, 1987, *Annual Report 1987*, 57. Emphasis added.

---

[24] Quoted in ADB, 2005, *Country Assistance*, 88.

later by the bank's Operational Evaluation Department (which had the very considerable advantages of hindsight) as being somewhat unfocused and "a statement which indicated more the absence of a clear-cut strategy than the deliberate pursuit of a strategic approach."[25]

Following the adoption of the 1987 country operational strategy, policy dialogue was seen as increasingly important. The establishment of the Indonesia Resident Mission strengthened the capacity of the bank to enter into policy dialogue. The government and ADB continued earlier policy discussions on such matters as fertilizer and pesticide subsidies. Other policy issues taken up included financial sector reforms, capital market development, and food crop sector policy reform.

Policy dialogue between ADB and Indonesia worked both ways. Responding to calls for ongoing reform in the bank, in 1987 ADB's President Masao Fujioka invited an external panel of five experts to make recommendations about the role of ADB in the 1990s. The panel came from within and outside Asia although, reflecting the ADB Charter, it was "Asian in its basic character." The chair was Saburo Okita, a distinguished Japanese economist. There were two other well-known development economists from Asia, Amartya Sen from India and Mohammad Sadli from Indonesia. Sadli was one of Indonesia's most senior and respected policymakers. In appointing Sadli to the panel, Fujioka's aim was to ensure that the views of ADB's largest borrower would be reflected in the proposed report.

In conducting their work the panel met delegations from many countries. In early 1989 they issued their final document, *Report of a Panel on the Role of the Asian Development Bank in the 1990s*. The panel report reflected the changes in thinking about development at the time. The report, consistent with Indonesian views about the roles of international agencies, confirmed that ADB should be a sound financial institution whose overriding aim was to promote development in its developing member countries. Development was defined broadly to include not only sustainable economic growth but also social and environmental goals. This approach, the panel emphasized, would mean striking a balance:

> From Asia's recent experience, one lesson stands clear. For successful and sustained development, nothing is more important than the achievement of the right balance—between the scope and roles of the public and private sectors, between government planning and the

[25] Ibid., 88.

judicious use of market mechanisms, between policies that directly promote growth and those that pay attention to social questions.

The panel members, reflecting Asian ideas about the best approach to development issues, were thus deliberately distancing themselves from the neoliberal pro-market policies espoused in some quarters in the late 1980s.

The panel offered specific recommendations. The recommendations were influential in shaping ADB's work well into the 1990s, including in Indonesia. One main suggestion was that while the bank should continue on-lending for public sector infrastructure investments, it should offer more support for social sectors such as public health, including family planning, and education. The panel also suggested that ADB should do more to address poverty, should support social investments that provided direct benefits to the poor, and should pay special attention to the impact of projects on employment, especially informal employment. Later, following the Asian financial crisis in 1997–1998, when preparing loans to respond to the crisis, the bank made a special effort to build these recommendations into its activities.

The suggestions of the panel also reflected the thinking of the World Commission on Environment and Development (Brundtland Commission) released in 1987. The Brundtland Commission had urged that the international community make "a fundamental commitment to sustainable development." Environment Minister Emil Salim who, like Sadli, was a well-known senior economist and policymaker in Indonesia, was one of the commissioners who took part in the preparation of the Brundtland report. During the 1990s, ADB would increasingly design its programs to incorporate attention to environmental issues, including in Indonesia, and would draw on Salim's experience in formulating environmental policies.

In the meantime, discussions about policy issues in the financial sector led to agreement on a package of reforms resulting in approval of a Financial Sector Program Loan (FSPL) of $200 million. The FSPL, approved in 1988 with soft-loan support from ADB's Asian Development Fund resources, reflected the bank's approach of giving more attention to policy issues in the financial sector supported with program loans.[26] The loan supported the government's approach to the promotion of liberalization in the banking sector by providing for the entry of new financial institutions,

---

[26] ADB, 2005, *Country Assistance Program Evaluation*, 164.

streamlining the legal framework, and encouraging other reforms. Loan proceeds from the FSPL were expected to provide balance of payments support and to assist in meeting the increased import demand resulting from the continuing deregulation in the trade and industry sectors.

The bank's 1987 country operational strategy was reviewed in 1989 when Indonesia's Fifth Five-Year Development Plan (Repelita V), for 1989–1994, was released. The adjustments needed in ADB's approach were relatively small and mainly involved widening the approach taken to support the government's aim of promoting restructuring to diversify into an economy not based on oil. Reflecting the broad development strategy set out in Repelita V, the revisions to the bank's strategy in 1989 emphasized diversification—diversifying the production base of the Indonesian economy; diversifying the balance between the public and the private sector; and diversifying ADB's programs into social sectors such as health and education.

In support of this approach, the bank's pipeline of activities steadily grew (Table 5.2). There were significant investments in power and roads as well for the bank's long-established support for agriculture. The large power loan approved in 1990 (Power XX) was the 20th activity that ADB had provided for the sector. The following year, another large power loan ($300 million) was agreed to. At the same time, the World Bank was providing assistance for similar activities. In total, the power sector in Indonesia in the two decades to the early 1990s received a major flow of capital from these multilateral development banks.[27]

There was ongoing support for the road sector as well: The $150 million Eleventh Road Sector Project approved in 1991 was designed to help improve roads at both the national and provincial levels, especially in the eastern part of Indonesia.

In the agriculture, irrigation, and plantation sectors, over 10 loans were approved in the five years to 1991. Reflecting the government's aim of promoting development across the whole of Indonesia and not just in Java, the bank supported a range of activities in outer islands. In 1989 ADB approved a concessional low-interest loan for agricultural development in Nusa Tenggara Timur and Nusa Tenggara Barat provinces of eastern

---

[27] ADB, 2003, *Impact Evaluation Study*. For additional details of the loans that the State Electricity Company (PLN) undertook from the 1960s and earlier, see Sambodo, 2016, *From Darkness*, 76.

Indonesia. The aim of the loan was to help increase agricultural production and farm incomes. The project was designed to improve irrigation facilities and encourage water users' associations to adopt improved management arrangements for irrigation systems.

All of these efforts were supported with measures to mobilize cofinancing. Almost $200 million of cofinancing was arranged in 1989, and over $100 million was agreed to in 1990 (Table 5.4). Cofinancing programs with Japanese institutions such as Eximbank of Japan were an important source of finance although ADB looked to work with other partners as well. A relatively small arrangement for cofinancing was arranged, for example, with the Asian Finance and Investment Corporation (AFIC) in 1989. The AFIC was an organization established by ADB as a merchant bank in Singapore with the aim of strengthening links with the private sector. There were, as well, numerous other cofinancing agreements the bank entered into with the aim of encouraging the flow of capital into ADB-supported activities in Indonesia.

Table 5.4: ADB Cofinancing in 1989 and 1990

	ADB loan (million)	Cofinancing (million)	Source of cofinance
1989			
Ninth Port	22.0	12.6	Eximbank of Japan
Financial Sector Program Loan[a]	200.0	50.0	CFS guarantee[b]
Tenth Road	120.0	50.0	Eximbank of Japan
Leasing assistance[c]	20.0	7.0	Asian Finance and Investment Corporation[b]
Local cost financing of ongoing ADB-assisted projects	–	77.0	Eximbank of Japan
1990			
Integrated Irrigation Sector	200.0	8.0	Netherlands
Power XX	235.0	110.0	Eximbank of Japan

ADB = Asian Development Bank.

Notes:
[a] Bank loan approved in 1988.
[b] Complementary Financing Scheme of ADB which involved the prearranged sale to commercial lenders of participation in an ADB loan.
[c] Private sector loan.

Source: ADB annual reports for 1989 and 1990.

Adjustment Continues

There were marked changes in the approach to economic policy in Indonesia after 1992. At the international level, the fall of the Berlin Wall in 1989 and the collapse of communism in the Soviet Union soon after opened the way for the global development community to discard the Cold War framework that had influenced foreign aid policies for over 40 years since World War II. Quite soon, both European donor countries and the US began to emphasize new priorities in their approach to international development programs. In Indonesia, too, the approach to development priorities was changing. Within Indonesia, there was growing confidence that the structural adjustment programs adopted in the late 1980s had been effective. The steps that had been taken to move economic management toward a new post-oil period had begun to pay off.

There were good reasons for Indonesian policymakers to be optimistic in the early 1990s. Anwar Nasution referred to the "great optimism during the early years of 1987–91."[28] This optimism continued to underpin the approach to policymaking in Indonesia during the next five years. Overall economic growth was strong and some international donors were talking of scaling back their aid programs because the assistance no longer seemed to be needed.

There was even talk of Indonesia becoming an "Asian Tiger." Indonesia was included in a select sample of countries surveyed in the well-publicized World Bank study of *The East Asian Miracle* in 1993.[29] The World Bank spoke of the "seemingly miraculous growth in just eight economies" in the region, including Indonesia in the seemingly miraculous group. In fact, optimism about the economic prospects grew in Indonesia during the five years to 1996. In his August Independence Day speech in 1995 to mark the 50th anniversary of Indonesian Independence, President Soeharto said that the original Sixth Five-Year Development Plan (Repelita VI) target for real growth of gross domestic product (GDP) during the period 1994–1999 of 6.2% per annum was too low. He lifted the target to 7.1%.

Three main issues attracted the continuing attention of policymakers during this period: the need to promote further structural reform; the implications of moving toward a more market-oriented approach to

---

[28]   Nasution, 1991, Survey, 3.
[29]   World Bank, 1993, *East Asian Miracle*, 1.

economic management; and the risks arising from the rapid changes taking place in the financial sector.

There was widespread agreement among observers that the pro-market reform process since the late 1980s had been successful. Numerous packages of policy changes had been introduced and the practice of announcing changes in tariffs and regulatory arrangements continued on into the early 1990s.[30] One main result of this approach had been a remarkable jump in growth in the labor-intensive manufacturing sector. Thee Kian Wie summarized these developments as follows:[31]

> As a result of the manufactured exports surge, Indonesia's manufacturing sector since the late 1980s emerged as the major engine of growth and the major source of export earnings, at least until Indonesia was hit in 1997/98 by the Asian financial and economic crisis. To a large extent the rapid growth of the manufacturing sector since the late 1980s was due to the rapid growth of manufactured exports, particularly labour-intensive exports (textiles, garments, and footwear) and resource-intensive exports (particularly plywood and other processed wood products).

The share of manufacturing in total GDP expanded rapidly during the early 1990s. By 1994, in his annual Independence Day speech, President Soeharto spoke of industrialization as being the main engine of growth for the nation. Repelita VI forecast that the non-oil and gas manufacturing sector would grow at over 10% during the five-year period 1994–1999.[32]

The growing importance of the manufacturing sector was reflected in another key structural change. The steady decline in the previously dominant share of agriculture in the Indonesian economy reached a turning point in the early 1990s when agriculture's share in the labor force fell, for the first time, below the 50% mark. A few years later, the absolute number of workers employed in agriculture began to decline as well. With these structural changes, the process of economic development in Indonesia moved toward a new post-agriculture stage. And although the focus of attention in the 1990s was on the growth of the manufacturing sector,

---

[30] A brief summary of some of the changes during this period is in Sastromihardjo, Indonesia's Foreign Investment Program, 85.
[31] Thee, 2012, Indonesia's Economy, 156.
[32] Republic of Indonesia, 1994, Repelita VI, 111.

before too long policymakers would begin to discuss the implications of expansion in the services sector.

A second issue concerned the implications of moving toward a more pro-market approach in economic management. The pro-market approach to reform in the manufacturing sector was widely seen as successful. There was less agreement about the outcome of liberalization in the financial sector.

Pro-market reform policymakers, especially the economic technocrats within the government such as Radius Prawiro and J.B. Sumarlin, believed that there was a need for continuing economic reform.[33] Too many parts of the economy, they argued, were protected from international competition, and there were too many sectors where local or national monopolies ("conglomerates") restricted the operations of markets.

There was also much talk, both within Indonesia and overseas, of the need to promote the private sector. It was often said that the private sector was "the engine of growth," that the involvement of government in commercial activities should be reduced, and that more should be done to encourage foreign investment in Indonesia. In fact, during the early 1990s, there was a marked shift toward adopting these kinds of policies in Indonesia. The distinction, it might be noted, between the promotion of the private sector, on one hand, and the promotion of effective pro-market policies on the other, was not always clear. But certainly efforts to promote foreign investment bore fruit. Foreign investment approvals boomed: For the 10-year period 1976–1985, approvals averaged $950 million per annum while during the next decade the average increased more than elevenfold to $11.1 billion of approved investment per annum.[34] By the mid-1990s, foreign direct investment (FDI) approvals were rising very rapidly—from a seemingly impressive $8.1 billion in 1993 to over $23 billion in 1994 and to almost $40 billion in 1995. It is hardly surprising that in some quarters, there was concern about the rapid rate of growth.

As part of the pro-market approach, steps were taken to support private firms and investors, both within Indonesia and from overseas, to invest

---

[33] See, for example, the comments by Radius Prawiro about deregulation and structural change during this period in Prawiro, 1998, *Indonesia's Struggle*, 298.

[34] Prawiro, op. cit., 275. These data are only indicative. It refers to approvals of foreign investment, not actual levels of investment. Nevertheless, it reflects the increased interest on the part of foreign investors at the time.

in infrastructure. In the power sector, for example, new agreements were entered into to allow the private sector to provide power to industrial estates. Not surprisingly, the process did not always go smoothly. There were sometimes questions about the results of tendering processes in the electricity sector which reflected deeper concerns about the shift toward increased reliance on a market-oriented approach in the infrastructure sector.[35]

The shift toward the private provision of power was significant. For one thing, it reflected the changes taking place in international thinking in development circles which, increasingly, promoted a pro-market approach during the 1990s. This approach later evolved into the "Washington Consensus" which summarized pro-market views said to be widely held within the International Monetary Fund (IMF), the World Bank, and the US Treasury. For another thing, the shift was a harbinger of a rapid expansion of investment in the private power sector. Between 1990 and 1997, Indonesia's State Electricity Company (PLN) signed a total of 26 agreements with private investors for power generation. The agreements represented about 11,000 megawatts (MW) of power and at least $13 billion in investment. The majority of the projects were led by foreign investors. As will be seen below, when the Asian financial crisis struck in 1997, this program ran into severe difficulties.[36]

The risks arising from the rapid change in the financial sector were a third issue attracting much discussion. On one hand, the reforms of the late 1980s had led to a rapid expansion in the banking system. On the other hand, numerous worrying signs had emerged. Some of the large state-owned banks had rising levels of bad debt. Too many of the newly established small private sector banks seemed to have lax standards of lending. These concerns were reflected in *Asian Development Outlook* in 1992:[37]

> The acceleration of growth, which followed the financial reforms of the 1980s not only in the banking sector but also in other financial institutions and the securities market, has strained the Indonesian regulatory and institutional structure and brought attention to the inadequacies of the tax and legal framework. ... The supervisory capacity of Bank Indonesia, Ministry of Finance and BAPPEPAM

---

[35] Hill, 1992, Survey, 22.
[36] Wells, 2007, Private power, 341.
[37] Prudent Financial Regulations in Indonesia, Box 1.4, ADB, 1992, *Asian Development Outlook*, 35.

(the stock exchange supervisory agency) is overextended and the legal and regulatory structures are inadequate. As a consequence, risk in the financial sector has increased so that the establishment of prudential safeguards to improve stability and enhance public confidence in the financial system has become a matter of priority.

Numerous other commentators pointed to the need to improve prudential safeguards in the financial sector.

Attempts to regulate the banking sector were to some extent undermined by the large capital flows which were occurring at the time. One of the main concerns was about the vulnerability of the Indonesian financial system to these large, and perhaps variable, international capital flows. The policy dilemmas reflected two fundamental features of the Indonesian economy: an open capital market, and the underdeveloped nature of Indonesian financial markets.[38]

The concerns about vulnerability reflected a debate that had been taking place in Indonesia for over two decades.[39] On one hand, liberalization of the financial system had enabled Indonesia's domestic financial markets to link in more easily with international markets. This arrangement had made it easier for Indonesia to tap into foreign savings and encourage private capital flows to supplement domestic savings. On the other hand, the Indonesian financial system was more exposed to external shocks. These shocks included fluctuations in international interest rates, currency realignments, and contagion from events in other countries.

A related concern was the level of Indonesia's international debt. This issue, too, had been a subject of debate among Indonesian policymakers since the 1960s. In the early 1990s Indonesian economic policymakers, with the support of international agencies such as the IMF and the World Bank, took the view that the level of Indonesia's international debt was safely contained within appropriate limits. But others were less certain. This second group harbored fundamental doubts about the capacity of the Indonesian bureaucracy and government to monitor debt levels or to respond quickly enough in a time of crisis. At the end of the 1990s, when the Asian financial crisis broke out, it would become clear that their doubts were well-founded.

---

[38] Monetary Management in Indonesia, Box 2.2, ADB, 1992, *Asian Development Outlook*, 116.
[39] Nasution, 1995, Survey, 4.

As ADB's third decade of work in Indonesia drew to a close, there remained much debate about the direction of national economic policy and the accompanying risks. On one hand, economic growth was rapid (put at over 7% per annum in both 1995 and 1996) and policies to promote structural reform, especially growth in labor-intensive manufactures, had proved very successful. On the other hand, some observers argued that there were signs the boom was getting out of hand.

These concerns were summarized in the ADB *Asian Development Outlook* survey for 1996 and 1997:

> The Indonesian economy continued to grow strongly in 1995 and, driven by strong private consumption and investment demand, can be expected to maintain that momentum over the next two years. As the economy is operating at a very high level of capacity, macroeconomic policy is critical to the maintenance of stable growth and to the avoidance of overheating. Although inflation shows signs of moderating, it remains high; and the current account deficit, which deteriorated in 1995, must be addressed in a timely manner.

Looking ahead, the *Asian Development Outlook* pointed to the need to design policies to manage the large amounts of capital flowing into Indonesia:

> The main challenge for macroeconomic policy in the next two years is to ensure growth with reasonable price stability and manageable fiscal and current account deficits. … Management of large flows of capital is another critical issue which the monetary authorities will continue to face. Running a tight monetary policy with high rates of interest is the appropriate action when inflationary pressures are present. However, given that international rates are steady or falling, such a policy invites capital inflows which, in turn, need to be sterilized. Experience in 1995 indicates that these flows are very susceptible to external events such as the Mexican financial crisis and appreciation of the yen, and unfavorable perceptions of domestic policy changes.

As will be seen below (Chapter 6), the challenge of managing capital flows would soon become a major issue for Indonesian policymakers during the Asian financial crisis in 1997 and 1998.

Donor Activities in the 1990s

The relationship between Indonesia and the international donor community evolved during the 1990s. There were changes both in international thinking about aid programs and in the relationship that Indonesia was aiming to maintain with the donor community.[40]

At the beginning of the 1990s, the international community remained confident in its donor relationship with Indonesia. Looking ahead, it seemed likely that foreign aid would continue to play a significant role until the end of the decade despite Indonesia's strong growth and approach to reform. It was accepted that development funds, especially from the World Bank, ADB, and Japan, would focus on main sectors such as infrastructure and human research development. It was also expected that as income per capita in Indonesia rose, the concessionality of international assistance would decline.

The role of foreign aid in Indonesia during the 1990s was therefore expected to change in several ways. First, there were signs that a two-level system of assistance was developing between the larger donors and a group of smaller donors. The official flows from the larger donors (Japan, the World Bank, and ADB) generally took the form of loans, in a mixture of both concessional and non-concessional flows, for budget support and for significant infrastructure projects as well as for other agreed activities. In contrast, funds from the smaller donors were generally provided as grants and focused on training or on smaller specific project activities, sometimes in less developed provinces or working in cooperation with Indonesian nongovernment organizations.

It seemed likely that this two-level system would continue to reflect the outlines of the patterns of aid delivery to Indonesia. The larger donors generally had sufficient funds to support significant projects in infrastructure and human development sectors, often in Java, while the smaller donors preferred to provide funds for more modest activities to support social, educational, and environmental goals.

A second change was that the level of concessionality of Indonesia's partners was tending to decline over time. In the late 1960s and early 1970s, nearly all assistance had been provided either as grants or as

---

[40]   The discussion here draws on the discussion in Muir, 1991, Survey, 24.

highly concessional loans. The level of concessionality had varied over time, reflecting changed conditions in Indonesia. For example, the level of conditionality of official flows rose significantly in the late 1980s. Following the sharp fall in the price of oil in 1986, partners increased their support for Indonesia as economic adjustments were made to cope with the strain of the "twin deficits" in fiscal and balance of payments policy.

Nevertheless, the long-term trend reflected declining conditionality. When former Japanese Foreign Minister Michio Watanabe visited Jakarta in September 1991, he told reporters that it was now "not unreasonable" for Indonesia to obtain "higher levels" of assistance (that is, less concessional forms of aid) because Indonesia had almost reached the classification of a newly industrialized country. Comments of this kind from representatives of the international community indicated that concessionality was likely to continue to decline during the coming decade.

A third change which led to significant shifts in relations between Indonesia and partner countries over time was that the international community began to develop a revised and expanded set of priorities for the provision of aid to developing countries in the early 1990s. Following the fall of the Berlin Wall and the collapse of communism, both European countries and the US began to adopt new approaches on a wide range of issues. This was an important change which was reflected in the relationship between the international donor community and Indonesia.

During the 1980s, a number of donor countries had been critical of the Government of Indonesia's approach to certain human rights issues within Indonesia. These criticisms became more pronounced during 1990 when Dutch Minister for Development Cooperation J.P. Pronk, known for his blunt views about human rights issues, became chair of the IGGI.

At the same time, Indonesia was becoming more confident. It was not evident at the time, but the aim of Indonesian policymakers was to reduce Indonesia's dependence on foreign aid. This approach underpinned Indonesia's relations with the international community for several reasons. First, the level of international debt was a constant focus of attention in discussions about economic policy in Jakarta. While most aid flows to Indonesia did not have a significant impact on the national debt burden, there was still a widespread perception that aid flows added to national debt. Second, it was sometimes suggested that economic policymakers in Jakarta were too ready to adopt policies recommended by the donor community. While there is ample evidence that this suggestion was not correct, policymakers in Jakarta nevertheless needed to take care to be seen to be listening to these views.

These issues underpinned Indonesia's decision in late March 1992 to announce that it was time for the IGGI, as an international aid coordination group chaired by the Netherlands, to be disbanded. In making the announcement, the Government of Indonesia indicated that it would welcome the opportunity to continue to meet with development partners on a regular basis. As the government saw it, however, it would be best for any new aid group to be coordinated through multilateral channels. This approach reflected the response of the government to statements from Pronk who had been critical of Indonesia's human rights record in Timor-Leste during 1991. Indonesia's view, emphasized by President Soeharto in a statement in December 1991, was that Indonesia would not accept the linking of aid to issues in Timor-Leste. Following the disbandment of the IGGI, a new international consultative group, the CGI chaired by the World Bank, was established.[41]

Despite these changes in the relationship with the international community, donor support for Indonesia remained strong. Donors agreed to over $4.9 billion in pledges at the first meeting of the new CGI in 1992. Pledges then remained at over $5 billion each year for the rest of the decade. Support from the international community was also reflected in statements at the CGI meetings. In 1993, the chair of the meeting, Gautam Kaji from the World Bank, described Indonesia as "one of the success stories of the developing world." He noted, however, that further reform was needed, urging that there be "further policy changes in trade and industrial deregulation and in investment facilitation." He pointed to the changes occurring in neighboring countries in Asia, noting that:

> The global trading environment, and that of East Asia in particular, are becoming more competitive. Countries such as the People's Republic of China and Vietnam are emerging to claim a share of the global market and to compete for the increased flow of private capital and foreign direct investment. It is a tougher contest today than it was even two years ago. The challenge to the government

---

[41] A summary of Indonesia's concerns with the evolving relationship with the IGGI at the time is in Kementerian Perencanaan Pembangunan Nasional, Badan Perencanaan Pembangunan Nasional, 2003, "Keberadaan dan Peran," 35. See also Manning, 1992, Survey, 5, and Hill, 1992, Survey, 14.

is to implement policies that allow Indonesia to succeed in this competitive environment.

Other donors echoed these views, noting that Indonesia's non-oil GDP had risen by around 6.7% per annum in the previous decade, while urging that the process of reform continue.[42]

Responding to these comments, Indonesia's Coordinating Minister for Economy, Finance and Development Supervision Saleh Afiff spoke of the ongoing process of reform and the need to "raise the productivity of workers, capital and firms, and increase our competitiveness in international markets." He outlined four elements of the strategy that Indonesia would follow to promote these goals:

> First, we will continue to give a very high priority to the maintenance of macroeconomic stability through careful fiscal and monetary management. ... Second, we will continue the process of trade and investment deregulation, and support these changes with an improved legal framework. ... Third, we need to make stronger efforts to manage our natural resources and prevent degradation of the environment. ... Fourth, we continue with our massive investments in human resources and physical infrastructure.

With these and other similar statements during the 1993 meeting, the Indonesian delegation indicated a commitment to the economic reform process.

At meetings of the CGI during the next few years, the international community continued to provide similar levels of support to Indonesia. The Government of Indonesia, for its part, remained committed to an ongoing process of reform. At the fifth meeting of the CGI in 1996, Afiff was able to note that economic growth in Indonesia in 1995 had reached 8% and that some observers were even concerned that the economy was showing signs of overheating.[43] There were, the minister acknowledged, risks associated with such a rapid rate of economic growth, and with the surge in investment, partly funded by private-sector offshore borrowings, which underpinned the growth.

---

[42] See the reports in World Bank (IBRD), Second Meeting, November 1993.
[43] World Bank, 1996, Consultative Group, 2.

Afiff explained that various steps had been taken to counter the risks. These steps included strengthening monetary policy, building up foreign exchange reserves, and introducing greater flexibility into management of the foreign exchange rate. But in addition, he said, Indonesia was hopeful of continuing support from the international community:[44]

> ...we feel we are at a particularly difficult stage. The current surge in investment is not likely to fall off soon, and the difficulties in the current account are not likely to decline rapidly. Thus we are facing a situation that will require significant forbearance and support from our development partners. The government is trying to increase its claim on domestic resources through increased tax effort and raising charges in other areas as rapidly as possible, but there are limits to how fast we can increase the flow of funds in these areas. ... As we have stated in the past we would like to reduce foreign commercial borrowing by the government. At the same time, we need concessional assistance in critical areas. The private sector is not nearly ready to provide sufficient funds for human resource development, public infrastructure, poverty alleviation, and regional development.

Thus, by 1996, the relationship between Indonesia and the international community had developed into a strong partnership. Both Indonesia and the international community remained committed to the relationship. At the close of the 1996 CGI meeting in Paris, the World Bank was able to report that during the meeting, "participants noted that the aid relationship with Indonesia offered one of the best models of a productive partnership between a development country and the donor community."[45] This was fortunate because, as we shall see in the next chapter, by the end of 1997 Indonesian policymakers were drawing heavily on international support as the Asian financial crisis engulfed economies in the Southeast Asian region.

ADB Programs

Into the mid-1990s, ADB continued to design its program in Indonesia to support the priorities set out by the government in Repelita V (1989–1994). This approach sometimes involved balancing suggestions from Western donor countries against the development plans set out by Indonesia.

---

[44]   Ibid., 5.
[45]   World Bank, 1966, Donors Reaffirm.

Nevertheless, the bank aimed to prepare a pipeline of loans that would be both approved by the ADB Board and be consistent with Indonesia's preferences as the borrower.

In the early and mid-1990s, ADB focused its lending on the provision of physical and human infrastructure as well as on activities supporting economic reform. Funding for physical infrastructure in the public sector remained a priority but efforts were also made to encourage the private sector to invest in infrastructure.

The bank's program in the electricity sector reflected this approach. In each of the four years from 1992–1995, large loans were approved for the power sector (Table 5.5). The Power XXII Project loan agreed to for

Table 5.5: ADB Lending to Indonesia, 1992–1996

Loan	Sector	$ million	Loan Terms
1992			
Telecommunications Project	Telecom	185	OCR
Water Pollution Control Project	Water	8	OCR
Second Financial Sector Program Loan	Finance	250	OCR
Power XXII Project	Power	350	OCR
Upland Farmer Development Project	Agriculture	30	ADF
Smallholder Tree Crop Processing Project	Plantation	75	OCR
Biodiversity Project (Flores and Siberut)	Biodiversity	24	ADF
Junior Secondary Education Project	Education	105	OCR
Central Java and Yogyakarta (DIY) Urban Development	Urban	150	OCR
Marine Resource and Evaluation Planning	Marine	33	OCR
1993			
East Indonesia Airports Project	Airports	110	OCR
Second Development Project Loan Project	Finance	200	OCR
Third Local Roads Project	Roads	200	OCR
Second Telecommunications Project	Telecom	195	OCR

continued on next page

Table 5.5   *continued*

Loan	Sector	$ million	Loan Terms
Flores Emergency Reconstruction Project	Emergency	26	ADF
Mangrove Rehabilitation and Management (Sulawesi)	Environment	8	ADF
Higher Education Project	Education	140	OCR
Sustainable Agriculture Development (Irian Jaya)	Agriculture	28	OCR
Power XXIII Project	Power	275	OCR
Eastern Island Urban Development Sector Project	Urban	85	OCR
1994			
Second Irrigation Sector Project	Irrigation	100	OCR
Rural Health and Population Project	Health	40	OCR
Vocational and Technical Education Project	Education	85	OCR
Sumatra Power Transmission Project	Power	272	OCR
West Lampung Emergency Reconstruction Project	Emergency	18	ADF
Microcredit Project	Finance	25	ADF
Eastern Island Roads (Sector) Project	Roads	180	OCR
Capacity Building Project in Water Resources Sector	Water	27	OCR
1995			
Sulawesi Rainfed Agricultural Development Project	Agriculture	30	ADF
Rural Water Supply and Sanitation Sector Project	Water	85	OCR
Gas Transmission and Distribution Project	Gas	218	OCR
Private Junior Secondary Education Project	Education	49	OCR
Senior Secondary Education Project	Education	110	OCR
Farmer Managed Irrigation Systems Project	Irrigation	26	ADF
Sumatra Urban Development Sector Project	Urban	130	OCR

continued on next page

Table 5.5   *continued*

Loan	Sector	$ million	Loan Terms
West Java Urban Development Sector Project	Urban	70	OCR
Power Development and Efficiency Enhancement	Power	337	OCR
1996			
North Java Flood Control Sector Project	Water	90	OCR and ADF
North Java Road Improvement Project	Roads	150	OCR
Engineering Education Development Project	Education	102	OCR
Industrial Technology and Human Development	Education	80	OCR
Basic Education Project	Education	85	OCR
Bapedal Regional Network Project	Regional	45	OCR
Integrated Pest Management for Smallholder Estates	Plantations	44	OCR
Family Health and Nutrition Project	Health	45	OCR
Segara Anakan Conservation and Development Project	Conservation	45	OCR and ADF
South Java Flood Control Project	Water	103	OCR
Regional Development Account Project	Development	50	OCR
Metropolitan Bogor, Tangerang and Bekasi Urban	Urban	80	OCR

ADB = Asian Development Bank, ADF = Asian Development Fund, OCR = ordinary capital resources.
Source: ADB annual reports, various years.

$350 million in 1992 was a landmark loan. It was the single largest loan that ADB had approved for any borrowing country. It would remain the largest activity on the bank's books until the emergency $4 billion Asian financial crisis loan for the Republic of Korea was agreed to in 1997. The Power XXII loan was supported with over $1 billion of cofinancing from the World Bank, Germany, and export credits.[46]

---

[46] ADB, *Annual Report 1992*, 180.

A major review of ADB's work in Indonesia since the late 1960s was set out in the *Indonesia Country Operational Strategy* (COS) prepared in 1994.[47] The COS noted that since 1969, Indonesia had received over $10.4 billion in loans and TA from the bank (Table 5.6). The sectoral balance of the bank's activities had changed since the late 1960s. Over the 25-year period between 1969 and 1994, almost 65% of ADB assistance had been provided for agricultural and physical infrastructure (energy and roads). A further 25% had been allocated to social and other sectors. Modest lending had taken place in the health, water supply, and industry sectors. Not surprisingly, the average loan size had grown markedly over time (Table 5.7). During the First Five-Year Development Plan (Repelita I) period from 1969–1974, when ADB had been establishing a pipeline of work in Indonesia, the loan size had been quite small, averaging around $5 million for each project. By the time of Repelita V, the average loan size had grown to over $100 million.

The sectoral focus of ADB's program over this period was tailored to reflect Indonesia's development priorities. Earlier, agriculture had been important. But over time, as the structure of the economy changed, the share of agriculture in total outputs had slowly declined. This structural change was reflected in ADB's lending program. In the early years, agriculture had received the largest share of bank assistance. However as Indonesia moved toward industrialization, manufacturing and parts of the service sectors became increasingly important. During the 1980s and 1990s, there was a shift in the focus of ADB programs toward investment in such sectors as transport, energy, finance, urban development, and education.

The bank's traditional approach had been to provide assistance through support for specific projects (Table 5.8). Especially since the mid-1980s, however, sector and program lending approaches had been agreed to. The COS noted that "both the Government and the Bank found important advantages in the program and sector lending approaches, which warrant their continued use in the country program."[48]

Looking ahead, the 1994 COS recommended that ADB's approach in Indonesia should emphasize three objectives: support for economic growth, for human resource development, and for the sustainable use of natural resources. The COS allowed for other priorities by noting that concerns for issues such as poverty reduction and for improving the status

---

[47] ADB, 1994, *Indonesian Country Operational Strategy.*
[48] Ibid., 16.

Table 5.6: ADB Approved Lending to Indonesia by Sector, 1969–1994

	Repelita I 1969–1974	Repelita II 1974–1979	Repelita III 1979–1984	Repelita IV 1984–1989	Repelita V 1989–1994	Total 1969–1994
			$ million			
Agriculture	70	132	728	900	1,063	2,893
Physical infrastructure	41	314	575	609	2,165	3,704
Energy	30	162	455	96	1,160	1,903
Transport	11	152	120	513	1,005	1,801
Social infrastructure		52	369	682	1,499	2,602
Education		39	185	254	844	1,322
Health				81		81
Water supply		12	76	40	47	174
Urban		1	108	307	608	1,024
Other		104	46	435	676	1,261
Finance		30		260	650	940
Industry		74	46	150		270
Multisector				25	26	51
Total ($ million)	111	602	1,718	2,626	5,403	10,460
			Percentages (%)			
Agriculture	63	22	42	34	20	28
Physical infrastructure	37	52	33	23	40	35
Energy	27	27	26	4	21	18
Transport	10	25	7	20	19	17
Social infrastructure		9	21	26	28	25
Education		6	11	10	16	13
Health				3		1
Water supply		2	4	2	1	2
Urban		…	6	12	11	10
Other		17	3	17	13	12
Finance		5		10	12	9
Industry		12	3	6		3
Multisector				1	…	…
Total (%)	100	100	100	100	100	100

ADB = Asian Development Bank, Repelita = Five-Year Development Plan.
Source: ADB, 1994, Indonesia Country Operational Strategy, 15.

Table 5.7: ADB Approved Lending and Technical Assistance to Indonesia, 1969–1994 ($ million)

		ADB Loans ($ million)				Average Loan Size ($ million)	Technical Assistance ($ million)
Repelita	Period	OCR ($ million)	ADF ($ million)	Total ($ million)	No.		
I	1969–1974	12	99	111	22	5	20
II	1974–1979	562	38	600	31	20	24
III	1979–1984	1,693	25	1,718	42	41	47
IV	1984–1989	2,386	240	2,626	41	64	64
V	1989–1994	4,877	327	5,203	47	111	107
Totals		9,530	729	10,258	183		262

ADB = Asian Development Bank, ADF = Asian Development Fund, OCR = ordinary capital resources, Repelita = Five-Year Development Plan.
Source: ADB, 1994, Indonesia Country Operational Strategy, 14.

Table 5.8: ADB Approved Lending to Indonesia by Mode, 1969–1994

	Repelita I 1969–1974	Repelita II 1974–1979	Repelita III 1979–1984	Repelita IV 1984–1989	Repelita V 1989–1994	Total 1969–1994
			$ million			
Project lending	111	554	1,484	1,533	3,289	6,971
Sector lending			187	551	914	1,652
Program lending				375	500	875
Other lending		46	46	202	577	871
Of which:						
Credit lines		33	26	155	500	715
TA loans		13	19	12		44
Private sector				35	77	112
Total	111	600	1,718	2,661	5,280	10,371
			Percentages (%)			
Project lending	100	92	86	58	62	67
Sector lending			11	21	17	16
Program lending				14	9	8
Other lending		8	3	8	11	8
Of which:						

continued on next page

Table 5.8   *continued*

	Repelita I 1969–1974	Repelita II 1974–1979	Repelita III 1979–1984	Repelita IV 1984–1989	Repelita V 1989–1994	Total 1969–1994
Credit lines	5	2	6	9		7
TA loans	2	1	1			...
Private sector			1	2		1
Total (%)	100	100	100	100	100	100

ADB = Asian Development Bank, Repelita = Five-Year Development Plan, TA = technical assistance.
Source: ADB, 1994, Indonesia Country Operational Strategy, 16.

of women were seen as integral parts of the three objectives. Nevertheless, the strategy flagged "economic growth as the centrepiece of the strategy." Economic growth was seen as needed for three main reasons: to help promote capital mobilization, to create jobs, and to lift living standards.

The priorities of the COS both reflected the work that ADB had been doing in Indonesia and pointed to activities that the bank should focus on during the rest of the 1990s. As well as supporting large investments in the power sector, the bank's traditional focus on roads was seen as remaining important. Large road loans were approved in 1993 and 1994, the latter being to support an Eastern Islands Roads Sector Project to help finance the improvement of roads in 13 eastern island projects. This project was part of the bank's program of responding to requests from the government to look for opportunities to support development in the relatively poor provinces of eastern Indonesia. In 1996, the largest loan approved was for the North Java Road Improvement Project. The project was designed to help improve the road network in the densely populated corridor across North Java stretching from Jakarta through Semarang to the large eastern city of Surabaya.

The 1994 COS also emphasized the advantages of promoting the private sector. The Sixth Five-Year Development Plan (Repelita VI) for the 1994–1999 period had noted the need for an expanded role for the private sector. The COS suggested that the bank should look for ways to support this goal. In the electric power sector, ADB policy dialogue had focused on issues such as the commercialization of activities of the State Electricity Company (PLN) and the expansion of private sector involvement in the supply of electricity. The COS observed that although private sector participation in the power sector had expanded significantly, "the actual implementation of the policy framework warrants assistance from the Bank, as does the fine-tuning of that framework."[49] The COS also recommended that ADB should lend support for restructuring, including the possible breakup of PLN into a series of regional utilities.

Measures to strengthen the finance sector were also seen as steps toward promoting the private sector. The COS suggested that bank strategy in the financial sector should promote improved financial intermediation and help develop the environment for an increased role for the private sector. Three loans were approved for programs in the finance sector between 1990 and 1996. A number of TA activities were also prepared to support policy reform (Table 5.9). The large Second Development Finance Loan ($200 million) was approved in 1993 with the aim of promoting the development of export industries and improving financial intermediation. It was designed as an umbrella loan with the plan that the loan proceeds would be re-lent to nine participating financial institutions. As things turned out however, utilization of the loan was slower than expected for various reasons including the problems that arose following the impact of the Asian financial crisis.[50]

Table 5.9: Advisory Technical Assistance for the Financial Sector, 1990–1996

Title	Amount $ '000	Date approved
Strengthening of Term Lending Capabilities of Participating Private Commercial Banks under Bank's Development Finance Loan	100	June 1990
Development of the Venture Capital Industry	92	June 1990
Development of the Leasing Industry	92	June 1990
Securities Market Development—Phase II	592	July 1991
Secondary Mortgage Facility	96	June 1996
Institutional strengthening of Regional Development Account	600	December 1996
Total	**1,572**	

Source: Asian Development Bank, 2005, *Country Assistance Program*, 164.

[49] Ibid., 36.
[50] ADB, 2004, *Second Development Finance Project*.

ADB supported a range of other activities to help the commercialization of state-owned enterprises and to promote the private sector.[51] In 1994, bank project reports discussed the possibility of amalgamating local government-owned water companies (PDAMs) into regional water authorities. The same year, ADB strategy focused on encouraging the privatization of the more successful urban water supply enterprises and targeting assistance to lower-income communities by cross-subsidizing user fees. But little progress was made in promoting these reforms.

Nor did ADB's other efforts to support the expansion of the private sector yield quick results. In the early 1990s, a range of loans was approved for activities by private borrowers (Table 5.7).[52] Taken together, these activities were small and reflected the practical difficulties that ADB ran into in trying to expand the bank's work in the private sector.

Despite this emphasis on promoting the private sector, ADB's experience in encouraging private sector growth in Indonesia was at best a mixed success. And, more broadly, wider attempts by other agencies including the World Bank and the government were only partially successful. In retrospect, it can be seen that the institutional infrastructure for the rapid development of a strong private sector in Indonesia was lacking: The legal framework was uncertain, and few of the official regulatory agencies had the resources to function well. In reviewing the experience of attempts to promote private sector involvement in the power sector in Indonesia in the 1990s, Wells concluded that:[53]

> If investors prove unwilling to accept arrangements that are more favorable to Indonesia than those of the 1990s, the country would do better by borrowing and building infrastructure itself. ... If Indonesia can do no better in new arrangements, privatization is simply too costly. Borrowed funds and state ownership, with all their problems, would be preferable.

These cautionary comments would appear to be relevant for programs designed to expand the role of the private sector to other parts of the Indonesian economy as well.

---

[51] ADB, 2005, *Country Assistance Program*, 156.

[52] These included (among others) loans to P.T. Wiraswasta Gemilang (1993 for $17 million, loan without government guarantee), P.T. Sunnymas Prima Agung (1993 for $9 million, without government guarantee), and P.T. Bandjarmasin Agrojaya Mandiri (1996 for $32.5 million, loan without government guarantee).

[53] Wells, 2007, Private Power, 362. See also Sambodo, 2016, *From Darkness*, 79, for a discussion of the contractual problems that arose in the power sector when private investors were encouraged to support projects in the generation sector in the 1990s.

While the main focus of ADB's work was on programs within Indonesia, the bank was also supporting regional activities that Indonesia was participating in. In 1993, the Indonesia–Malaysia–Thailand Growth Triangle was established as a subregional activity to promote economic cooperation. In 1995, the Brunei Darussalam–Indonesia–Malaysia–Philippines East ASEAN Growth Area (BIMP-EAGA) was launched to address inequalities in development (Box 5.3). Progress on expanding activities within these and other regional programs has taken time because limited resources are available. Nevertheless, these agreements are part of the broader network of linkages across Southeast Asia which strengthen regional cooperation.

Calm Before the Storm

The benefits of economic reform during this period led to rapid development reflected in expanding job markets and a widening range of consumer goods becoming available. Domestic and foreign investment underpinned a boom in the labor-intensive manufacturing sector which, in turn, was the driving force behind many of the employment gains in the period 1985 to 1995. During the decade, employment in the textiles, clothing, and footwear sector in Indonesia grew by over 10% per annum. Young women from rural areas in Java, especially, benefited from the job opportunities that opened up in new firms producing textiles, clothing and footwear. These firms produced for domestic as well as export markets. The result was a rapid expansion in the supply of lower-cost consumer goods in Indonesia in the early 1990s. Poverty had been falling markedly as well during the previous two decades. In the mid-1970s, more than 50 million people (around 40% of the population) had been living in poverty. By 1996, the poverty level had been reduced to an estimated 22.5 million people (around 11% of the population).

In 1993, Kimimasa Tarumizu spoke of critical challenges in the Asian region as he reviewed trends in his last annual meeting speech as the fifth president of ADB. The challenges Tarumizu listed were certainly relevant for Indonesia. He listed the urgent need for development of human resources, the importance of improved economic performance, the fact that poverty remained pervasive across Asia, and that environmental degradation had become a matter of great concern, especially since the Earth Summit in Rio de Janeiro in 1992.

Nevertheless, as the third decade of ADB's work in Indonesia came to a close, prospects seemed encouraging. There were, it was true, signs of strain in some sectors. However these signs of strain seemed to reflect pressures of growth rather than failures of policy. The challenge for policymakers seemed to be one of managing rapid growth. But this was the calm before the storm. Very soon, as the next chapter shows, the Asian financial crisis would engulf Indonesia. As the crisis widened, ADB would need to quickly design flexible programs to respond to Indonesia's needs for assistance.

Box 5.3: Northeast Indonesia: Development through Cooperation

Northeast (NE) Indonesia—comprising East Kalimantan, West Kalimantan, and North Sulawesi—is perhaps the most underdeveloped area of the country. Most of its residents are poor and are engaged in farming, forestry, or fisheries.

The marginalized socioeconomic conditions prevailing in NE Indonesia are in large part because recent development plans have directed proportionately greater resources to the development of Java. To promote regional equity, the Government of Indonesia in its latest national Five-Year Development Plan, Repelita VI, has accorded priority status to NE Indonesia. A major strategy in this regard is the government's promotion of economic cooperation with neighboring economies.

Indonesia is currently participating in regional economic ventures, such as the Indonesia–Malaysia–Singapore (IMS) and Indonesia–Malaysia–Thailand (IMT) growth triangles. Drawing on these experiences, the Indonesian Government agreed to participate in an initiative to explore potential areas of cooperation within the Brunei Darussalam–Indonesia–Malaysia–Philippines East ASEAN Growth Area (BIMP-EAGA).

The development of NE Indonesia, however, largely depends on overcoming the constraints associated with the past neglect toward the subregion. To address these constraints, three major programs under the BIMP-EAGA scheme are being proposed by an ADB technical assistance study: human resource development; infrastructure development; and development of productive sectors.

ADB = Asian Development Bank, Repelita = Five-Year Development Plan.
Source: Summarized from ADB, *Asian Development Outlook 1996–1997*, 80.

Workers clear open areas as part of the Second Bandung Urban Development
Project, approved in 1985.

Coordinating Minister of Economics, Finance, Industry and Development
Supervision Ali Wardhana (*second left*) opens the ADB Indonesia Resident
Mission in 1987, witnessed by Finance Minister Radius Prawiro (*second right*) and
ADB President Masao Fujioka (*right*).

A resident of Sermo village passes by Sermo Dam in Kulon Progo, Yogyakarta, which was built as part of the Integrated Irrigation Sector Project (1990).

Students gather in front of a high school in Jakarta that received support under the Senior Secondary Education Project (1995).

CHAPTER 6

Asian Financial Crisis
(1997–1998)

Dealing with the Asian financial crisis of 1997–1998 was a new and unique experience for ADB. Though it had been called on in the past to assist in reconstruction efforts following natural or man-made disasters, such as earthquakes, floods, typhoons, and civil wars, it had never been confronted by anything as abrupt, massive, and volatile as this crisis.

Asian Development Bank, Special Evaluation Study of the ADB's Crisis Management Interventions in Indonesia, 2001.

At the beginning of 1997, the broad economic outlook for Indonesia seemed encouraging. To be sure, there were numerous challenges that needed attention. However there was little sign that a major financial crisis was about to unfold.

While there was some worrying pressure on the Thai baht in foreign exchange markets in mid-May, the indications were that the Thai monetary authorities were taking effective steps to respond. And there were—as usual—reports of poor management in the financial and corporate sectors in Indonesia. But these were not new problems. These well-known issues in Indonesia did not seem to present any immediate threat to the Indonesian financial system.

Appearances were misleading. By the end of the year, policymakers in Indonesia, the Republic of Korea and Thailand would be swept up in the eye of a powerful financial storm. Markets in other countries in the region would also be disrupted by financial contagion. By December 1997 the international community would be attempting, with no more than mixed success, to coordinate large emergency response programs in the three main crisis-affected countries. And while the Republic of Korea and Thailand would recover relatively quickly, the impact of the crisis would be much more severe in Indonesia and recovery would be slow.

Before the Crisis

Financial crises do not appear from nowhere. Many things are clearer in hindsight. Numerous factors contributed to the Asian financial crisis in Indonesia. In retrospect, it can be seen that trends earlier in the decade contributed to the combination of circumstances that underpinned the remarkable events that became known as the Asian financial crisis. These included, first, the zeal with which pro-market policies (including pro-market financial policies) were promoted following the fall of the Berlin Wall in 1989 and, second, the rapid increase in debt levels that occurred during the 1990s in Indonesia as domestic investors borrowed enthusiastically in international markets (and, it should be noted, creditors just as enthusiastically lent to them) to support activities, some of them highly speculative, at home.

In the post-Cold War policy environment, during the 1990s there was increasingly an emphasis in development thinking, especially in industrial countries, on the importance of markets. Much of the discussion focused particularly on financial markets and on the need for financial market liberalization. This was reflected, for example, in the official American statement at the Asian Development Bank (ADB) annual meeting in 1993 (delivered by Jeffrey R. Shafer) that:

> I want to especially mention financial markets. They are important in their own right; they are also crucial for realizing the full potential of every other sector. The financial sectors of some countries in this region are not keeping up with the needs of rapidly maturing economies. Financial reform is now underway and facilitating domestic resource mobilization, but the pace is sometimes snail-like, especially when it comes to market opening. It is as important to realize the gains from trade and competition in the financial sector as it is in manufacturing.

In hindsight, the "incessant prodding" (as Toyoo Gyohten described it) of the advocates of globalization appeared to have encouraged some developing countries in Asia to open their capital markets prematurely.[1] At the time, there was much support in international agencies such as the International Monetary Fund (IMF) for moves to liberalize capital markets. But there was less emphasis in these discussions for the need for countries

---

[1]   Gyohten, 2006, 10.

such as Indonesia to sequence the process of capital liberalization carefully so as to ensure that timely changes to other aspects of financial policy— such as the liberalization of foreign exchange markets and the regulation of domestic financial markets—were introduced as well. There was, as policymakers in Indonesia such as Anwar Nasution have pointed out, a failure to consider carefully the appropriate regulatory arrangements that might be needed during the process of liberalizing financial markets.

Partly in response to the encouragement to liberalize, developing countries in Asia such as Indonesia began to open their capital markets. In 1994, the ADB *Asian Development Outlook* reported that:[2]

> Since the late 1980s, regulatory reforms have been undertaken by many Developing Member Countries and financial markets are now faced with far fewer regulatory controls and thus there is greater scope for operational flexibility. Liberalization measures have eased many of the restrictions on foreign participation and ownership in most economies.

These changes encouraged an upsurge of international investor interest in opportunities in developing Asia. A financial boom began to develop in cities such as Bangkok, Jakarta, Manila, and Singapore. In Jakarta, the stock market rose by 115% in 1993. During the next few years, both short-term portfolio capital and longer-term foreign direct investment (FDI) capital flowed into the region. FDI flows to four of the main Association of Southeast Asian Nations (ASEAN) countries, Indonesia, Malaysia, the Philippines, and Thailand, increased rapidly in the several years before the crisis from $9.4 billion in 1994 to $14.6 billion in 1996.[3]

A striking feature of the three countries which required large amounts of assistance during the crisis—the Republic of Korea, Indonesia, and Thailand—was that they all took on relatively large amounts of short-term debt. These three economies were the only ones in the region with a ratio of short-term foreign debt to official reserves of more than 100% at the end of 1996.[4] It was not recognized at the time, but this situation led to a serious "double mismatch" problem when investors in Asia borrowed large amounts of short-term debt in a foreign currency (usually US dollars)

---

2   ADB, 1994, *Asian Development Outlook*, 18.
3   ADB, 1999, 258.
4   Sussangkarn, 2010, 1.

and used the funds to promote relatively long-term and illiquid projects which often provided income flows only in local currencies. The result was that when Asian currencies were unexpectedly devalued in 1997 and foreign lenders called in the short-term debts, investors in the region were faced with the double mismatch problem. They were both short of the immediate liquidity needed to repay debts and, simultaneously, needed to find much larger amounts of local currency than expected to repay foreign obligations denominated in US dollars.

To add to the difficulties, in the countries most seriously shaken by the crisis, both the financial and corporate sectors were deeply affected. In Indonesia, numerous non-financial corporate firms had borrowed overseas. When the crisis broke out, these firms soon found themselves in difficulties. In other cases in Indonesia, financial sector institutions, especially banks, had acted as intermediaries, taking on foreign debt and then relending the funds in local currencies. As a result, the banking sector was quickly drawn into the crisis with widespread financial effects across the Indonesian economy.

The Crisis Erupts

The Asian financial crisis, it is generally agreed, began in Thailand. Some signs of economic difficulties began to appear in Thailand in early 1997. But at the time, the difficulties did not seem to be especially important.[5] By mid-1997, however, the speculative pressure against the baht was mounting. On 2 July, the Thai authorities recognized the inevitable, devalued the baht, and allowed the currency to float (Box 6.1). The baht immediately entered a period of sustained depreciation. In hindsight, the decision to devalue the baht on 2 July 1997 marked the start of the Asian financial crisis.[6]

The crisis in Indonesia was in turn triggered by contagion from Thailand.[7] Although economic conditions seemed firm in the first half of 1997, the rupiah began to weaken in the second week of July 1997 following the

[5] ADB, 1997b, Box 2.2.
[6] The notion that a major financial crisis can be said to have commenced on any particular day is somewhat arbitrary but many observers mention 2 July as the day that the Asian financial crisis began. Writing just a few months later, for example, Lindblad (1997, 4) said, "It all started in Bangkok on 2 July 1997. The baht was floated and immediately depreciated by 18%." See also ADB, 1999, *Asian Development Outlook 1999*, 21.
[7] Blustein, 2001, provides a vivid account of the crisis in Indonesia.

Box 6.1: Asian Financial Crisis in Indonesia: Key Dates

Date	Event
1997	
14 May	Thailand tried to defend the Thai baht against speculative attacks using foreign reserves.
2 July	A managed float of the Thai baht was announced. News of the devaluation drops the value of the baht by as much as 20%, triggering widening turmoil in Asian financial markets.
14 August	Indonesia abandoned its system of closely managing the exchange rate and allowed the rupiah to float, triggering a loss of confidence and a plunge in the currency.
31 October	A $23 billion IMF-led rescue package for Indonesia (with participation of ADB, the World Bank, and various nations) was announced.
1 November	The Government of Indonesia closed 16 banks.
19 November	Deputy finance ministers met in Manila and issued the Manila Framework statement.
9 December	The rupiah fell sharply following concerns about the financial situation in Indonesia and rumors that President Soeharto was gravely ill.
19 December	ADB agreed to a $4 billion emergency loan for the Republic of Korea, and $1.3 billion emergency assistance for Thailand.
22 December	Moody's Investors Service downgraded the sovereign debt of four countries—Indonesia, the Republic of Korea, Malaysia, and Thailand.
1998	
7 January	Indonesian, Malaysian, Philippine, and Thai currencies fell to new lows, pulling down stock markets across the region.
9 January	US President Bill Clinton called President Soeharto to insist that an IMF-proposed program be followed.
15 January	IMF managing director visited Indonesia to sign an agreement with President Soeharto.

continued on next page

Box 6.1 *continued*

14 February	54 banks were deemed uncreditworthy and brought under the authority of the IBRA.
3 March	Senior US officials said that the US would not support the IMF's next loan disbursement to Indonesia without adequate progress in reforms.
8 April	The IMF approved a new $3 billion package for Indonesia.
21 April	The Indonesian central bank raised the one-month interest rate to 50%.
21 May	President Soeharto resigned; B.J. Habibie became president.
28 May	The Bank of Central Asia was put under IBRA control after a massive run.
24 June	The Government of Indonesia signed an agreement with the IMF, the fourth in nine months.
25 June	ADB approved a $1.4 billion loan to Indonesia.
23 September	Paris Club rescheduled $4.2 billion of sovereign debt of Indonesia.
31 December	Indonesia's GDP was estimated to have fallen by around 13% during 1998.

ADB = Asian Development Bank, IMF = International Monetary Fund, IBRA = Indonesian Bank Restructuring Agency, GDP = gross domestic product.

Source: ADB and IMF documents. A more detailed timeline is in IMF, 2003, 91, Appendix A1.2.

floating of the baht. Faced with what appeared to be some concern in financial markets, on 11 July the Indonesian authorities announced that the range that the rupiah was allowed to trade in would be widened.

Initially, the decision to widen the range was seen as almost a routine exercise. Similar arrangements had been made a number of times before. Previously, when changes of this kind had been announced, the rupiah had strengthened. But ominously, on this occasion the rupiah began to weaken. J. Soedradjad Djiwandono, who was governor of Bank Indonesia at the time, has noted that it soon became apparent that a "contagion effect was in progress" because the "herd instinct" of international creditors, worried by events in Thailand, was to move their investments out of Asia.[8] To the surprise of Indonesian monetary authorities, the beginnings of capital flight began to appear.

During July there was increasing pressure on the rupiah. By the first week of August, the currency had weakened somewhat from around Rp2,300 to Rp2,600 against the US dollar. Other countries in the region had decided to allow their currencies to float freely so on 14 August it was announced that the rupiah would be allowed to float as well. At the same time, a package of other monetary and fiscal measures was implemented which was intended to strengthen confidence and bolster financial markets.

But the efforts to strengthen confidence did not work. Indeed, the new measures announced by the Government of Indonesia seemed to have the perverse effect of unnerving investors further. The rupiah quickly fell to Rp2,900. The situation was becoming worrying. And then, quite quickly, a new problem developed. Not only were there signs of a loss of confidence in the rupiah in international markets but there were indications of a loss of confidence at home as well. Runs on domestic banks began to occur in the second half of August. Within Indonesia a "flight to safety" from bank accounts into cash was underway. The crisis was spreading. In just a few weeks, numerous Indonesian banks were in financial difficulties. At the end of August, more than 50 domestic banks failed to comply with the minimum official reserve requirements of the banking system of 5%.

The government responded quickly. On 3 September, an additional policy package of fiscal and other measures was announced. But confidence, often somewhat fragile in Indonesia, was beginning to evaporate. As before, these measures failed to stabilize financial markets. The rupiah fell further before recovering temporarily to a level of Rp3,200. Meanwhile, there were signs that the crisis was continuing to widen. Economic distress was beginning to spread across into the corporate sector.

Realizing that the problem of confidence was becoming serious, the government looked to the IMF for support. The hope was that a substantial international program would help restore trust across the markets. After some brief delays to discuss details, on 31 October, a package totaling $23 billion was announced which included support from

---

[8] Djiwandono, 2000, 52. An authoritative account of the evolution of the crisis and Bank Indonesia's role is in Djiwandono, 2005, *Bank Indonesia*. See also Goeltom, 2008, *Reassessing the IMF Programme*.

ADB, the World Bank, and a range of bilateral participants.[9] To strengthen the package, a letter of intent (LOI) setting out agreed policy reforms was signed between Indonesia and the IMF.

Although the storm clouds were gathering quickly, it was still hard to believe that an economy which had done well for almost 30 years was facing such severe difficulties. And the international community, especially in official circles, tended to rely on the IMF to judge what was happening in financial markets in the region. In early November, therefore, both Indonesian policymakers and advisers in international agencies such as the IMF continued to hope that a well-judged approach would restore confidence.[10] Some years later, an IMF evaluation report on events at the time would note that, "At this stage, the IMF believed that the crisis was a moderate case of contagion in which the exchange rate had overshot."[11] But it soon became clear that there was nothing moderate about the crisis.

One of the requirements of the LOI signed on 31 October was that 16 insolvent banks in Indonesia be closed. The aim of imposing firmer discipline in the banking sector was to show that lax financial arrangements were not acceptable and that the government intended to enforce the rules. But rather than strengthening confidence, the sudden closure of the banks added to growing panic in the markets.

During the following weeks the crisis worsened. It soon began to appear that the government could not restore confidence in financial markets. This perception fueled a wider crisis of confidence in the overall ability of the government to manage the broader affairs of the nation. It did not help that in early December, President Soeharto became sick. Reports about his ill-health attracted wide attention in the media. The financial crisis, then, was reinforced by a widening crisis in the corporate sector, all of which was magnified by a growing political crisis. The rupiah began to fall rapidly below the Rp 5,000 level and soon reached Rp 6,000. During early January, the rupiah entered a dizzy fall toward Rp 10,000 against the US dollar. Confidence had collapsed.

Faced with this rapid deterioration in the situation and much public confusion about the direction of economic policy, the government and the IMF agreed that a second LOI was necessary. On 15 January 1998, in a widely

---

[9]   Details of the package are provided in Djiwandono, 2000, 54.
[10] Grenville, 2004, 4.
[11] IMF, 2003, 13.

publicized and rather dramatic ceremony attended by IMF Managing Director Michel Camdessus, President Soeharto personally signed a new LOI outlining a greatly strengthened, and highly controversial, structural reform program.[12] However the January program was never presented to the IMF Executive Board in Washington because it failed to halt the spiraling collapse of the exchange rate. On 23 January, the rupiah sank past Rp 15,000 against the US dollar. All attempts to stabilize the panic in the markets had failed.

During the next few months the economic and political situation in Indonesia continued to deteriorate. On 4 April 1998, the IMF and the government agreed on another assistance package totaling $3 billion which was disbursed in several stages over the next few months. However the uncertainty in markets continued. In May the political crisis reached a peak when President Soeharto resigned.

The new president, B.J. Habibie, quickly introduced a series of political and economic reforms. The wide range of reforms introduced during his tenure in office ushered in a period of change which became known as the *Reformasi* (Reforma Era) period. The *Reformasi* approach—which embodied a willingness to reconsider many aspects of the approach to governance that had become established during the previous New Order Era—was carried on by the two successive presidents, Abdurrahman Wahid and Megawati Soekarnoputri.

Habibie's period in office turned out to be short. The series of liberalizing political changes he introduced were well received by many Indonesians but dismayed other, more traditional groups. He announced that free elections would be held in 1999, the first in Indonesia for over 40 years. But economic recovery was very slow. In 1998, the economy experienced a severe recession with national output estimated to have fallen by around 12%. As things turned out, it was almost a decade before real income per person in Indonesia climbed back to precrisis levels and sustained economic growth began to take hold once more.

The political situation was also difficult. Established political parties were keen to rebuild their influence in the post-Soeharto period so when

---

[12] Extensive details are provided in an IMF evaluation report prepared in 2003 (IMF, 2003, 15). A comprehensive timeline of events is provided in the IMF evaluation report (IMF, 2003, 91). A memorandum accompanying the LOI set out the policies that Indonesia intended to follow as part of the agreement with the IMF (IMF, 1998).

President Habibie presented an accountability speech before the People's Consultative Assembly (MPR) in October 1999, it was rejected and he resigned as president. The new president was Wahid, universally known as Gus Dur. It was then during the presidency of Wahid, and of Megawati who succeeded him, that the international community, including ADB, designed a range of programs to help promote Indonesia's recovery from the Asian financial crisis.

Donors and the Crisis

On the eve of the Asian financial crisis in early 1997, the international donor community did not have plans to introduce any significant changes to the established programs of assistance to Indonesia. Indeed, there was some discussion as to whether it was not time to scale back the overall level of assistance to the country. Some commentators pointed out that private sector flows to Indonesia had been strong during the 1990s, that economic growth had been robust, and suggested that perhaps there was less need for aid to Indonesia than had been the case in the past. However the World Bank, in presenting the annual survey of the Indonesian economy to a meeting of donors at the Consultative Group on Indonesia (CGI) meeting in Tokyo in mid-1997, argued that the provision of foreign assistance was still important (Box 6.2).

At the Tokyo CGI meeting on 16–17 July there was no sense among delegates that a crisis was looming. The float of the Thai baht had been announced just two weeks earlier but the events in Thailand did not seem likely to affect markets in Indonesia. Rather, the mood of the international community was supportive of Indonesia. The most recent World Bank survey of developments in Indonesia, issued just shortly before the CGI meeting, reported that, "On the basis of broad macro indicators, Indonesia's economy has performed very well recently."[13] To be sure, the World Bank also noted that significant risks remained and warned that a reversal of capital flows could cause problems. Nevertheless, in mid-1997, the donor community remained confident that economic management in Indonesia remained effective.

---

[13]   World Bank, 1997, *Sustaining High Growth*, xxi.

Box 6.2: World Bank's View on the Need for Aid to Indonesia in Mid-1997

"Although the private sector has provided a growing share of Indonesia's external financing needs in recent years, official foreign assistance will still be important for several reasons. First, it represents virtually the only source of stable, long-term funding for public investments which are not attractive to the private sector. These include education, public health, and most infrastructure, especially in the Outer Islands. Second, official assistance often comes with strong project appraisal and preparation as well as technical assistance. Third, private finance is only available in a few infrastructure sectors. Fourth, there is a risk involved in relying too heavily on private finance for public investments, as highlighted, for example, by the Mexican crisis. Finally, the long-term nature and risk diversification associated with official assistance improves the structure of debt and the debt service profile, thus reducing exposure to the risk of sudden shifts in private capital flows."

Source: World Bank, May 1997, *Indonesia: Sustaining High Growth with Equity*, tabled at the 1997 Consultative Group on Indonesia meeting in Tokyo in July 1997.

As was usual after meetings of the CGI, the headline figure for total pledges received considerable publicity. This was particularly the case following the float of the Thai baht because there were already some widening signs of uncertainty in financial markets in Southeast Asia. At the Tokyo meeting, total CGI commitments amounted to around $5.3 billion. This amount scarcely differed in nominal terms from the level that had become customary since the CGI had been established in 1992.

The donor community and other international observers were aware of the fact that flows of international assistance were only part of the broader amounts of total capital flows to Indonesia. Private flows—such as foreign direct investment and increasing amounts of portfolio investment—also helped finance the deficit on current account. Nevertheless, considering the state of the current and capital accounts, the view of both Indonesian policymakers and international observers at the time was that Indonesia's financial and economic position was sound and that there was no need to consider making any adjustments in the program for assistance to Indonesia. Very soon, however, the international community would need to revise these views.

The pressures on the rupiah, which mounted in August and September, initially seemed to reflect short-term fluctuations in financial markets. Usually the donor community had relied on monetary authorities—such as Indonesia's central bank, Bank Indonesia; and the IMF—to respond to events in financial markets. Bilateral donors, therefore, monitored the changes in Indonesia but did not see any need to adjust their established aid programs.

As seen earlier, the Indonesian authorities, in turn, looked to the IMF for support. However the IMF's $23 billion program announced on 31 October and subsequent efforts in November and December failed to restore stability. Perhaps the main weakness of the response to the financial crisis in Indonesia at this stage was that few policymakers understood how fragile the financial system was. The IMF later concluded that:[14]

> The initial program was designed on the assumption that the crisis was essentially a moderate case of contagion and the implementation of a relatively conventional IMF-supported program would bring the rupiah back into a reasonable range. These expectations were belied and, towards the end of December, it became clear that the crisis in Indonesia was much more severe than elsewhere in the region.

As events unfolded in late 1997 and early 1998, most bilateral donor agencies relied almost entirely on the multilateral financial institutions to restore economic stability. The problem for most bilateral donor agencies was that the crisis was unfolding in financial markets. But the management of financial markets was not an area of economic activity that most bilateral agencies had experience of. And it was only later, in 1998 and in 1999, that policymakers began to give more attention to the widening impacts of the crisis beyond the financial sector. As a response to these impacts, the donor community, including ADB, prepared a range of programs to support adjustment and recovery. In the event, as will be seen below, the impact of the crisis was severe and recovery was slow.

ADB Response

ADB, like the rest of the international community, was unprepared for the scale and pace of the crisis. And like the other two major multilateral

---

[14]   IMF, 2003, 65.

institutions, the IMF and the World Bank, ADB needed to respond both rapidly and in a flexible way.

Considering that ADB is known as a prudent institution which normally prefers to take time to consider new activities carefully, the speed and manner of the bank's response to the Asian financial crisis was remarkable. Pragmatic considerations took over from normal cumbersome procedures in responding to the rapidly evolving crisis.

Managing ADB's response to the events in Indonesia proved very challenging. ADB played a strong and active role during the crisis in Indonesia, providing both funds and technical advice. However, the task proved difficult and ADB's program was delayed. Problems arose because, first, the international community itself was divided on important issues of policy and, second, there were sharp disagreements within the Government of Indonesia which were exacerbated by the rapidly deteriorating political situation.

ADB's approach, following international practice, was to rely on the IMF to take the lead in setting out conditions for support for a crisis-oriented program to help Indonesia. An ADB team arrived in Jakarta shortly after the main IMF mission from Washington in October 1997. However difficulties of coordination soon arose between the different teams working for the IMF, World Bank, and ADB. Partly, the problems of coordination were practical ones. Staff from the three institutions worked out of different offices which meant that the coordination of dozens of meetings at unpredictable hours proved difficult. To complicate matters, the IMF team was subject to close guidance from senior IMF management in Washington, DC. who often wanted to hold lengthy phone conferences into the early hours of the morning in Jakarta.

Partly, too, there were disagreements between the multilateral teams about policy and the approach to take in negotiating with the Indonesian authorities. The IMF team, in answering to a disciplined hierarchy in Washington, found that it had little leeway in these matters when discussing the issues with World Bank and ADB colleagues. Before too long, the leaders of the ADB team were sufficiently irritated as to write to the head of the IMF team in Jakarta expressing their frustration.[15] Further, not surprisingly, the disagreements between the teams from the three institutions were sometimes apparent to their Indonesia colleagues. One

---

[15]   Blustein, 2001, 104.

Indonesian official is reported as chiding a World Bank staffer that, "The patient is dying, and the three doctors are fighting."

The problems of coordination between the IMF and ADB were later outlined in a frank IMF evaluation report of policy responses during the financial crises in Indonesia and the Republic of Korea.[16] After noting that there had been differences in approach between the IMF and World Bank teams in Jakarta, the IMF report observed that:[17]

> The relationship with the ADB was also difficult...Citing confidentiality...the IMF staff did not keep the ADB team fully informed of issues being discussed with the Indonesian authorities. The relationship was cool at best and continued to deteriorate until the end of January 1998, when the ADB temporarily pulled out of the collaborative relationship with the IMF over disagreement on the creation of the IBRA [Indonesian Bank Restructuring Agency]. The first ADB program loan, for US$1.4 billion, was not approved until June 1998. Subsequently, working relationships were established again. ADB staff was involved in financial sector work with MAD [the Monetary and Exchange Affairs Department of the IMF], and took the lead in the audits of the "non-IBRA banks."

Despite these difficulties, the three multilateral organizations worked as well as possible within the fraying administrative and political conditions to prepare programs of assistance.

In December 1997 and January 1998 an ADB mission visited Indonesia to prepare plans for the large $1.4 billion loan to support the Financial Governance Reforms: Sector Development Program. The program was almost set in place when the plans were disrupted by the overriding agreement signed between President Soeharto and the managing director of the IMF, Michel Camdessus, on 15 January 1998 in Jakarta. Subsequent delays, and the need for the ADB program to be redesigned, meant that this first main ADB crisis-related loan for Indonesia was delayed and was not agreed to by the ADB Board until 25 June 1998.[18]

---

[16] The IMF report also discussed the crisis in Brazil which occurred in 1998–1999. See IMF, 2003.
[17] IMF, 2003, 82.
[18] McCawley, 2017, *Banking on the Future*, 218. An extensive discussion of the political economy of the design and implementation of the Financial Sector Governance Reforms Sector Development Program is in Abonyi, *Policy Reform in Indonesia*.

During 1998 and 1999, ADB approved five fast-disbursing loans for
$2.8 billion (Table 6.1). These loans, collectively referred to as crisis-
support loans, were regarded as part of the initial IMF package of
$23 billion in October 1997 underpinned by an LOI. Particular features
of ADB's approach were a focus on measures to improve the operations
of capital markets and on loans to provide social protection to the poor.[19]
Apart from specific objectives for each of the five loans, a common purpose
underpinning all of the loans was to provide liquidity and budgetary
support to Indonesia.[20]

The recovery in Indonesia took much longer than in Thailand or the
Republic of Korea. The ADB program in Indonesia extended well past
2000. The implementation of ADB activities in the post-crisis period in
Indonesia was affected by a "big bang" radical decentralization of the
government in Indonesia between 1999 and 2001, which complicated the
delivery of assistance. A later ADB country evaluation study noted that this
change had caught the bank unawares because "ADB was unprepared for

**Table 6.1: Main Crisis-Related Loans provided by ADB to Indonesia
during the Asian Financial Crisis**

Date	Loan	Amount ($ million)
25 June 1998	Financial Governance Reforms Sector Development Program	1,500
9 July 1998	Social Protection Sector Development Program	306
23 March 1999	Power Sector Restructuring Program	400
25 March 1999	Health and Nutrition Sector Development Program	303
25 March 1999	Community and Local Government Support Sector Program Development Program	322

Notes:
1. Date is the date of ADB Board approval.
2. Amount is the amounts provided by ADB; in some cases additional cofinancing was
   provided by other institutions.

Source: ADB annual reports for 1997, 1998, and 1999.

---

[19]　See the ADB *Special Evaluation Study on the Interventions in Indonesia* (ADB, 2001) for a
　　discussion of ADB's approach.
[20]　ADB, 2001.

the flexibility required to adjust to the needs of a rapidly changing client."[21] In 2003, Indonesia finally graduated from the main IMF stabilization program, the last of the three main crisis-affected countries to do so.[22] But it took several more years before stronger economic growth began to gather pace.

Issues from the Crisis

The 1997–1998 crisis imposed very severe economic and social costs in Indonesia and other countries in the region. The result was that there was, among other things, much criticism of the role that international agencies played, especially the IMF. These criticisms led, over time, to major reconsiderations within the international community about the appropriate way to respond to a financial crisis.

Not surprisingly, the reconsiderations were further stimulated by the 2008 financial crisis in the United States (US) and Europe. As far as the Asian financial crisis of 1997–1998 was concerned, discussion focused on three main issues: analyzing the causes of the crisis, considering the nature of policy responses, and formulating programs to mitigate the social impact of the crisis. There was also a fourth issue: the long-term damage that the experience during the crisis left in developing countries in Asia and their views toward engagement with the international economy.

Causes of the Crisis

Following the crisis there was widespread discussion about the factors that triggered the financial collapse. Two main views emerged.[23] A "weak fundamentals" approach pointed to a range of underlying problems (such as structural and policy distortions, and weak governance) that had been present in Indonesia and the other crisis-affected countries before the problems emerged. According to this view, the crisis was essentially caused by these weak fundamentals even though, later, the collapse of market confidence led to excessive capital flight and an economic collapse.

An alternative "investors' panic" approach emphasized the unexpected shifts in market expectations and the loss of confidence following regional

---

[21]   ADB, *Country Assistance Program*, 2005, 10.
[22]   ADB, *Country Assistance Program*, 2005, 4.
[23]   Zhuang and Dowling, 2003, Lessons.

contagion.[24] This view recognized that certain structural and governance problems had existed in Indonesia and other crisis-affected countries but pointed to the strong macroeconomic performance before the crisis. This approach suggested that the nature of the crisis was more due to "herd behaviour" and market panic than to the underlying fundamental problems.

Both of the approaches contribute to an understanding of the crisis. That there were structural and policy weaknesses, both in Indonesia and as well as in other developing countries in Asia, had been widely recognized for many years. In view of the way the crisis in Indonesia widened into an overall crisis of governance, it seems clear that in Indonesia at least, the fundamental problems exacerbated the financial ones. But it is also evident that the immediate trigger for the crisis in Indonesia was imbalances in financial markets. The collapse of investor confidence in Indonesia led to sharp and unexpected flights of capital. These flights of capital quickly caused serious problems in other parts of the economy.

The Asian financial crisis in Indonesia, therefore, began as a *capital account* crisis in the balance of payments, not a traditional *current account* crisis. One of the problems during the early stages of the crisis was that the nature of short-term capital flows was not fully recognized, either by borrowers and lenders in the markets or by international organizations. To be sure, once capital had begun to flee, there was a tendency for the problems to widen into the corporate sector and into a crisis of confidence in the government. However, in retrospect, it is clear that the sanguine view of the benefits of free capital flows which were widely held before the crisis underestimated the difficulties of managing capital flows in developing countries in Asia.

The international debate about capital flows, and about the appropriate way of facilitating flows, evolved considerably following the crisis.[25] In recent years, there has been a rethinking in the international policy community about the role of capital flows. The current consensus is that perhaps large flows of uncontrolled "hot money" can be destabilizing and that careful thought is needed on how to manage these flows. That sudden changes in capital flows can complicate macroeconomic management was reinforced in mid-2013 during the "taper tantrum" in Indonesia when talk of an impending "taper" in US monetary policy led to capital flight.

---

[24] See, for example, McLeod, 1997, 35.
[25] Villafuerte and Yap, 2015, Managing Capital Flows.

Policy Responses

The policy approaches supported by the international community during the Asian financial crisis were strongly criticized in some quarters. Criticisms focused on both the short-term macroeconomic policies adopted as well as on the longer-term structural adjustments expected to be implemented in the crisis-affected countries.

The main criticisms of short-term macroeconomic policy were that the international community, as part of the conditionalities set for emergency loans, insisted that excessively tight monetary and fiscal policies be imposed in the affected countries. The results of this approach, critics argued, were that aggregate demand was unduly restrained although the economies in the region were already in recession; the balance sheets of banks and non-financial corporations were greatly damaged; and widespread unemployment was created, spreading needless social costs to millions of poor people in Asia.

It is hard to know, even with the benefit of many years of hindsight, just what combination of macroeconomic policies was needed at the time. The fiscal policies suggested by the international community were probably too contractionary, but whether or not the monetary policy suggested at the time was too restrictive is hard to determine. Today, 20 years later, discussion of these issues is complicated by the experience of the adoption of extremely expansionary monetary policies in Organisation for Economic Co-operation and Development (OECD) countries following the 2008 financial crisis; it is hard to understand why international financial advisers recommended contractionary policies during the Asian financial crisis but expansionary policies following the 2008 crisis.

There was also controversy about the stringent conditions that the international community attached to the emergency loans for Indonesia. Two main issues related to the nature of the conditionality programs, and of the realities of attempting to introduce widespread structural reforms at the time. As far as the nature of the programs is concerned, debates revolved around whether it was sensible for the international monetary community to urge that very ambitious structural reforms be adopted. The practical policy realities of the approach drew criticism as well. Critics suggested it was quite unrealistic to expect that structural adjustment programs of this kind could be introduced when Indonesia was passing through a period of extreme difficulty.

Mitigating the Social Impact

It was soon recognized that the economic and social consequences of the crisis would be severe. Unemployment began to rise and social impacts such as the growing numbers of children dropping out of school and the rising levels of malnutrition began to attract attention. The international community quickly realized that programs would be needed to help.

ADB made special attempts in Indonesia to address issues of poverty during the crisis.[26] A range of safety net programs were designed including a Social Protection Sector Development Program and a Health and Nutrition Sector Development Program, totaling $600 million (Box 6.3). Later evaluation

Box 6.3: Social Safety Net Programs

Social Protection Sector Development Program (SPSDP) and Health and Nutrition Sector Development Program (HNSDP), totaling $600 million, aimed to provide a social safety net to the poor affected by the crisis. These programs supported continuing the operations of schools and maintaining adequate health supplies during the crisis. By providing funds directly to the beneficiaries through post offices, they also established new approaches and mechanisms for building social safety nets and minimizing waste.

The investment components of the programs were successful in helping meet basic needs during the crisis. The programs provided employment opportunities, subsidized rice, free school, and health care. After the Asian Development Bank finished its assistance to these programs, the Government of Indonesia continued to fund the main activities.

Implementation of the policy component was slower than envisioned, due to the extensive conditionalities and the tight 12-month time frame for the second tranche release of funds. The programs were implemented under the decentralized structure, and faced administrative problems and capacity constraints at lower levels of government. Since HNSDP followed SPSDP, the feedback available from SPSDP was incorporated in the design and scope of HNSDP.

Source: ADB, 2005, *Country Assistance Program*, 13.

---

[26] For a survey of the social impact of the crisis and some suggestions for ADB responses, see Sigit and Surbakti, 1999, *Social Impact.*

studies indicated that the investment components of these programs were seen as successful in responding to the social issues caused by the crisis.

Nevertheless, poverty-oriented projects often had mixed results. Accurate targeting of poor households is not easy, especially during a crisis. In Indonesia local officials who distributed subsidized rice sometimes adopted rather rough and ready eligibility criteria, or just gave a share to everyone who demanded assistance.[27] Another problem was that for the poor, the opportunity cost of participating in the assistance programs was sometimes high because they were expected to take time to travel, line up for rations, and participate in discussions. The risk, under these circumstances, was that the benefits of the international programs would be captured by village elites.[28]

Views in the Region

During the 1997–1998 crisis, the international community expected Indonesia as well as the other crisis-affected countries to agree to strict adjustment policies as a condition for receiving assistance. Arrangements for these conditions were controversial, not least in Indonesia.[29] One of the long-term consequences of this difficult experience was a strengthening of the feeling that the dominant Bretton-Woods international financial institutions were, too often, influenced by a Western policy agenda.

Heightened apprehension about the role of the Bretton-Woods institutions and of the risks involved in undertaking international borrowings continued to influence discussions about public policy in Indonesia well after the crisis ended. These concerns served to encourage the view that the Washington-based international institutions tended to implement "one size fits all" prescriptions and that stronger regional institutions were needed to better reflect the interests of developing countries in Asia.

Concerns about borrowing were encouraged, too, by the sharp change in the pattern of capital flows to Indonesia after the crisis. In the several decades before the 1997–1998 crisis, Indonesia had generally imported capital to support high levels of investment and promote development programs. Following the crisis, Indonesia became much more cautious

---

[27] ADB, 2001, 13.
[28] ADB, 2001, 15.
[29] Soesastro and Basri, 1998, and Lee and Rhee, 2012.

about relying on the use of international capital. As a group, after the Asian financial crisis, Asian developing countries became net savers of capital rather than net borrowers. This led to the apparent paradox of "capital flowing uphill" from capital-scarce developing countries in Asia to capital-abundant OECD countries, especially the US.[30]

These changes in investment and savings patterns in Indonesia after the financial crisis were reflected in a rise in foreign exchange reserves held in Indonesia and other Asian countries after 2000. During the 1990s, foreign exchange reserves held across developing Asia rose by around 13% per annum. But in the eight years after 2000, the growth rate increased sharply to over 20% per year. During this latter period (2000–2008), regional reserves rose fourfold from around $700 million to nearly $3.4 billion.[31]

This rapid buildup of foreign exchange reserves led to much discussion. The changes in investment and savings were clearly the result of various factors. Some policymakers emphasized a "savings glut" view that suggested that Asia (especially the People's Republic of China) was flooding the world with excess savings. An alternative view pointed to an "investment slump" which noted that investment levels in some Asian countries had fallen markedly following the Asian financial crisis. The difference between the two views was important because of their differing implications for policy.[32]

Both views cast light on the changing patterns of savings and investment in Indonesia after the crisis. However, it seems clear that strong precautionary instincts encouraged by the difficult experience of the financial crisis were an important contributing element to the rise in savings. Following the crisis, policymakers in Indonesia were understandably inclined to self-insure by building up foreign exchange reserves. One measure of the damage caused by the crisis was that for the next two decades it was difficult for Indonesia to balance the need to promote investment at home with the need to build up savings abroad to bolster financial security against highly uncertain international capital flows.[33]

---

[30] Kramer, 2006; Prasad, Rajan and Subramanian, 2007.
[31] Park and Estrada, 2009.
[32] Kramer, 2006.
[33] A survey of the relationship between overall growth and investment patterns in Asia in the decade after the Asian financial crisis is provided in "Ten years after the crisis: The facts about investment and growth" in "Part 1 Developing Asia and the world," ADB, 2007, 46–65. See also the discussion about the problems caused by surges of short-term capital flows into developing countries in Asia in ADB, 2010, 39.

Lessons for ADB

There were lessons for ADB from the experience of the Asian financial crisis. One key question which many policymakers and observers wondered about for a long time after the crisis was why it was not foreseen. How was it that a regional development bank such as ADB, with many years of experience in working in Asia, did not anticipate the problems in Indonesia?

The answer is that before the crisis spread across the region in 1997, there was little reason for policymakers to expect that financial markets and institutions would be as fragile as turned out to be the case. The contagion of collapse of confidence across multiple markets was an entirely new feature of financial markets in Asia. Throughout the 1990s, governments across Asia, including in Indonesia, had been repeatedly urged by the international community to liberalize the management of financial markets in the region. With some hesitancy, Indonesian policymakers came to adopt this advice.

What was not foreseen was that the *sequencing* of liberalization was vital. In retrospect, it is clear that liberalizing financial markets *before* financial institutions were strengthened was a mistake. Strong and effective markets—including financial markets—can only operate well when there are strong and effective institutions to underpin those markets. The need to *sequence* reforms in Indonesia's financial market was not understood, including by international advisers. This lack of understanding of the importance of introducing reforms in the right sequence was a main factor that contributed to the failure to foresee the crisis.[34]

Other important lessons were discussed in some detail in several ADB evaluation reports including a *Special Evaluation Study of the Asian Development Bank's Crisis Management in Indonesia* released in 2001.[35] Several of the main lessons related to preparedness, to be ready to work with other partner institutions, and to plan to address both short-term and long-term priorities.

---

[34] Abonyi discusses the weaknesses that existed in the financial sector and the way that "liberalization of the financial sector in the 1980s and 1990s generally did not pay sufficient attention to the supervision and regulation required for a more open system." Abonyi, 2005, 9.

[35] ADB, 2000, *Crisis Management Interventions*.

It was clear from the experience of the crisis that the bank needed to be better prepared to respond to financial crises in the region. Dealing with the Asian financial crisis was a new challenge for ADB. The bank was not at all ready to deal with a crisis of such proportions, nor did it have ready the financial and policy tools that were needed. Nevertheless, the bank responded quickly, sending out staff to design new programs and participate fully in the international programs.

ADB also needed to develop new forms of assistance. The bank's traditional forms of lending such as project and program loans were not suitable financial instruments to use to respond to the crisis.[36] To be effective, the usual design of ADB's program loans needed to be adjusted to allow for large amounts of up-front funds to be disbursed almost immediately.

A second lesson was that the complexity of large-scale financial crises requires highly effective coordination across numerous international and national institutions. In the case of the Asian financial crisis, the size of the financial packages needed was too large to be within the means of a single agency such as the IMF. To support the IMF, the participation of other agencies such as the World Bank, ADB, and major bilateral aid agencies was necessary.

A third lesson for ADB was that it is necessary to address longer-term issues as well as short-term immediate priorities. One of the new challenges that ADB faced was that support provided during an emergency financial crisis is quite different to normal development assistance. On one hand, the short-term priorities are extremely urgent. Much of the financial support needs to be disbursed rapidly with the aim of bolstering market confidence. On the other hand, longer-term social costs such as growing unemployment and marked increases in poverty need to be addressed as well. ADB responded to these latter issues in Indonesia through the provision in 1999 of the sector development program loans for health and nutrition and for community and local government support.

There was a fourth lesson for ADB. This was the need for ADB to take steps to strengthen the region against crises of this kind. ADB responded both by supporting the development of new policies, and by establishing new programs within the bank.

---

[36]   ADB, 2001, *Study on Program Lending.*

Not surprisingly, the Asian financial crisis led to much consideration among policymakers as to what had gone wrong. ADB supported this region-wide process of reflection by sponsoring numerous seminars and by promoting the publication of books and articles. In 2003, for example, the ADB Institute published a study on *Post-Crisis Development Paradigms in Asia*,[37] and collections of articles by ADB staff and scholars such as *Asian Capital Market Development and Integration: Challenges and Opportunities*[38] were prepared. The annual issues of ADB's *Asian Development Outlook* regularly discussed the progress being made in the region to improve policies and institutions. Reviews of policy reform focused on numerous issues. Many observers emphasized the "investors' panic" view of the crisis. Other commentators noted that the "weak fundamentals" approach suggested that structural changes, such as measures to promote corporate reform and better governance as well as overcome the non-performing loans region in crisis-affected countries, were also necessary.[39]

ADB also established a range of new programs to help underpin the policy reform process. In early 1999 a Regional Economic Monitoring Unit (REMU) was formed in the bank to support ASEAN to carry out regional surveillance of economic policies and to operate a new Asia Recovery Information Center (ARIC). In 2000, the REMU began production of publications such as the *ASEAN Economic Outlook* and *East Asian Economic Monitor*. The same year, on the sidelines of ADB's annual meeting in Thailand in May, the Chiang Mai Initiative (CMI) was established to set up a network of bilateral swap arrangements among ASEAN, Japan, the People's Republic of China, and the Republic of Korea (ASEAN+3) and form a regional financing facility. Later, in 2010, the CMI evolved into the Chiang Mai Initiative Multilateralization.

Eventually the impact of the Asian financial crisis receded. Nevertheless, it was a decade before the ADB *Asian Development Outlook 2007* was able to note that "an air of normality has returned."[40]

---

[37] Yoshitomi and ADBI staff, 2003.
[38] ADB and Korea Capital Market Institute, 2014.
[39] ADB, 2000, Corporate and Financial Sector, 20.
[40] ADB, 2007, 46.

CHAPTER 7

Recovery
(1999–2006)

The Asian financial crisis delivered a deep blow to Indonesia. The slow, drawn out recovery from the crisis occupied much of the attention of senior economic policymakers for most of the rest of the fourth decade of ADB's work in Indonesia. The need to tailor programs to promote recovery was reflected in the work of the international community and in the Asian Development Bank's (ADB) activities during this period.

Aftermath of the Crisis

Three effects of the crisis, especially, left a mark. One was the fall in investment as a share of gross domestic product (GDP) from around 30% in the decade before the crisis to about 24% between 2000–2006. This sharp drop in investment, reflecting uncertainty and policy drift, hampered efforts to stimulate recovery.

Second, the need to reduce the level of national debt as a share of GDP was seen as an urgent priority. One of the consequences of the financial crisis was that the Government of Indonesia needed to provide emergency support to the banking system. The result was that government debt rose sharply. Starting from a moderate level of 23% of GDP in 1996, by 2001 the government had become burdened with debt that exceeded 90% of GDP.[1] Debt service payments also rose quickly to about 40% of government revenues, forcing authorities to introduce harsh expenditure cuts across the rest of the budget. These spending cuts put considerable pressure on the government's ability to maintain key spending on development and poverty reduction programs. Further, concerns about the level of government debt affected investor confidence, making it harder to attract long-term foreign direct investment.

---

[1] World Bank, 2001, 1.12.

Third, relations between Indonesia on one hand, and the International Monetary Fund (IMF) and the World Bank on the other, became strained.[2] In the short term, these strains were apparent in disagreements between Indonesian authorities and the Washington financial institutions about such things as arrangements for the disbursement of loan funds. In the longer term, there was abiding concern in some quarters in Indonesia, especially in parliamentary circles, about the relationship with the IMF.

Difficulties of Recovery

Political uncertainties also hampered economic recovery. Both President B.J. Habibie (in 1998 and 1999) and President Abdurrahman Wahid (1999–2001) experienced difficult relations with the Indonesian parliament. In late 1999, Booth noted that the economic recovery was "vulnerable."[3] Booth provided a summary of the key medium-term challenges as outlined by Boediono, the minister for national development planning, in August 1999. Addressing an economic conference in Jakarta, Boediono stressed that the crisis:[4]

> ...had left a 'costly economic legacy', not just in the form of a devastated banking sector and a deeply-indebted nonbank corporate sector, but also in the form of severe constraints on the public finances, which would in turn limit the capacity of government to spend more on infrastructure rehabilitation and expansion, and on education and health care. In order to overcome the fiscal constraint, the government would have to work hard at increasing government revenues (by several points of GDP), while at the same time prioritising expenditures on infrastructure maintenance, on basic health care and on education.

In addition, Booth noted, Boediono emphasized the urgency of fundamental reform in the legal and judicial systems. Two years later, in mid-2001, there had been but little improvement in the situation. Mari Pangestu and Miranda Goeltom noted that:[5]

---

[2] Sadli, 2001, 11.
[3] Booth, 1999, 3.
[4] Booth, 1999, 34.
[5] Pangestu and Goeltom, 2001, 141.

Market confidence has declined further because of increasing political uncertainty and inconsistent implementation of policy. Mistrust between key institutions such as the IMF and Indonesian policy makers has deepened with the emergence of problems of governance and transparency, controversial suggestions for new bond issues, delays in the divestment of assets controlled by IBRA (the bank restructuring agency), and disagreement over proposed amendments to the central bank law. International support for Indonesia has waned, and there is a clear tendency on the part of the IMF to involve itself more and more in the micro management of economic policies.

After President Megawati Soekarnoputri took office in July 2001, the sense of crisis in government in Indonesia receded and signs of economic recovery became clearer. Initially, relations with the international community improved. The Government of the United States (US) sent a senior representative, US Trade Representative Robert Zoellick, to Jakarta to deliver a letter of support from President George W. Bush and to invite President Megawati to visit Washington in September. Relations with the IMF improved too. A new letter of intent with the IMF was signed on 13 December.

Nevertheless, the international environment became more difficult for Indonesia after the 11 September 2001 terrorist attack in New York. Concerns about security soon began to receive increased attention from Western governments and there was growing pressure on major Islamic countries to support efforts to curb terrorism. The Government of Indonesia, facing social and political constraints at home, found it difficult to respond quickly to this change in the international mood and, in early 2003, needed to balance domestic protests about the looming outlook for war in Iraq against the foreign policy objective of maintaining good standing abroad. Widespread publicity after the Bali bombing attack on 12 October 2002 in which over 200 people died also attracted international attention to threats in Indonesia.

Strengthening Economy

Throughout 2003 and into 2004 the economy strengthened. Nevertheless, numerous commentators noted that the growth rate, which was moving up toward an annual rate of 5%, was still well below the precrisis average of over 7% per year. By 2004, real income per capita had still not recovered to precrisis levels. The delayed nature of the recovery prompted a debate about the government's economic strategy and fiscal policy. The 2004 budget, announced in August 2003, had emphasized the need to maintain a prudent fiscal policy. Reflecting the priority given to the need to reduce government debt levels, the budget targeted a reduction in borrowings from international sources such as the Consultative Group on Indonesia (CGI).

Critics of the budget suggested that the budget was too conservative and had failed to provide sufficient fiscal stimulus. However, Boediono, who had been appointed minister of finance in the Megawati Cabinet in August 2001, argued that in the country's straitened circumstances, the only way to finance any substantial increase in spending would be through an increase in debt. But this approach, he maintained, would be contrary to both the budget strategy and to the government's longer-term fiscal objectives. The government's broad strategy, he noted, had been set out in a white paper[6] outlining a "Package of Economic Policies Approaching and Beyond the Ending of the Program of Cooperation with the International Monetary Fund." The best form of economic stimulus, Boediono argued, would be private investment spurred by improved macroeconomic fundamentals.

The election of Susilo Bambang Yudhoyono (widely known as SBY) as president in 2004 boosted hopes for improved governance and economic management. The economic agenda outlined by the new government appeared promising: Programs listed included efforts to improve the investment climate to maintain economic stability, and to raise public welfare and eradicate poverty. However, the initial response to this program was somewhat restrained with some observers wondering whether the objectives were realistic. But attention to these early discussions about the programs of the new Yudhoyono administration was overtaken by other events. On the morning of 26 December 2004, a massive tsunami struck Aceh and swept out across the Indian Ocean. Over 167,000 people were taken in Indonesia and perhaps another 60,000 died in Sri Lanka and India as well as in other neighboring countries such as Thailand and Maldives.[7] During much of 2005 and into 2006, Indonesia's relationship with the international community was focused on responses to the tsunami.

While the recovery in Aceh was attracting much international attention, the Indonesian economy was continuing to strengthen. In 2006, at the

---

[6] Government of Indonesia, 2003.
[7] Jayasuriya and McCawley, 2010, *The Asian Tsunami*, 3.

end of ADB's fourth decade of work in Indonesia, the overall picture of macroeconomic management was encouraging. Numerous sectoral imbalances remained, and numerous social and environmental issues remained urgent. But the key goal of economic recovery from the Asian financial crisis which had occurred almost a decade earlier had largely been attained.

The Donor Community

Much of the recovery period after the Asian financial crisis (a period which, broadly speaking, covered the five years 1999–2004) was marked by changeable relations between Indonesia and the international community. Both Indonesia and the international community tried to maintain mutually effective programs. There were, however, a range of factors both inside Indonesia and across the international community which made these years a difficult time for the delivery of international assistance.

One complicating factor was political uncertainty. Boediono, one of Indonesia's most well-known economists who was vice president between 2009 and 2014, observed that "much of Indonesia's modern history is about powerful interactions between politics and economics."[8] It proved to be the case during Indonesia's recovery after the Asian financial crisis.[9] During 2000 and into 2001, for much of the period of the presidency of Wahid, political controversies complicated the management of government.[10] The donor community was uncertain as to how to deliver programs in this environment. The relationship between Indonesia and international partners became more confident when Megawati became president in July 2001 although some ministers in her cabinet were known for their outspoken views about Indonesia's relations with the donor community.

A second issue was the resentment in Indonesia about the influence that international agencies, especially the IMF, had over key policy issues following the Asian financial crisis. This resentment arose, partly, because of misunderstandings between the IMF and policymakers in Indonesia

---

[8]   Boediono, 2005, 315.
[9]   Some of the uncertainties in this period are discussed in Boediono, 2002, The International Monetary Fund.
[10] Wimar Witoelar discusses the period in detail in Witoelar, 2002, *No Regrets*.

during and after the Asian financial crisis. As an IMF evaluation report put it:[11]

> The IMF overestimated the extent of country ownership, particularly in structural reforms. While most of the measures were endorsed by the economic team and popular with the general public, the programs lacked the ownership of those who counted the most in the decision-making apparatus in Indonesia. Greater understanding of the political economy dynamics might have contributed to a different program design.

There were other factors which made the relationship between the IMF and some Indonesian policymakers problematic as well. The IMF report observed that the interaction of politics and economics "that made the Indonesian crisis so toxic" meant the process of designing financial packages for Indonesia was difficult.[12] And in some cases, the preparation of parts of the international assistance program was rushed. The result was that some key stakeholders felt that their views had not been taken into account.

A third element in this complex picture was the way that the changing international environment complicated the delivery of aid to Indonesia. As international concerns about terrorism and security became more pronounced during 2002, a number of Western countries issued warnings about travel to Indonesia, cut back expatriate staffing levels to focus on essential tasks, and scaled back aid activities. Multilateral agencies also began to restrict travel by staff to Indonesia.

Nevertheless, despite the uncertainties, the government and international partners continued to meet regularly through the CGI forum and to discuss how to promote economic recovery. Agreed programs of assistance were postponed on a number of occasions but were usually taken up again after a delay.

Differences with the Donor Community

There were stops and starts to the programs supported by both the World Bank and IMF in 1998 and 1999 and during the next few years.

---

[11]   IMF, 2003, *IMF and Recent Capital Account Crises*, 86.
[12]   Ibid., 86.

In 1998, for example, significant reschedulings of World Bank lending were arranged with the aim of funding new crisis-related activities.[13] But the relationship between the government, on one hand, and the IMF and the World Bank on the other, became strained in September the following year over various matters. There had been controversy about apparent financial malpractices involving a bank, Bank Bali. And the rapid deterioration in the social and security situation in Timor-Leste following an overwhelming vote in favor of independence at the end of August 1999 had attracted worldwide attention.

Indonesia faced much international criticism as a result of the Bank Bali affair and the Timor-Leste crisis. In early September 1999, the IMF announced that an official mission to Indonesia in mid-September had been postponed. This decision, in effect, placed IMF lending to Indonesia on hold. At the same time, US President Bill Clinton issued a statement cutting off military ties to Indonesia, citing events in Timor-Leste as needing immediate attention. A few days later, World Bank President James Wolfensohn lent his voice to the international criticisms and said that the World Bank program to Indonesia would be suspended. ADB, too, followed suit and held back lending for a period.

These actions taken by the international community were announced at a time when the Government of Indonesia itself was in the midst of political crisis. Just one month later, in October, President Habibie was forced to resign and President Wahid took office. Given the uncertainty in Jakarta during this time, and the difficulty that new and inexperienced ministers had in settling into government, it was not possible for Indonesia to respond quickly to the concerns of the international community.

Relations continued to be difficult between the government and the international community, especially the IMF, for the next several years. The IMF, not surprisingly for an international financial institution that was often called upon to make short-term loans on an emergency basis, was inclined to take a somewhat legalistic agreement-focused approach in disbursing funds to Indonesia. As each milestone in the detailed financing schedule approached, IMF staff carried out reviews to decide whether agreed targets had been met. Since there were many delays on the Indonesian side, IMF staff often declared themselves unhappy with progress. The international community, in turn, generally supported the

---

[13] World Bank, 1999, 11.

IMF, which meant that Indonesia's difficulties with the IMF influenced the wider set of relations across the donor community in Indonesia.

The Indonesian view of the situation was rather different. There was a perception on the Indonesian side that although the government had indeed signed up to various agreements with the IMF and the World Bank, these agreements had often been imposed unilaterally. Various key Indonesian ministers were therefore openly critical of the commitments that had been entered into with the IMF. In 2001, for example, senior Coordinating Minister for Economic Affairs Rizal Ramli publicly suggested that the IMF had been pressing too hard for reforms in Indonesia when conditions were extremely difficult. Rizal had himself signed the relevant letter of intent with the IMF yet he remained openly unhappy with the way things had worked out.[14]

Two of Indonesia's leading economists, Mari Pangestu and Miranda Goeltom, reviewed the difficult situation in mid-2001. They observed that "one difficult issue after another has emerged" in relations between the government and the IMF.[15] Pangestu and Goeltom discussed the "waning international support" from the international community for Indonesia and noted that:[16]

> The IMF insisted that the 2001 budget be revised to reflect worsened macroeconomic conditions. As a further reflection of the level of mistrust, it requested that it be permitted to review the revised budget before it was submitted to the [parliament] for approval.

Pangestu and Goeltom added that:[17]

> The deepening of the level of mistrust is leading to even more 'micro management' by the IMF and other donors. The IMF not only determines the reforms to be undertaken and the target deadlines, but in a number of instances has had to prescribe also how the reforms should be implemented. ... The dilemma of the donors and multilateral agencies is how to balance the desire for such a hands-on approach, given the level of mistrust and the extent of delays, against the risk that such an approach is unlikely to be effective, given the

---

[14] Sadli, 2001, 11.
[15] Pangestu and Goeltom, 2001, 143.
[16] Ibid., 145.
[17] Ibid., 146.

resentment that excessive intervention creates among Indonesian policy makers. Presumably the IMF and other donors would change their approach if trust could be rebuilt, but this is likely to happen only with a new set of key players.

Despite the difficulties, both the government and international partners were keen to ensure that wherever possible, aid programs continued to be delivered. Following the Asian financial crisis, it had soon become clear that the social impacts of the crisis were severe and that a social safety net system of some kind needed to be established. By late 1999, the main elements of the system were seen as consisting of:[18]

(i)   a food security program to guarantee availability and affordability of food;

(ii)   a labor-intensive public works program to reduce unemployment and encourage productive activities;

(iii) a social protection program to protect access to health and education facilities; and

(iv)   promotion of the *ekonomi kerakyatan* (people's economy), especially through support for small and medium enterprises.

It was hoped that funding for these programs would be available from the government's development budget and from CGI contributions. During the next few years, numerous partner agencies including ADB worked to design programs to strengthen a social safety net along these lines.

However, despite donor support for recovery programs such as social security nets, by 2003 there was an emerging consensus both on the Indonesian side and among partner agencies that it would be best if Indonesian authorities took greater control of their own affairs. Indeed, events were clearly pointing in this direction. Within a few years, as will be seen in Chapter 8, by 2007 the government had decided that it would no longer be necessary to rely on the CGI for the coordination of international assistance to Indonesia.

---

[18]   Cameron, 1999, Survey, 28.

A Changing Mood

Although Indonesia signed another letter of intent with the IMF in March 2003, by this time there was a growing nationalist mood in political circles in Indonesia. A debate was intensifying on the question of what form of engagement, if any, Indonesia should have with the IMF after the agreed arrangements expired at the end of 2003. This discussion came more sharply into focus in May when a senior IMF staff member publicly outlined three options for Indonesia upon the expiry of the existing program: a Standby Agreement; a Precautionary Standby Agreement; or exiting the standby framework but continuing to engage in a "post program dialogue." A fourth option, not canvased by the IMF staff but one explicitly favored by some in Indonesia, was to have an even cleaner break by exiting all borrowing arrangements with the IMF as quickly as possible and declining the option of further regular policy dialogue. A little later, in August, a senior official in the Coordinating Ministry for Economic Affairs, Mahendra Siregar, announced that a team would be established to prepare a strategy to exit the IMF program by the end of 2003.[19]

This changing mood at the political level was reflected within official circles where a discussion was taking place about Indonesia's *ketergantungan* (dependency) on financing from overseas and on the CGI. During 2003, National Development Planning Agency (Bappenas) officials prepared a detailed report on the future of Indonesia's relations with the CGI. The report, issued in December 2003 as *Keberadaan dan Peran Consultative Group for Indonesia (CGI): Kajian dan Rekomendasi Kebijakan* (The Place and Role of the Consultative Group for Indonesia [CGI]: Study and Policy Recommendations) presented a comprehensive overview of Indonesia's relations with the donor community since the late 1960s.[20] The Bappenas study considered the implications of *ketergantungan* at some length and outlined a series of steps that might be taken to strengthen Indonesia's bargaining position in dealing with the donor community (Box 7.1).

The Bappenas study also provided a valuable stocktake of the support that the international community had provided to Indonesia since the late 1960s. Since the Inter-Governmental Group on Indonesia (IGGI), and later the CGI, had begun holding donor meetings, the international community had pledged (in current dollars) just over $110 billion to Indonesia (Table 7.1).

---

[19]   Uning, 2003, Pemerintah Tak Akan.
[20]   Kementerian Perencanaan Pembangunan, 2003, *Keberadaan*.

Box 7.1: Bappenas' 2003 Recommendations on Indonesia's Relations with the CGI and the Donor Community

(1) **Clarify the position of the CGI and focus on its function as a forum for aid communication.**

The CGI continues to be needed to help Indonesia obtain international financing and to coordinate aid arrangements. The agenda of CGI meetings should be focused on efforts to cover deficits and to improve effectiveness in using international funds.

(2) **Introduce reforms into the work processes and leadership arrangements of the CGI.**

For the time being, while the CGI is still needed, reforms are needed so that the work of the CGI is not donor-led but, rather, moves in the direction of Indonesian-led arrangements. Since there are many participants in the CGI and they are oriented toward the views of creditors and donors, moves toward a country-driven aid coordination system will present challenges. First steps will involve changes in leadership arrangements at midterm CGI review meetings so that Indonesia cochairs meetings rather than participates in a supporting capacity to the World Bank.

(3) **Strengthen the focus and agenda of meetings.**

The Government of Indonesia should be more active and exercise initiative in setting meeting agendas. Agenda items should focus on issues concerning finance and the aid provided by CGI participants. The chair of the Indonesian delegation, exercising joint leadership of the meeting, can help direct discussion. While wider issues may be considered, discussion would best focus on issues concerning ways to encourage private capital inflows and not just official capital flows.

(4) **Reorganize and strengthen Indonesia's role in working groups and in setting the work agenda.**

Working groups support the CGI's aid coordination activities. The groups are needed where there are direct links with contributions from CGI participants in sectors such as infrastructure, health, and education, which receive substantial financing. The government should exercise initiative and leadership within the working groups. Serious attention is needed on the Indonesian side to commitment and capacity building when participating in the working groups. There is no need for issues not linked to funding to be discussed within the working groups.

continued on next page

Box 7.1 *continued*

(5) **Establish a policy forum outside of the CGI.**

Indonesia should establish a policy forum as a basis for discussions with the international community about Indonesia's development policies and strategic policy directions. The agenda for discussions in the forum would be decided by Indonesia. The forum would be free of the monitoring and reporting overtones that are part of the CGI processes. And a wider group of countries than are included in the CGI could participate, such as ASEAN countries, the PRC, and Russia.

(6) **Strengthen, intensify, and maintain commitments to bilateral cooperation.**

Outside of the CGI framework, Indonesia should strengthen bilateral cooperation with those multilateral and bilateral donors who provide significant pledges of finance. If this were done, creditors and donors would not need to rely on the CGI forum in a way that weakens Indonesia's bargaining power.

(7) **Improve the management of foreign loans and overseas aid.**

The government must aim to introduce continuous improvements in the management and utilization of foreign debts and aid. The accumulation of debt must be weighed against the need for more resources as well as the absorptive capacity to utilize and manage the debt. Additional efforts are needed to cope with well-known difficulties which lead to increased costs such as delays in execution and problems in absorption.

Bappenas = National Development Planning Agency, CGI = Consultative Group on Indonesia, ASEAN = Association of Southeast Asian Nations, PRC = People's Republic of China.

Source: Translated and summarized from Kementerian Perencanaan Pembangunan, 2003, *Keberadaan*, 94.

Over time, the multilateral share of these pledges had risen quite markedly. Within the multilateral share, ADB's support had risen from quite low levels in the early 1970s to over 26% at the end of the period (Table 7.2). Within the bilateral share, Japan was by far the largest donor.

Although the recommendations set out in the Bappenas report were not put into place immediately, the review of aid relations clearly indicated

Table 7.1: Total Pledges at IGGI and CGI Meetings, 1967–2003
(\$ million)

	Bilateral		Multilateral		Total	
	(\$ million)	%	(\$ million)	%	(\$ million)	%
1967–1969	523	98	8	2	531	100
1: 1969–1974	2,870	82	634	18	3,507	100
2: 1974–1979	3,062	47	3,482	53	6,544	100
3: 1979–1984	3,962	38	6,420	62	10,381	100
4: 1984–1989	5,798	40	8,804	60	14,602	100
5: 1989–1994	10,042	43	13,586	57	23,628	100
6: 1994–1999	12,245	42	16,770	58	29,015	100
1999–2003	8,824	39	14,046	61	22,870	100
Total	**47,327**	**43**	**63,752**	**57**	**111,078**	**100**

IGGI = Inter-Governmental Group on Indonesia, CGI = Consultative Group on Indonesia.
Note: The numbered ordering of the six periods in this table reflects the successive five-year planning periods. The First Five-Year Development Plan (Repelita I), for example, covered the period 1969–1974. Successive Repelita each covered five-year periods. In 1999, the practice of preparing Repelita was discontinued.
Source: Kementerian Perencanaan Pembangunan, 2003, *Keberadaan*.

Table 7.2: Pledges at IGGI and CGI Meetings by Share, 1967–2003
(% share)

	Bilateral		Multilateral			
	Japan	Other	World Bank	ADB	Other Multilaterals	Total
1967–1969	32.0	66.4	1.5	0.0	0.0	100
1: 1969–1974	24.2	57.6	14.7	3.2	0.3	100
2: 1974–1979	13.5	33.3	42.4	10.6	0.1	100
3: 1979–1984	14.1	24.0	43.6	15.3	3.0	100
4: 1984–1989	21.3	18.4	39.7	17.8	2.8	100
5: 1989–1994	29.0	13.5	32.7	21.7	3.1	100
6: 1994–1999	31.3	11.3	27.9	23.8	5.6	100
1999–2003	26.2	12.3	30.7	26.8	3.9	100

IGGI = Inter-Governmental Group on Indonesia, CGI = Consultative Group on Indonesia.
Note: The numbered ordering of the six periods in this table reflects the successive five-year planning periods. The First Five-Year Development Plan (Repelita I), for example, covered the period 1969–1974. Successive Repelita each covered five-year periods. In 1999, the practice of preparing Repelita was discontinued.
Source: Kementerian Perencanaan Pembangunan, 2003, *Keberadaan*.

that a shift in thinking was taking place in Jakarta. The broad approach in the report was reflected, too, in the 13th meeting of the CGI held in Jakarta in December 2003. In his statement to the meeting, the Coordinating Minister for Economic Affairs, Dorodjatun Kuntjoro-Jakti, said that it was time for a new approach that maximized Indonesian leadership of the CGI while increasing efficiency in the use of finances.

Two major events during 2004 brought further changes to the programs that the international community supported in Indonesia. The first occurred in October, when Yudhoyono took office as the sixth president of Indonesia. He quickly indicated that improved international relations would be a part of the new approach of his administration. The early outlines of policies supported by the Yudhoyono government pointed toward reform of economic programs and emphasized the need to increase investment, especially in infrastructure sectors such as transport and power.

The second event, however, dramatically changed priorities for the international community in Indonesia. On 26 December, around 8:30 a.m. local time, a huge tsunami swept across coastal areas of Indonesia's northernmost province, Aceh.[21] The tsunami destroyed main parts of Banda Aceh, the provincial capital. Within perhaps half an hour, over 167,000 Indonesians had died. As the tsunami spread outward around the tip of North Sumatra and to Thailand, South Asia, and eventually even to Africa, many thousands more were swept away.

The response to the tsunami took up much of the attention of the donor community in Indonesia throughout 2005 and 2006. The earlier discussions about compliance with IMF conditionality were quickly put aside. Rather, donors focused on the challenge—a new one for the international community in Indonesia—of providing humanitarian aid in the wake of a large-scale disaster.

ADB's Role

ADB's program in Indonesia changed markedly after the 1997–1998 financial crisis. The years between 2000 and 2004 were a transition period for both Indonesia and for development partners such as the bank. It took until around 2005 for ADB's activities to return to a more normalized country program—and even then, the priorities of the international community

---

[21] Jayasuriya and McCawley, *Asian Tsunami*, 2010, 1. See also Kompas, 2005, *Bencana Gempa*.

Table 7.3: Notable Events, 1997–2006

Item	Comment
1997	
Asian financial crisis	ADB responded to coordinated efforts to address the crisis in late 1997
1998	
Asian financial crisis loans	ADB approved a series of crisis-related loans
1999	
ADB Board approved a new Poverty Reduction Strategy	The ADB strategy was reflected in the bank's responses to the Asian financial crisis in Indonesia
2000	
Several ADB concessional loans were approved	ADB supported concessional lending to help recovery from the Asian financial crisis
2001	
ADB lending was reduced	Indonesia cut back on all international borrowings with the aim of reducing the level of national debt
2002	
Financial Governance and Social Security Reform loan	A major program loan which was one of a series of ADB loans to support reform in the financial sector
2003	
ADB lending remained at a reduced level	The Government of Indonesia continued to give priority to the goal of reducing the level of national debt
2004	
State audit reform sector	Large loan to support audit reform and improved governance
Asian tsunami in December	The international community began to mount a major relief effort in response to the tsunami
2005	
Tsunami relief and rehabilitation	The government and the international community expanded rehabilitation and reconstruction programs in Aceh and other areas
Asian Tsunami Fund established	First ADB fund established to focus on disaster relief
2006	
Bantul earthquake loan	ADB's expanded support for assistance after disasters continued following a large earthquake in the Yogyakarta region in Java

in Indonesia were largely influenced by the effort of responding to the humanitarian needs in Aceh following the 2004 tsunami (Table 7.3).

During the Asian financial crisis in 1997 and 1998, ADB, working with other external development partners, adopted an interim operational strategy (IOS).[22] The interim strategy supported the government's recovery program with a focus on providing social protection to the poor and strengthening the new decentralization program. In view of the crisis in the banking and corporate sectors, the IOS emphasized the need to address problems in the financial sector along with reforms to restructure the banking sector and state-owned enterprises. Support from ADB was made up of quick-disbursing loans supplemented by nonlending steps to provide assistance (such as a review of the loan portfolio, acceleration of disbursements, and policy advisory support).

In November 1999, the ADB Board in Manila had approved a new bank-wide Poverty Reduction Strategy. There were immediate implications for ADB's activities in Indonesia.[23] Much of ADB's work during the 1990s before the Asian financial crisis had been focused on infrastructure and other projects designed to tackle poverty. In the post-crisis operations in Indonesia, ADB moved to give special attention to poverty-oriented activities.

Following the crisis, ADB worked to strengthen a social safety net program in Indonesia. Targeting, however, was a difficult problem. Further, ADB activities were probably too widely dispersed to be effective in any one area because many of the bank's activities were spread out over a number of provinces. Later, at the end of 2005, a major ADB evaluation of the its program in Indonesia for the period 1990 to 2004, the *Country Assistance Program Evaluation for Indonesia* (CAPE) set out a summary overview of ADB's activities during and after the financial crisis.

The view set out in the CAPE was that ADB had responded quickly during the Asian financial crisis and had done so in a way that was relevant but which, in some areas, "lacked the modalities to address the crisis."[24] The bank remained engaged, rightly, to support recovery and the transition to decentralization. But this engagement had affected the quality of ADB's portfolio in Indonesia because there had been an increase in problem loans and excessive commitment fees paid by the

---

[22]   ADB, 2005, *Country Assistance Program*, Appendix 5.
[23]   ADB, 2005, *Country Assistance Program*, 13.
[24]   Ibid., paragraph 25, p. 9.

government. Moreover, ADB's internal practices were slow to react to rapidly changing client needs and to augment staff resources and skills. Rather, the bank responded within the framework of its traditional programs. In hindsight, new instruments were needed. ADB continued to lend about $1 billion annually until 1999.

Surveying ADB's approach during the transition years of 2001–2004, the CAPE suggested that the bank's approach in Indonesia had strengths and weaknesses. ADB's work had remained "relevant" but the bank had been slow to channel adequate resources and delegate authority in response to Indonesia's new needs. However, after a new country strategy and program (CSP) had been approved in 2002, ADB had given more consideration to implementing operations suited to the key needs of decentralization. Staff resources, for example, had been strengthened in Jakarta and ADB had become more vigilant about detecting corruption. ADB had also remained an active member of the CGI. On the other hand, the CAPE observed that some international development partners considered that working with ADB was cumbersome. Further, the operating environment for donors in Indonesia had changed markedly following the dramatic moves toward decentralization in 1999 and 2000. Like most other international agencies working in Indonesia, ADB had taken time to respond to the changes.

Subsequently, ADB lending declined markedly to about $500 million annually. Indonesian policymakers had cut back on international borrowings with the aim of reducing the debt ratio. It became harder to process loans once the new decentralization arrangements had been announced.[25] Nevertheless, ADB gave priority to supporting the international program led by the IMF. This approach required that bank loans be approved quickly. ADB approved several large program loans or sector development programs totaling $2.8 billion with attached ambitious reform agendas.

Given the pressure to support the government's budgetary needs at the time, the bank was under pressure to move quickly. The 2005 CAPE review suggested that more attention should have been given to the time needed to review the commitments that the government had agreed to and to consider the realism of enacting legislation at a time when the Indonesian parliament had assumed a more assertive

---

[25] The experience of ADB during this period is discussed in ADB, 2001, *Special Evaluation Study.*

role. A *Special Evaluation Study of the Asian Development Bank's Crisis Management Interventions in Indonesia* prepared in 2001 concluded that the investment components of the social safety net program loans which addressed immediate needs were appropriate. However, the study suggested that it was a moot point whether it was appropriate to try to promote long-term reforms when the main objective was to respond to a crisis. The study noted that one of ADB's quick-disbursing policy loans supported the introduction of nationwide policy reforms in such areas as education management and the mobilization of new resources. The study suggested that it would seem that programs of this kind "would rank lower on the scale of relevancy" in the midst of a crisis.[26]

These broad trends reflected the annual programs that ADB implemented during the recovery period which extended until close to the end of the fourth decade of the bank's work in Indonesia.

ADB Programs

In 2000, ADB's program in Indonesia reflected a new strategy designed to respond to priorities that had become clear following the financial crisis. The new strategy focused on reducing poverty and regional inequalities and supporting steps toward better governance. The bank's annual report for 2000 set out the challenges that needed to be addressed in Indonesia:[27]

> In 2000, published reports suggested that as many as one million people had been displaced because of violence or threats of violence. The peace and order situation has been a major factor in discouraging investment, both domestic and foreign. The focus on improving good governance is a result of the crisis since in many respects the weakest link in Indonesia's past development strategy was governance.

ADB's approach during 2000 was to continue with policy dialogue with the government while, at the same time, supporting activities which addressed immediate priorities. Policy dialogue about issues of reform in the financial and power sectors were arranged in forums such as the CGI, governance partnership meetings, and in discussions on program loan implementation.

---

[26]   Ibid., paragraphs 18 and 19.
[27]   ADB, 2000, Annual Report, 78.

A range of loans was approved during 2000 (Table 7.4). The largest (for $200 million) was for an Industrial Competitiveness and Small and Medium Enterprise Development Program. The activity was to help promote competition in the industrial sector. The bank's support for the loan reflected the request of the government that ADB take the lead in coordinating aid to the small and medium enterprises sector. Two technical assistance grants were included to promote deregulation and competition.[28]

Several other loans with soft-loan ADF components were also approved. One of these, the Decentralized Health Services Project, reflected the

Table 7.4: ADB Lending to Indonesia, 2000–2006

Loan	Sector	$ million	Loan Terms
2000			
Industrial Competitiveness of SMEs	SME	200	OCR
Community Empowerment for Rural Development	Multisector	115	OCR and ADF
Marine and Coastal Resources Management	Water	50	OCR and ADF
Technological and Professional Skills Development	Education	180	OCR
Road Rehabilitation (Sector) Project	Roads	190	OCR
Decentralized Health Services Project	Health	65	OCR and ADF
2001			
Decentralized Basic Education	Education	100	OCR and ADF
State-Owned Enterprise Governance and Privatization	Public sector	400	OCR
2002			
Poor Farmer Income Improvement with Innovation	Agriculture	56	OCR and ADF
Coral Reef Rehabilitation and Management	Water	33	OCR and ADF
Sustainable Capacity Building for Decentralization	Decentralization	42	OCR and ADF

continued on next page

---

[28] ADB, 2010, *Indonesia: Industrial Competitiveness.*

Table 7.4 *continued*

Loan	Sector	$ million	Loan Terms
Financial Governance and Social Security Reform	Finance	250	OCR
Small and Medium-sized Enterprises Export Development	SME	85	OCR
Renewable Energy Development Sector Project	Power	161	OCR
Power Transmission Improvement Sector Project	Power	140	OCR
2003			
Participatory Irrigation Sector Project	Irrigation	73	OCR and ADF
Neighborhood Upgrading and Shelter	Housing	88	OCR and ADF
Second Decentralized Health Services Project	Health	100	OCR and ADF
2004			
State Audit Reform Sector Development	Public sector	225	OCR and ADF
2005			
Community Water Services and Health	Rural water	65	OCR and ADF
Road Rehabilitation II	Roads	151	OCR
Local Government Finance and Governance Reform	Decentralization	330	OCR and ADF
Tangguh Liquefied Natural Gas	Energy	350	Private, no guarantee
Rural Infrastructure Support Program	Multisector	50	OCR and ADF
Development Policy Support Program	Public sector	200	OCR
2006			
Infrastructure Reform Sector Development Program	Multisector	426	OCR and ADF
Sustainable Aquaculture for Food Security and Poverty	Fisheries	33	ADF
Madrasah Education Development	Education	50	ADF
Second Development Policy Support Program	Public sector	200	OCR

SMEs = small and medium enterprises, ADF = Asian Development Fund, OCR = ordinary capital resources.
Note: Some small loans not included.
Source: ADB annual reports, various years.

bank's focus on the need to address social issues following the crisis. The project had the twin objectives of improving health and family services across seven provinces and promoting access of the poor, especially women, children, and infants, to these services. An evaluation of the project conducted in 2013, four years after the project closed, concluded that the project had been successful and that "primary, district, and provincial health services have developed to improve access for a greater number of people, including those in remote and rural areas, because of project support."[29] The project was also regarded as providing significant benefits in terms of maternal health and gender outcomes:[30]

> Overall, the project has had an impact on women's health. It developed a subsidy scheme for traditional birth attendants to give pregnant women skilled antenatal care and delivery, which continues and has improved the overall coverage of skilled health care for women. As such, the project played an important role in raising awareness about women's reproductive health issues and incorporating gender in community health services.

The evaluation noted, however, that Indonesia continued to face some key hurdles in the health sector, that "a large segment of the population is still in dire need of modest health services," and that ADB should consider additional steps to provide assistance in the sector.[31]

A second loan with a soft-loan component agreed to in 2000 provided support to the Community Empowerment for Rural Development (CERD) project.[32] This activity, like the Decentralized Health Services Project, was designed to assist low-income families following the 1997–1998 financial crisis. The CERD project was expected to increase the incomes of poor families directly through promoting microenterprises and small-scale firms in rural areas. An additional component of the project was intended to improve links to markets, and to social and health services, by improving rural infrastructure. Activities were to be carried out in six provinces—three in Kalimantan and three in Sulawesi.

The CERD project aimed to empower communities and to strengthen village and local officials' capacity to work under the new decentralized

---

[29] ADB, 2013, *Decentralized Health Services*, v.
[30] Ibid., 30.
[31] Ibid., vii.
[32] ADB, 2009, *Indonesia: Community Empowerment*.

framework of government in Indonesia. To promote empowerment, community-based groups were established, including women's groups, in over 500 villages in the six provinces. The groups involved over 20,000 villagers, of whom over 8,000 were women. By the time the project was completed in 2007, many types of rural infrastructure had been constructed (roads, bridges, small dams, village markets, and numerous village buildings). The ADB Internal Evaluation Department judged that the project had been "relevant, effective, and efficient" and rated the activity as successful.[33]

The following year, in 2001, ADB adopted a new country operational strategy (COS) for Indonesia. The COS gave increased emphasis to long-term development issues. For the bank, this was a step toward moving beyond a short-term focus on responses to the 1997–1998 financial crisis. The COS drew upon a Poverty Reduction Partnership Agreement (PRPA) signed between the government and ADB in April 2001. The PRPA reflected the lessons of the crisis. The crisis had shown how vulnerable millions of Indonesians were to sudden macroeconomic shocks. ADB's programs since the crisis had also supported a range of interventions intended to help reduce the impact of the shocks through promoting expanded social service delivery.

The bank's 2001 COS was an important document. For the first time, themes that would guide ADB's approach in Indonesia throughout the post-crisis transition period were identified. The COS indicated that the bank would focus on five priorities:

(i)   reducing poverty and improving governance;

(ii) supporting decentralization;

(iii) protecting the environment;

(iv) promoting human development; and

(v)   strengthening the economy through infrastructure investment and private sector development.

These themes were carried forward in the ADB Country Strategy and Program (CSP) for 2003–2005 issued the following year.

---

[33]   Ibid., 7.

ADB President Tadao Chino made an official visit to Indonesia in September 2001. In Jakarta, shortly after President Megawati had taken office, Chino spoke of the bank's strong commitment to supporting the government's efforts for reform, fighting poverty, and promoting sustainable development. Chino's emphasis on support for the government's own programs reflected the bank's traditional approach of focusing on the priorities of member countries rather than on trying to set ADB's preferred reform goals for borrowing countries. And Chino's attention to poverty was consistent with both the priorities in the bank's Poverty Reduction Strategy adopted in November 1999 as well as his own well-known commitment to supporting anti-poverty programs in the bank's work.

One main priority for Chino during his visit was to review ADB's level of lending to Indonesia. Indonesia had cut back on all international borrowings following the financial crisis so ADB's approvals had fallen markedly. Total approvals had dropped from $1 billion in 1999 to $800 million in 2000, and would fall again to $500 million in 2001. In addition to the government's own concerns about borrowing, the bank itself was finding it difficult in the uncertain climate in Jakarta to prepare loan proposals. Indonesia's own reform goals were in a state of flux, and the rapidly decentralizing system of government greatly complicated the situation.

In 2001, only two ADB loans were approved for Indonesia. The loan for the State-Owned Enterprise Governance and Privatization Program supported measures to privatize selected state-owned firms. The goal was to release public resources for poverty and social development programs and to promote strengthening of the private sector. The Decentralized Basic Education Project reflected the emphasis on decentralization in Indonesia; the loan was to provide resources for local governments, communities, and schools in rural areas and urban districts.

But during the next several years, it proved difficult for the bank to sustain a higher level of lending (Table 7.1). Loan approvals in 2002 rose significantly to over $700 million but then fell away markedly in the following two years. In terms of expanding the level of operations, this was a challenging period for both ADB and other agencies in the international community.

New Strategy

Toward the end of 2002, the new CSP for the three-year period 2003–2005 was released.[34] The strategic focus of the CSP (Box 7.2) carried forward the priorities listed in the 2001 COS. Reflecting ADB's long-standing policy of working cooperatively with borrowing countries in Asia, the CSP had been tailored to support the plans set out by the government in the National Development Program (PROPENAS), issued earlier in October 2000.[35] PROPENAS had adopted a thematic approach

---

Box 7.2: Strategic Focus of ADB's Country Strategy and Program, 2003–2005

ADB's Country Strategy and Program document for the three-year period 2003–2005 outlined five main objectives as the strategic focus for the period.

(i)   Improve governance, strengthen the capacity for long-term sustainable development, and emphasize anticorruption and legal and judicial reform.

(ii) Meet local needs through decentralization and identify local development partners that prioritize good governance and poverty reduction. Sharpen ADB's geographic focus, increasing program effectiveness.

(iii) Promote human development by improving the provision of social services and access by the poor to them, particularly in education and health, and addressing gender inequities, especially at the local level.

(iv) Mainstream management of the environment and encourage sustainable use of natural resources. Develop transparent, market-oriented, participatory policymaking tools. Provide expanded livelihood options for those now dependent on natural resources.

(v)   Increase the potential for poverty-reducing growth through investments in infrastructure, strengthened corporate governance, and expanded private sector development.

ADB = Asian Development Bank.
Source: ADB, 2002, *Country Strategy*, v.

---

[34]   ADB, 2002, *Country Strategy*.
[35]   Details of the formulation and adoption of PROPENAS are in the important history of development planning in Indonesia in Mustopadidjaja et. al., 313–341.

rather than setting out sectoral priorities in the way that Indonesia's earlier five-year Repelita planning documents had done. In the PROPENAS thematic approach, good governance and the rule of law had been set out as central themes. The five PROPENAS national goals were:

(i)   national cohesion and social stability;

(ii) good governance and the rule of law;

(iii) economic recovery and sustained growth;

(iv) development of the social sectors and human welfare; and

(v)   regional autonomy, rural and urban development, and structural programs to reduce poverty.

The approach outlined in the bank's 2003–2005 CSP was designed to support these goals. The CSP also set out an annual target lending range of $600 million to $1.2 billion over the three-year period to 2005. But, realistically, the CSP noted that lending at the higher end of the range was not likely.

There were underlying difficulties affecting the operations of both ADB and numerous other international agencies in this post-crisis period. Significant changes were taking place which affected both the demand for, and supply of, foreign assistance.

On the demand side, as seen earlier, the government had introduced sharp cuts in development spending (Figure 7.1). These reductions had the flow-on effect of reducing Indonesia's capacity to participate in foreign assistance activities where international partners expected that matching rupiah funds would be available. Further, public commentary within Indonesia had become less accepting of the benefits of foreign aid after the financial crisis when the national debt had risen sharply. The CAPE, for example, reported that:[36]

> During consultations with the CAPE Mission, NGOs expressed several concerns regarding ADB's development agenda in Indonesia. Policy-based loans have generated more controversy than other ADB loans since they target changes in the structure of the economy, industry, or sector. Policy impacts often mean privatization, deregulation, or liberalization.

---

[36] ADB, 2005, *CAPE*, 56.

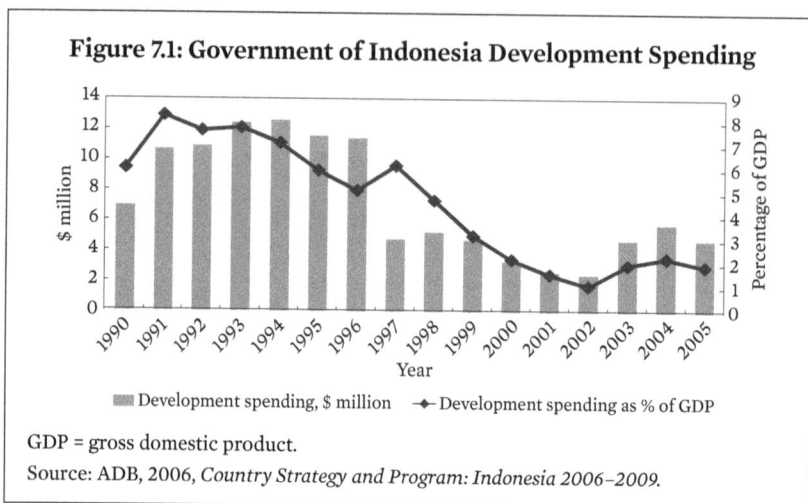

Figure 7.1: Government of Indonesia Development Spending

GDP = gross domestic product.
Source: ADB, 2006, *Country Strategy and Program: Indonesia 2006–2009*.

There were also more practical problems which hampered the preparation of an expanded pipeline of ADB activities. A survey of views across the government conducted for the 2005 CAPE brought forth a range of suggestions of ways in which the bank could become a more relevant partner (Box 7.3). The suggestions reflected concerns across the government that had been holding back bank programs for some time. Commenting on the fall in lending during this period, the 2005 CAPE noted that: "A less than enthusiastic attitude to external development partner finance at the National [Development] Planning Agency…has aggravated this sharp reduction in project lending.[37]

The problems were not only on the demand side. International agencies for their part, including ADB, were finding it difficult to supply assistance to Indonesia. Summarizing problems that most international agencies were trying to deal with at the time, ADB's CSP noted that higher levels of lending would only be possible if the government introduced a workable on-lending policy to support local governments, if implementation problems were eased, if the government facilitated investments to reduce poverty, and if structural reforms were accelerated.

Despite the challenging environment, the government and ADB were able to agree on a balanced mix of loans in 2002. Concessional low-interest loans

---

[37]   ADB, 2005, *CAPE*, 123.

Box 7.3: Government's Views on How ADB Can Become More Relevant

Longer Time Frame for Project Preparation. Compared with the pre-decentralization era, a longer project preparation period is required to consult with different local stakeholders and build consensus on project design aspects between various institutions including technical ministries, the Ministry of Finance, local governments, and the Asian Development Bank (ADB).

Quality at Entry and Project Readiness. The Government accords high priority to quality at entry and project-readiness criteria, and would like to negotiate loans only if the project design has matured. This would ensure that the Government does not pay unnecessary commitment fees.

Improving Portfolio Management. ADB should place more emphasis on supervising implementation of the ongoing portfolio and restructuring problem projects. The problems of ongoing projects should be addressed by adapting the approaches to the evolving context, rather than canceling loans and designing new projects. The Indonesia Resident Mission (IRM) could play a larger role in portfolio management

Increase Government Ownership of Policy Reforms. Program loans must be grounded on government ownership and leadership. Conditionalities must be realistic and should not include items that require legislative actions, which are beyond the control of the administrative branch of Government. Flexibility to negotiate conditionality, given the context of the country, should be allowed.

Improving the Effectiveness of Technical Assistance. There needs to be a demand-driven approach to identifying technical assistance (TA) with adequate inputs from the executing agencies (EAs) on the selection, contracting, and supervision of consultants. Excessive reliance on international consultants who are not familiar with the local context and consultants working to fulfill ADB terms of reference rather than the requirements of the EA must be avoided, as they diminish the country ownership of TA grants and undermine their utility.

Roles of the Indonesia Resident Mission. Government and external development partners (EDPs) emphasized the importance of resident mission-based operations management, delegation of responsibilities, and staffing (sector contact points). As several EDPs have moved toward country-based decision-making, ADB should do the same to facilitate EDP coordination. The staff of IRM need to have the skills and experience to spearhead initiatives and interact effectively with other stakeholders.

continued on next page

Box 7.3 *continued*

Supporting the Enabling Environment for the Private Sector. ADB should increase its private sector operations in Indonesia, involving the strengthening of the enabling framework (legal, regulatory, and governance issues); financing private sector projects, and helping to catalyze private sector investments.

New Products and the Capital Market. ADB should be more innovative and offer a wider range of products to meet the needs of one of its major clients, for example issuing local currency bonds and providing local currency loans to reduce currency mismatch issues.

Source: ADB, 2005, *Country Assistance Program Evaluation,* 53.

were approved for the agriculture sector and to support decentralization programs (Table 7.5). A coral reef rehabilitation loan was also arranged to strengthen the capacity to manage coral reef resources. A loan for coral reef rehabilitation was a somewhat unusual activity for ADB but it reflected the bank's response to increasing concerns about links between economic growth in Asia and environmental degradation in the region.

The largest activity approved in 2002 was the Financial Governance and Social Security Reform (FGSSR) Program loan. The loan, which as it turned out would become one of a series of bank loans to support reform in the financial sector in Indonesia, followed on from the earlier major Financial Governance Reforms Sector Development loan for $1.4 billion approved in 1998. In 2000, the government had asked ADB to support the development of a blueprint for an integrated financial services financial institution. The FGSSR loan was ADB's response to this request. The FGSSR was designed to promote reform in the nonbank financial sector and help establish a major new regulatory agency, the Financial Services Authority (OJK). The bank later (Chapter 8) approved several more large loans to assist with reform in the financial sector.

Following the encouraging increase in lending in 2002, ADB approvals dropped away in 2003 and 2004. All of the loans approved during these two years, and most of the lending agreed to in 2005 and 2006, were on concessional terms. In 2003, the largest loan was for a project in the health sector. This loan was one of various activities that ADB supported after the major reforms to promote decentralization were announced in Indonesia in 1999 and in 2001.

Table 7.5: Decentralization Support Loans to Indonesia, 1998–2009

Loan		$ million	Loan terms
	Core Decentralization Support Loans		
1999	Community and Local Government Support Sector Development Program—Policy Loan and Program Loan	320	OCR
2002	Sustainable Capacity Building for Decentralization	42	ADF
2005	Local Government Finance and Governance Reform Sector Development Program and Project	330	OCR and ADF
2008	Second Local Government Finance and Governance Reform Program Cluster	350	OCR
	Sector-Based Decentralization Support Loans		
1998	Social Protection Sector Development Program and Project	300	OCR
2000	Decentralized Health Services	65	ADF
2001	Decentralized Basic Education	100	ADF
2003	Second Decentralized Health Services	100	OCR and ADF
2006	Infrastructure Reform Sector Development Program	426	OCR and ADF
2008	Infrastructure Reform Sector Development (Subprogram 2)	280	OCR
	Public Sector Management Loans with Decentralization Components		
2001	State-Owned Enterprise Governance and Privatization	400	OCR
2004	State Audit Reform Sector Program and Project	225	OCR and ADF
2005	Development Policy Support Program	200	OCR
2006	Second Development Policy Support Program	200	OCR
2007	Third Development Policy Support Program	200	OCR
2008	Fourth Development Policy Support Program	200	OCR
2009	Public Expenditure Support Facility Program	1,000	OCR
	Countercyclical Support	500	OCR
	Total Loans Supporting Decentralization	**5,239**	

OCR = ordinary capital resources, ADF = Asian Development Fund.
Source: ADB, 2010, *Asian Development Bank Support*, 27.

In 2004, only one loan was approved. This was for the State Audit Reform Sector Development Program. Yet the activity, which was part of the bank's support for governance reform, was an important one. It focused on the key area of strengthening audit controls across a wide range of government institutions in Indonesia.

Indonesia had long had a national audit agency. An early institution tasked to exercise audit-type supervision of national government agencies had been established in the late 1940s. But in the succeeding decades, the institution had found it difficult to operate effectively. In the Reform Era beginning in 1998 there was a widening appreciation of the importance of institutions such as the national audit agency. The bank's approval of the State Audit Reform Sector Development Program reflected support in Indonesia for improved governance mechanisms across the public sector.

The approval of the loan, as it happened, took place at a fortuitous time. A well-known economist, Anwar Nasution, had been nominated by President Megawati as chair of the Supreme Audit Board (BPK) earlier in 2004.[38] In December 2004, the new President Yudhoyono confirmed Nasution's appointment as chair of the BPK. Nasution, formerly the senior deputy governor at Bank Indonesia, had an established reputation as an independent official and as a professional economist. The appointment of Nasution, as ADB's loan was being approved, meant that the implementation of the bank's audit reform program got off to a good start. In the event, the project was judged a success. Later, in 2011, a bank completion report rated the activity as successful and noted that the project had "achieved the majority of outputs and outcomes with positive impacts…[and] contributed significantly to strengthening the audit institutions."[39]

But then, at the end of the year, on 26 December (Boxing Day), a huge tsunami struck the province of Aceh in northern Sumatra. During the next few hours, the tsunami spread outward to Thailand, India, Sri Lanka, and eventually to Africa. The exact death toll was never established but it is clear that almost 230,000 people were lost. In Indonesia, nearly 170,000 people died within an hour of the tsunami sweeping over large parts of coastal Aceh.[40]

ADB joined with the Government of Indonesia and the rest of the international community to respond quickly to the disaster both at regional and national levels. To support efforts at a regional level, the bank established an Asian Tsunami Fund (ATF) in February 2005. The fund provided resources for programs in all of the main countries where large-scale damage had occurred. The bank made an initial contribution to the

---

[38] Nasution, *Bukan Ekonom Biasa*, Ch 19.
[39] ADB, 2011, *Indonesia: State Audit Reforms*, 12.
[40] Nazara and Resosudarmo, 2010, Indonesia: The First Two Years.

ATF from internal funds of $600 million. Countries such as Australia and Luxembourg also contributed to the fund.

In Indonesia, ADB's main response was channeled through the Earthquake and Tsunami Emergency Support Project (ETESP) approved in April 2005. The cost of the project was over $320 million spread across activities for community infrastructure, livelihood support, physical infrastructure, and other programs. The initial ADB response, given the nature of the disaster, was prepared quickly:[41]

> Because of the exigencies of the disaster situation that required quick response, detailed subproject design and implementation arrangements were not fully developed. ... Nevertheless, the government and ADB decided to proceed with the emergency assistance on the basis of a broad framework for project preparation and implementation before detailed guidelines and procedures were established. While this may be a risky strategy, it was driven by the urgent need to mitigate the crisis by providing poor communities with immediate relief.

In April 2005, the government established a new Rehabilitation and Reconstruction Agency (BRR) to coordinate assistance activities. The bank's response over the next few years was tailored to support the work of the BRR.

In May 2005, ADB established offices in Medan in North Sumatra and in Aceh to help coordinate the work of teams of international and national advisers. ADB's efforts during the rest of 2005 and into 2006 focused on undertaking immediate rehabilitation and planning for longer-term reconstruction. By the second half of 2006, the bank had increased attention to the task of implementing reconstruction programs. During the next few years, numerous ETESP activities were undertaken including support for programs in agriculture, fisheries, micro-enterprises, health and education, rural water supplies, and housing. Implementation of these activities, however, was not always easy. At times, practical difficulties of implementation delayed work in the ETESP into 2007 and 2008.

ADB activities across a range of sectors in Indonesia picked up markedly in 2005 and 2006. Two large loans approved in 2005 were for the Local Government Finance and Governance Reform Sector activity and the

---

[41] Ibid., 14.

Tangguh Liquefied Natural Gas Project in the eastern part of Indonesia, in West Papua province. The first of these was designed to support steps toward the decentralization of government (Table 7.2). Key objectives included promoting the delivery of basic services by strengthening the framework for decentralization and developing the capacity of local governments.[42] Following the moves to decentralize government in 1999 and later, local governments had been assigned expanded responsibilities for many public service functions. But problems had emerged in the arrangements for decentralization. The ADB loan was designed to help overcome some of the main issues. The implementation of this kind of program was not easy but an evaluation completed eight years later concluded that the activity had been successful.[43]

The Tangguh project drew on the priorities outlined by the government in a major Infrastructure Summit in Jakarta in early 2005. The project was seen as an important step toward the revival of ADB's private sector operations in Indonesia.[44] The activity was also designed to strengthen bank support for the development of the gas sector. Earlier, in 1995, ADB had approved a loan for a Gas Transmission and Distribution Project in Sumatra. Work on the activity was delayed during the Asian financial crisis but after a redesign, the Sumatra project turned out to be very successful.[45]

The 2005 Tangguh project was a major greenfield development to extract gas from fields in the Berau and Bintuni bay areas and to produce liquefied natural gas (LNG) for shipping to export markets. Interests in the project were shared by a range of major international oil and gas companies including BP plc, China National Offshore Oil Corporation, Mitsubishi Corporation, INPEX Corporation, and others. The government had set energy security as a key development goal and the project itself was designated as a national project.[46]

In 2006, two more large loans were approved. The first was for an infrastructure reform program which, like the two main loans agreed to the previous year, supported the programs set down in the Indonesia

---

[42] ADB, 2013, *Indonesia: Local Government*.
[43] Ibid., 9.
[44] ADB, 2005, *Indonesia: Tangguh Project*, 3.
[45] ADB, 2006, *Indonesia: Gas Transmission*, 12.
[46] A discussion of energy security issues and energy policy in Indonesia is in Nugroho, 2011, *A Mosaic*.

Infrastructure Summit in January 2005. Following the summit, an infrastructure policy package had been released by the government which called for major private sector participation in infrastructure and suggested that public-private partnerships (PPPs) should be the preferred approach for increasing private sector participation.

To promote PPP reforms, the government asked ADB, the Japan International Cooperation Agency, and the World Bank to provide policy support. In response, ADB approved the Infrastructure Reform Sector Development Program to finance activities to expand PPPs and to strengthen private sector participation across nine sectors including transport, power, oil and gas, and telecommunications.

The other large project agreed to was the Second Development Policy Support Program. This activity followed on from the first Development Policy Support Program loan approved in 2005. It was part of a wider series of development policy loans which supported a common development policy agenda prepared by a joint team from the Government of Indonesia, the World Bank, the Government of Japan, and ADB. The broad aim of this series of loans was to support the goal of lifting Indonesia's economic growth rate toward 7% per annum by 2009. Toward this end, the loans together promoted economic reforms including improved macroeconomic management, encouraging investment, and improving the delivery of public services.

Responses to natural disasters remained a main focus of the bank in 2006. The international community in Indonesia was involved in the major rehabilitation and reconstruction effort in Aceh. ADB, too, was implementing dozens of activities in different sectors across the province. The tasks of monitoring, coordinating, and reporting on all of this work took up much time, as did participation in meetings of the Multi Donor Fund, an umbrella fund that had been established on the request of the Government of Indonesia to help coordinate the $7 billion response to the disaster.

And then, as if to emphasize the risks of natural disasters in Indonesia, in May 2006 an earthquake hit the provinces of Central Java and Yogyakarta in Java. The impact of the earthquake was centered on the district of Bantul to the south of the city of Yogyakarta. Over 4,000 of the total of around 5,700 people who died in the earthquake were estimated to have died in Bantul alone. ADB President Haruhiko Kuroda visited Yogyakarta and

Bantul several days after the disaster to meet with President Yudhoyono and discuss immediate bank assistance. In normal circumstances, ADB staff would have taken time to prepare a proposal for approval to present to the ADB Board. Given the urgent needs, however, ADB's initial offer of support was expected to be funded from the reallocation of funds from existing projects. This approach minimized red tape and allowed a fast response to the needs in Bantul.

Tumult Through the Decade

ADB's fourth decade in Indonesia was a tumultuous period for the nation. At the beginning of the decade, Indonesia was seen as having become one of the newest miracle economies of Asia (Chapter 6). But the Asian financial crisis of 1997–1998 brought huge damage to Indonesia—both to the economy, and to many parts of wider Indonesian society and the community.

The efforts to support reforms and restore financial stability after the crisis saw a modest recovery of sorts in the period to 2003. Poverty rose sharply during the financial crisis but then fell quite quickly, partly because a range of social safety net programs was introduced. And then, toward the end of ADB's fourth decade in Indonesia, beginning in 2004, the Indonesian economy began to recover in a sustained way. A boom in motorcycle sales reflected rapidly growing consumer confidence. Motorcycle registrations increased from around 12 million in 1997 to over 33 million in 2006. The jump in sales was especially marked toward the end of the period. In 2005 alone, motorcycle registrations grew by 24%. The expansion in domestic air travel was just as dramatic. Between 2000 and 2006, domestic passenger arrivals grew by over 25% per annum, rising from 8.3 million to nearly 34 million in the six-year period. The idea of increased connectivity across the nation for the growing middle class in Indonesia was rapidly becoming a reality.

ADB aimed to adjust its programs in Indonesia during the changing circumstances over the decade. In response to the Asian financial crisis, the bank supported reforms in the financial sector and provided finance to strengthen social safety nets. In the transition period between 2000 and 2004, ADB joined with the rest of the international community to focus on reforms in governance and to support decentralization. In 2005 and 2006, as economic recovery began to strengthen, ADB worked with the government and with other major partners in the international community to support economic reform and promote investment.

Looking ahead, as the decade came to a close, the challenge for economic policymakers in Indonesia was to lift the growth rate toward the 7% level that President Yudhoyono had set as a target. For ADB, the question was how best to provide well-designed assistance in a country undergoing rapid change. On one hand, Indonesia's needs for basic infrastructure in such sectors as water and sanitation remained urgent. On the other hand, emerging challenges in other sectors—such as environmental pressures, and social issues concerning employment, and the needs of women and children—were increasingly seen as important as well.

At the end of 2006, the role of the international donor community in Indonesia was also somewhat uncertain. The aim for Indonesian policymakers of establishing a clearer degree of independence within the CGI had not been forgotten. Indeed, as will be seen in the next chapter, quite soon in 2007 the Indonesian authorities would decide that after 40 years, the guidance of the international community through the work of consortia such as the IGGI and the CGI would no longer be needed.

In the fifth decade of ADB's work in Indonesia, the relationship between Indonesia and the donor community would become quite different to the one that had been sustained during the four decades since the late 1960s.

ADB President Mitsuo Sato (*second right*) meets with Indonesian President Soeharto (*left*) during a courtesy visit in 1997.

The Lahendong geothermal power plant in North Sulawesi was partly financed under the Renewable Energy Development Sector Project (2002).

Farmers work together at a site of the Participatory Irrigation Sector Project (2003).

A boat perches on top of buildings after being washed ashore in December 2004 when an offshore earthquake followed by a tsunami with waves up to 30 meters high struck Aceh and North Sumatra. ADB joined with Indonesia and the rest of the international community to quickly respond to the disaster.

ADB President Haruhiko Kuroda inspects the destruction near Banda Aceh in 2005 after the city was struck by a massive tsunami.

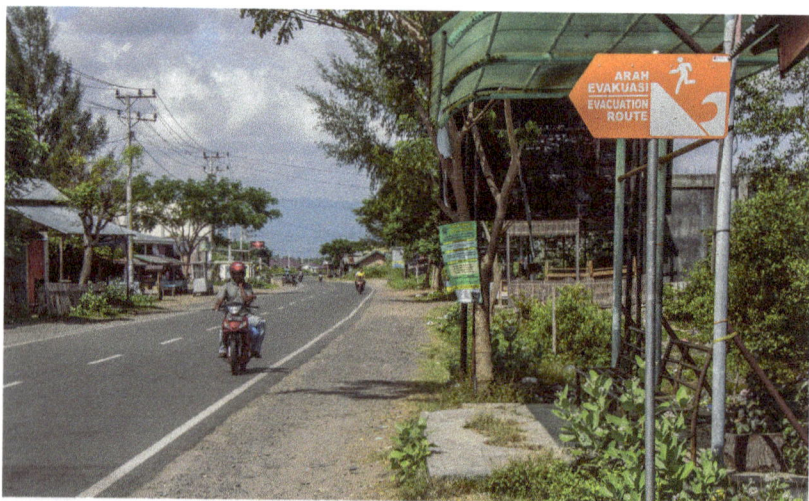

Through the Asian Tsunami Fund (ATF) and the Earthquake and Tsunami Emergency Support Project, both approved in 2005, ADB helped to reconstruct numerous roads and bridges, build 8,500 homes, and fund eight power projects in Aceh. The ATF was the first ADB fund established to focus on disaster relief.

Indonesia's President Susilo Bambang Yudhoyono (*center*) meets with ADB
President Haruhiko Kuroda (*third left*) in 2005.

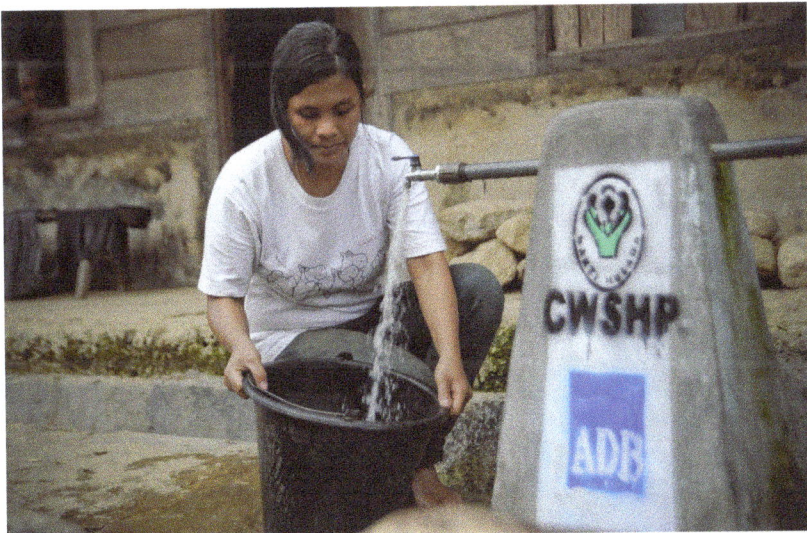

A local resident takes clean water from a public water facility in Barito Timur,
Central Kalimantan, financed as part of the Community Water Services and
Health Project (2005).

ADB President Haruhiko Kuroda (*left*) meets with Finance Minister and Governor for Indonesia for ADB Sri Mulyani Indrawati in 2005.

Pupils and a teacher talk together in the courtyard of a *madrasah* (Islamic school) that was supported under the Madrasah Education Development Project (2006).

CHAPTER 8

Middle-Income Country Issues (2007–2019)

In early 2007, at the beginning of the Asian Development Bank's (ADB) fifth decade of work in Indonesia, there was an optimistic mood with hopes of economic change across the country. President Susilo Bambang Yudhoyono (widely known as SBY) had been in office for two years and was promoting economic reform by announcing various packages with the aim of accelerating policy improvements in such areas as infrastructure, the financial sector, the investment climate, and small and medium enterprises.[1] Economic growth, too, which had been sluggish since the Asian financial crisis, was beginning to accelerate. It seemed, perhaps, that a sustained recovery was finally getting underway.

The international community, including ADB, needed to adjust to changing circumstances during the decade. Indonesia had been moving toward establishing a new set of relations with donors. The changes became clearer during the early years of the Yudhoyono administration. Increasingly, the National Development Planning Agency (Bappenas) and other key parts of the Government of Indonesia would take ownership of the management of Indonesia's dealings with international partners.

Strengthening Recovery

During 2007 and into 2008, macroeconomic performance in Indonesia steadily improved. Economic growth rose toward 7% per annum—a level which had not been seen since before the Asian financial crisis—and trends in other main variables such as inflation, the exchange rate, and the stock market reflected a strengthening economy as well. Investment, too, was expanding quickly; by early 2008, investment was growing at a rate of over 12% per annum.

Nevertheless, Indonesian policymakers were concerned about several issues. One was what many in Indonesia regarded as a major structural imbalance in the economy: the lack of strong growth in the manufacturing

---

[1] For a discussion of policy packages at the time, see Takii and Ramstetter, 2007, Survey, 297.

sector. Those who took this view were concerned that six decades after Independence, Indonesia's economy was still hampered by a "colonial structure" characterized by excessive dependence on a small number of export-oriented natural-resource based industries. During the colonial era, it was argued, the Indonesian economy had been dominated by export-oriented plantation sectors such as rubber, tobacco, sugar, palm oil, and tea and coffee. Later, after Independence, during the 1970s and 1980s, for a time the boom in the oil sector displaced the plantation industries as the dominant export-oriented resource-based sector. And then, from around 2005, yet another large commodity boom—this time in the coal and palm oil industries—was seen as distorting the structure of the economy. Many observers argued that distortions were holding back the development of an established labor-intensive manufacturing sector that would build balance and strength in the Indonesia economy.

The underlying issue in this long-running discussion about the structure of the Indonesian economy reflected the "Dutch disease" phenomenon, which regularly brought structural pressures to many industries across the country. When key export-oriented sectors in Indonesia experience booms, the real foreign exchange rate tends to appreciate (the Dutch disease effect) and other sectors of the economy exposed to international markets (such as some important manufacturing industries) are hard hit by the appreciation.

Concerns about the implications of a commodity boom for other tradable sectors such as manufacturing became pronounced when international prices for coal and palm oil rose sharply around 2008. Prices later eased somewhat, and the foreign exchange rate depreciated, making it easier for the manufacturing sector to compete with imported tradable goods. However, problems of sluggish growth in manufacturing continued to be seen as an important issue needing attention from policymakers.

There is, in fact, no easy way of cushioning sectors such as manufacturing from these fluctuations in the real exchange rate. Moreover, discussions about the need to assist manufacturing in order to promote employment are complicated by the fact that variations in the foreign exchange rate are only one of numerous factors that affect manufacturing firms. Even so, concerns about problems in the manufacturing sector were widely held.[2] There was a feeling that somehow, at least some of the resources

---

[2] Aswicahyono, Hill, and Narjoko, 2012, Industrialization, 194.

that became available from having a strong natural-resource based sector should be used to encourage the growth of a strong manufacturing sector. This approach, it was expected, would help provide jobs for the millions of young people entering the labor force.[3]

A second issue of concern was the need to promote investment in infrastructure.[4] Investment in infrastructure had fallen away sharply after the Asian financial crisis (Figure 7.1). Responding to the problem, the Yudhoyono administration arranged several infrastructure summits in Jakarta to try to encourage both domestic and international investment in such sectors as transport, power, and telecommunications. Nevertheless, it did not prove easy to build a pipeline of high-quality projects. Investment in infrastructure gradually began to pick up although recovery took some time. Efforts to promote expanded programs in infrastructure, which ADB supported, remained a priority throughout the Yudhoyono administration and were taken up by the next president, Joko Widodo, when he took office in October 2014.

The strength of the economic recovery was a third concern. Although economic conditions had clearly been improving, the overall rate of growth was still noticeably below that of the precrisis years in the 1990s. ADB's *Asian Development Outlook* for 2007, which presented an extended analysis of investment and growth trends in Asia 10 years after the 1997 crisis, summarized the issues:[5]

> Ten years after Asia's crisis, an air of normality would appear to have returned and incomes in the crisis countries now exceed their pre-crisis peaks. But a closer look shows that growth and investment rates have settled on a lower trajectory. On average in 2000–2006, growth in the five most directly affected countries (Indonesia, Korea, Malaysia, Philippines and Thailand) ran some 2.5 percentage points behind performance in 1990–1996. Viewed over longer periods, performance also seems to have slipped a gear. Investment rates have tumbled. Although investment may have been too high before the crisis, on a variety of measures it now seems to be low. Slower growth and low investment rates may be linked.

---

3   Ginting, Manning, and Taniguchi, 2018, *Indonesia: Enhancing Productivity.*
4   See the discussion on underspending on infrastructure in Kong and Ramayandi, 2008, Survey, 18.
5   ADB, 2007, *Asian Development Outlook*, 17.

Surveying these trends, policymakers agreed that further measures were needed to promote investment and to stimulate growth.

But during 2008 there was a marked slowing of growth in the major advanced economies. The global economic situation quickly deteriorated and soon became regarded as a global financial crisis. Initially it appeared that Indonesia was well-placed to weather the international troubles. Strong economic growth was sustained through the first part of the year and uncertainties in global markets did not seem to be reflected in local financial conditions. But following the much-publicized collapse of the major Lehman Brothers investment bank in the United States (US) in September 2008, global uncertainty increased and there were signs of capital flight from emerging countries such as Indonesia. For a time, in late 2008, it seemed that Indonesia might be caught up in the financial crisis affecting Organisation for Economic Co-operation and Development (OECD) countries.

As it turned out, the impact of the global financial crisis in developing Asia, including in Indonesia, was relatively mild.[6] There was even discussion of the way that growth in developing Asia had seemingly become decoupled from growth in advanced economies. Sustained growth in the People's Republic of China (PRC) helped bolster economic conditions across Asia. In Indonesia, a combination of fiscal stimulus measures, well-designed monetary policy and cash transfers to the poor helped soften the impact of the crisis.[7] Growth in Indonesia was sustained, albeit at a somewhat reduced rate of around 4% per annum into 2009. In October 2009, following mid-year elections, Yudhoyono and Boediono were inaugurated as president and vice-president for 2009–2014. Promoting investment in infrastructure and designing programs to mitigate the impact of climate change were nominated as key policy priorities for the second term of the Yudhoyono administration.

Growth remained strong for the first few years of the second term of the Yudhoyono presidency. Domestic demand was resilient, partly because much consumption spending in Indonesia is for basic necessities rather than for luxury goods so the scope for optional reductions in consumer expenditures is limited. Growth rose to over 6% in both 2010 and 2011. There was talk of perhaps soon achieving a much-discussed target of

---

[6]   Ginting and Aji, 2012, Macroeconomic management, 156.
[7]   Resosudarmo and Yusuf, 2009, Survey, 287.

7% per annum. Buoyed by the favorable environment, the government announced various programs to support economic growth. Two major initiatives were the National Medium-Term Development Plan (RPJMN) and the Masterplan for the Acceleration and Expansion of Indonesian Economic Development (MP3EI).

The RPJMN for 2010–2014, released in early 2010, was a major policy document which set out a strategy for development over the next five years. It outlined overall strategy, sectoral priorities, and regional plans in detail (Box 8.1).[8]

Box 8.1: The National Medium-Term Development Plan 2010–2014

The National Medium-Term Development Plan (RPJMN) 2010–2014 was set out in three books. These outlined national, sectoral, and regional development priorities.

Book 1 outlined the strategy, general policy, and macroeconomic framework which reflected the 11 national development priorities of the RPJMN. The overriding vision was "to realise an Indonesia that is prosperous, democratic, and just." The 11 priorities were: (1) bureaucratic and governance reform, (2) education, (3) health, (4) poverty reduction, (5) food security, (6) infrastructure, (7) investment and business climate, (8) energy, (9) environment and disaster management, (10) least developed, frontier, outer, and post conflict areas, and (11) culture, creativity, and technological innovation.

Book 2 set out sectoral development plans with the theme "to strengthen the synergy across development sectors" in order to support the priorities set down in Book 1. Some selected programs included constructing about 20,000 kilometers of highway across the country's five biggest islands, enhancing electricity generation capacity by around 3,000 megawatts per annum, and building transportation infrastructure based on a National Transportation System.

Book 3 outlined regional development plans by island: Sumatra, Java-Bali, Kalimantan, Sulawesi, Nusa Tenggara, Maluku, and Papua. The RPJMN noted that there was a dilemma between, on one hand, focusing on programs in

continued on next page

---

[8]   There is an extensive summary in World Bank, 2010, *Indonesian Economic Quarterly.*

Box 8.1 *continued*

leading regions, and on the other hand ensuring that minimum services were
delivered in lagging regions. The RPJMN listed five main steps to help tackle
these trade-offs in regional development policy:

1. Promote growth in regions seen as having good potential outside Java-
    Bali and Sumatra while, at the same time, maintaining the momentum of
    growth in Java-Bali and Sumatra.

2. Strengthen interregional linkages by increasing interisland trade.

3. Strengthen the competitiveness of regions by promoting leading sectors
    in each region.

4. Promote the development of lagging regions and regions with potential,
    and areas with high risk of disasters.

5. Support the development of regions oriented toward seafaring and sea-
    related activities.

Source: Summarized from World Bank, 2010, *Indonesian Economic Quarterly*, March.

The broad priorities of the RPJMN were reflected in a wide range of
supporting documents. One of the most important of these was the MP3EI.
The MP3EI, launched in May 2011, was the most comprehensive plan for
the expansion of infrastructure ever prepared in Indonesia (Box 8.2). The
aim of the program was to raise the rate of growth in Indonesia toward a
7%–9% range. The broad approach was to involve all main sectors of the
economy—central government agencies, local governments, state-owned
enterprises, and the private sector—to promote increased productivity.
The plan stated that "the private sector will be given a major and important
role in economic development" and that "the government will not only be
a regulator, it will also be a facilitator" to support growth.[9]

These key planning documents reflected the widespread agreement across
the government that better coordination of the work of the hundreds of
different official agencies across the nation was needed. On one hand,

---

[9] For a thorough discussion of the interaction between infrastructure investment programs
and regional development in Indonesia, see Susantono, 2015, *Infrastructure and Regional
Development*. Transport policy and infrastructure programs are discussed in Susantono,
2013, *Transportasi dan Investasi*.

Box 8.2: Masterplan for the Acceleration of Indonesian Economic Development

Plans for the implementation of the MP3EI included 8 main programs which consisted of 22 main economic activities. The implementation strategy of MP3EI aimed to integrate 3 main elements:

(1) developing the regional economic potential in six Indonesian economic corridors: Sumatra Economic Corridor, Java Economic Corridor, Kalimantan Economic Corridor, Sulawesi Economic Corridor, Bali–Nusa Tenggara Economic Corridor, and Papua–Kepulauan Maluku Economic Corridor;

(2) strengthening national connectivity locally and internationally; and

(3) strengthening human resource capacity and national science & technology to support the development of main programs in all of the economic corridors.

Implementation of MP3EI was expected to support and complement the existing development planning documents produced by the government, including the National Long-Term Development Plan (RPJPN) and National Medium-Term Development Plan (RPJMN).

MP3EI = Masterplan for the Acceleration and Expansion of Indonesian Economic Development.

Source: Republic of Indonesia, 2011, *Masterplan*, 10.

coordination of government policies had always been a challenge in Indonesia ever since Independence in 1945. Even when official planning documents such as the successive Five-Year Development Plans (Repelita) were prepared, it was often difficult to coordinate different parts of the disparate Indonesian bureaucracy. On the other hand, documents such as the RPJMN 2010–2014 and the MP3EI provided important signals about national priorities. At all levels of the government—national, provincial, and regional—the documents became reference points for planning about annual activities. The themes that they emphasized, such as the need to improve governance, promote productivity and growth, and strengthen inclusiveness, were issues that it became necessary for government agencies across the nation to acknowledge as important goals and to try to address.

Strong growth continued into 2011. But as so often in the past, concerns about the balance of payments continued to occupy the attention of economic policymakers. The traditional attention of policymakers had been directed to deficits on the current account. However in 2011 there were strong capital inflows which swamped the current account. These capital inflows led to marked increases in Indonesia's foreign exchange reserves and to pressures supporting an unwelcome appreciation of the rupiah.

These unwelcome pressures proved temporary. For a time, during 2012, the economic outlook remained encouraging. President Yudhoyono had earlier spoken of the need to promote three "pros" in economic management in Indonesia—policies that were pro-growth, pro-job, and pro-poor. Now he added a fourth—policies that were pro-environment.

Further changes in international markets soon provided new challenges. By 2013, capital inflows had abated and economic growth began to slow. And then an increase in global interest rates led to a reversal of capital flows. Capital outflows began to take place during 2013 and a "taper tantrum" occurred following speculation about changes in monetary policy in the US (a "tapering" of monetary policy) which led to a marked depreciation of the rupiah.[10] These fluctuations in capital flows and the resulting pressures on the rupiah were monitored very closely by authorities in Bank Indonesia. Memories of the extreme difficulties that had arisen during the Asian financial crisis were still fresh.

Overall economic growth began to slow markedly in 2013 as well. By 2014 annual growth had slipped from the 6% range to just over 5% and for the next five years hovered around this level. The slowdown in growth caused considerable concern for policymakers. It was generally agreed that the end of the international commodity boom which had buoyed Indonesia's rate of growth since around 2005 was a key factor contributing to the slower growth, and that ways needed to be found to stimulate domestic demand. Earlier, in August 2013, Finance Minister Chatib Basri had foreshadowed the challenges caused by changes in the international economic conditions, saying that: "The current global economic situation is not very promising … so the role of fiscal policy is quite clear. We have to provide stimulus for the economy."[11]

---

[10]   Basri, 2017, India and Indonesia.
[11]   Rahadiana and Thatcher, 2013, Indonesia says 2014 budget to focus on raising domestic demand.

Measures to stimulate demand and promote economic growth were introduced by the new president, Joko Widodo (widely known as Jokowi) who took office in October 2014. Between September 2015 and February 2016, the new administration announced 10 economic policy packages in an effort to promote deregulation and support investment in key sectors. Further packages of reform were announced during 2016. One area in which the government, and the new president himself, gave priority to was infrastructure. A range of new projects was announced, a number of which had been set out earlier in 2011 in the MP3EI infrastructure masterplan. Thus in promoting investment in infrastructure, there was a considerable degree of continuity between the outgoing and incoming administrations.

By the end of 2016, as ADB's fifth decade of work in the country came to a close, the Indonesian economy had experienced, first, a marked acceleration of growth since 2007, and then a slowdown. International economic conditions had become more difficult during 2016 because global demand was sluggish, the economic boom in the PRC was slowing, and commodity prices had declined. The expanding emphasis on infrastructure in Indonesia, which ADB prepared loan activities to support, was designed to help stimulate domestic demand as a balance to the changed conditions in international markets.

New Era for Donors

At the beginning of 2007, on 24 January, President Yudhoyono made an announcement that marked the end of a four-decade long relationship with the international community and Indonesia: The Consultative Group on Indonesia (CGI) would be dissolved and Indonesia would coordinate all relations with international partners directly, rather than through the auspices of the CGI. At the time, the CGI consisted of 21 member countries and 11 multilateral agencies and was chaired by the World Bank. It had met regularly for 15 years since the former grouping of donors, the Inter-Governmental Group on Indonesia (IGGI), had been dissolved on the request of Indonesia.

Although the president's announcement had not been expected by donors, it reflected a careful process of reviewing relations with the donor community which Indonesian authorities had been conducting for some time. The 2003 Bappenas report on the future of Indonesia's relations with the CGI issued as *Keberadaan dan Peran Consultative Group for Indonesia (CGI)* (Box 7.1) had signaled that the government was considering key aspects of the relationship with donor countries. Indeed, within the international community as well, there was a growing recognition that perhaps the time was approaching when Indonesia should take full ownership of the coordination of international assistance programs.

The president's decision was announced just after a visit by Rodrigo de Rato, managing director of the International Monetary Fund (IMF). Following the announcement, the president reminded the public that Indonesia had fully repaid its IMF loans and had completed the post-program monitoring reviews. The president's decision was widely welcomed, being seen as signaling a clear break from policies of the past.

Nevertheless, the influence of IMF policies was still widely felt in Indonesia. Some years later, Anggito Abimanyu, a senior policymaker, described Indonesia's relations with the IMF in the following terms:[12]

> Certainly, between 1999 and 2004 the management of the Indonesian economy was under the control of the IMF. But once the IMF loans were repaid and the CGI (Consultative Group on Indonesia) was disbanded, there was no further interference in our economic affairs from the IMF or from other multilateral or bilateral agencies. Nevertheless, the influence of the IMF program on the management of the Indonesian economy, through the impact of programs which swelled the national debt such as the recapitalization of the banking sector and the BLBI (Bank Liquidity from Bank Indonesia), has had a long-term impact. Because of these things, whether we like it or not, Indonesia's economy is still influenced by programs designed by the IMF. Whatever government holds office in the post-IMF program era must therefore swallow the bitter pill of the consequences of these programs and must manage the implications, regardless of whether they like the program or not. This situation helps give rise to the impression that the Indonesian economy is not yet really an independent economy.

Reflecting concerns of this kind, in 2007 senior economic ministers in Indonesia saw the changed approach in relations with the international community as a timely step for the country to make.[13] It was explained that Indonesia would still need foreign aid to fund development projects but that bilateral negotiations would be held with each partner country rather

---

[12] Abimanyu, 2011, *Refleksi dan Gagasan*, 5, translated from the original.
[13] Details here are drawn from Lindblad, J., and Thee K.W., 2007, Survey, 10.

than going through the annual process of responding to the commentary and sometimes pointed criticisms in the CGI forum. Coordinating Minister for Economic Affairs Boediono noted that the new approach had the support of Indonesia's three major creditors, the World Bank, ADB, and Japan. He added that it would now be possible for new loan agreements with each lender to be different rather than following the standardized approach under the CGI procedures. Moreover, on the Indonesian side, senior officials rather than ministers would conduct negotiations with officials from partner countries. Henceforth, Indonesian ministers would become involved only when serious problems arose.

Minister of Finance Sri Mulyani Indrawati also supported the change. Lindblad and Thee noted that the minister took the view that:[14]

> …the CGI budget was a product of the New Order, intended to help finance the government's budget deficit. But after the fall of [President] Soeharto, it had often been perceived as an instrument of political interference in Indonesia's affairs, for example, in relation to human rights. In the current era, however, the government could avoid such interference since it had other means to help finance its deficits, including issuing bonds domestically and internationally…

Moreover, Minister Sri Mulyani added, "China has recently emerged as a potentially important source of finance, offering large loans to Indonesia."

The international community decided to welcome the change. Donor countries and international agencies had been aware, for some time, that there was a mood in Indonesia to adjust the relationship with development partners. Several years later, in reviewing the changed arrangements, Baird and Wihardja concluded that: "The decision to abolish the Consultative Group on Indonesia (CGI) in January 2007 symbolised the end of Indonesia's 'aid dependence', and ushered in a new era of bilateral 'partnerships' with major creditors and donors."[15] After all, the two other major developing nations in Asia, the PRC and India, did not accept official aid flows through the monitoring arrangements of an international consultative group. The change in Indonesia was really no more than a reform which brought Indonesia into line with other large countries in the Asian region.

---

[14] Ibid., 10.
[15] Baird and Wihardja, Survey, 155.

Following the dissolution of the CGI, the international community continued to implement the agreed programs in Indonesia. Nevertheless, it soon became apparent that in the absence of the CGI, a clearer set of development policies was needed when Indonesia participated in international conferences and negotiations. In 2008, for example, international statements such as the Accra Agenda for Action and the Doha Declaration on Financing for Development were seen as important declarations that Indonesia should help prepare. The earlier 2005 Paris Declaration on Aid Effectiveness which had been based around five central pillars—ownership, alignment, harmonization, managing for development results, and mutual accountability—was widely seen as setting out key principles for the management of effective aid. As a step toward establishing a well-defined Indonesian approach to these issues, in January 2009 development partners and the government signed the Jakarta Commitment, a declaration with which signatories would work together to apply the principles of development set out in recent international agreements.[16]

The Jakarta Commitment, subtitled "Aid for Development Effectiveness," was created as a road map to help implement internationally agreed principles of aid effectiveness in Indonesia.[17] It was recognized that the aims of aid programs in Indonesia, and the best methods of delivering assistance, were changing. The Jakarta Commitment noted that on one hand, although Indonesia had moved into the middle-income range of developing countries, there were still key development challenges that needed to be addressed. The commitment spelled out three challenges seen as especially important: poverty reduction, service delivery, and decentralization. On the other hand, the flow of external assistance to Indonesia had been declining —and was expected to continue to decline. Indeed, the commitment anticipated that Indonesia would itself establish an international assistance program, noting that: "Indonesia will in time commit to providing assistance to countries in the region and beyond." The commitment therefore emphasized the need for Indonesia to focus on improving the effectiveness of external resources and stated that, "The main constraint facing Indonesia in addressing the challenges and achieving its planned development outcomes is not merely the lack of financial resources but rather the utilization of the resources."

---

[16]   Indonesia, 2009, *Jakarta Commitment*.

[17]   Indonesia's relationship with the donor community at the end of 2008 was reviewed in the comments about "Indonesia and the Donor Community" in Ashcroft and Cavanough, Survey, 358.

The Jakarta Commitment also outlined issues which would shape the way that Indonesia was prepared to receive international assistance over the next decade. One issue was alignment—that is, the degree to which Indonesia's development partners were prepared to align their programs to the priorities and the processes of the government. Alignment had become a major issue of concern to Indonesian policymakers because there were numerous instances of external assistance which had been supplied without careful discussion with Indonesian stakeholders. The commitment therefore proposed that "Development partners commit to providing all their development assistance to Indonesia based on country demands."

A second issue was the way that finance should flow from development partners to Indonesia. Ever since the major international effort to support Indonesia had begun in the late 1960s, donors had provided finance in a wide variety of ways—through supplying hard or soft loans, or in grant form, and to support projects or numerous different types of programs, technical assistance, emergency humanitarian aid, scholarships, and so on. From the Indonesian point of view, this kaleidoscope of aid forms, agencies, and financial arrangements, often provided with numerous different types of conditionalities attached, was very difficult to administer. The problems of fragmentation were especially acute in programs supported by smaller donors. As Indonesian policymakers saw it, a better arrangement was the multidonor trust funds system that had been used to support activities in Aceh and Nias after the tsunami humanitarian disaster in 2004.

The Jakarta Commitment addressed the issue of finance for development, suggesting that changes were needed:[18]

> Multi-donor trust funds have emerged as an important vehicle for development partners to support Indonesia's development—ranging from large multi-donor trust funds established to implement reconstruction programmes, capacity building activities and targeted development interventions such as the Multi-Donor Fund for Aceh and Nias, the Decentralization Support Facility and the Indonesian Partnership Fund for HIV/AIDS, to quite small and ad hoc trust funds [to] support very special activities. These trust funds have enabled development partners to respond flexibly and rapidly to Indonesia's priority needs…In using the multi-donor support modality, the

---

[18]   Indonesia, 2009, *Jakarta Commitment*, 3. Emphasis in the original.

> **Government and development partners will move away from
> project based approaches towards [a] programme based approach,**
> supporting government programs and linking the priorities of
> Bappenas, Ministry of Finance, and concerned line ministries.

The approach set out in the Jakarta Commitment, therefore, reflected
the strong preference of the government for more streamlined ways of
managing financial flows. In particular, the government was signaling
that the preference was for external assistance to be channeled through
government systems, increasingly bringing funds from partners onto
the national budget. Indonesia was becoming more confident, too, in
suggesting changes of this kind. Indonesian agencies were beginning to
become more accustomed to accessing alternative sources of finance such
as international bond markets. With the difficult experience of the Asian
financial crisis behind them, Indonesian agencies increasingly had new
options for raising finance that had not been available in the past.

Nevertheless, the management of financial flows from international
agencies to Indonesian organizations continued, at times, to cause
difficulties. On-lending of funds from partners to subnational
governments, including from ADB, had long been a part of government
finances in Indonesia. Yet the experience of on-lending had often been
disappointing.[19] It was hoped that stronger government ownership of
assistance programs under the Jakarta Commitment would help improve
the management of financial flows such as on-lending arrangements from
partner agencies.

A third issue which the Jakarta Commitment addressed was the issue of
aid effectiveness. The need to improve aid effectiveness had become a
global theme following the Paris Declaration on Aid Effectiveness in 2005.
Taking up this theme—which the international community had strongly
emphasized in many international meetings since 2005—the Jakarta
Commitment noted that:

> Indonesia's overarching concern is to maximise the effectiveness
> of all its resources committed to development, including external
> assistance. It is in this context that the aid effectiveness agenda
> becomes particularly relevant. External assistance is not simply a
> financial supplement to domestic resources, but complementary to
> these resources—playing a catalytic role in allowing Indonesia to access

---

[19]   Lewis, 2007, *On-lending in Indonesia*, 53.

international knowledge and best practice, to enhance institutional capacity and bring about strategic systems improvements.

With the aim of strengthening effectiveness, the commitment looked to partners to help strengthen Indonesia's capacity to implement development programs. And the commitment stated that "the **Government will articulate, and development partners will support the achievement of capacity development objectives and targets within sector plans and thematic strategies.**"[20] During the next few years, a range of efforts was introduced to improve aid effectiveness in Indonesia. An Aid for Development Effectiveness Secretariat was established within Bappenas to help focus efforts on the effectiveness program.[21] However, the capacity development constraints which the Jakarta Commitment referred to continued to hold back progress toward meeting the goals set out by the government.

A number of issues emerged as needing attention for the international community following agreement to support the Jakarta Commitment. One was the way that development partner countries coordinated their activities—both in their sectoral programs, and across different regions of Indonesia. Arrangements for coordination in supporting Indonesia's decentralization efforts, for example, called for partners to coordinate their work within agreed sectors and across different provinces in Indonesia.[22] A range of agencies, including ADB, had been active in supporting Indonesia's decentralization programs since the late 1990s. Winters noted that:

> After the passage of the 1999 laws, donors stepped in with significant amounts of technical assistance. In 1999, the Asian Development Bank alone produced three technical assistance projects. A 2002 "matrix of actions" produced by the Decentralization Working Group of the CGI lists projects from ADB, CIDA, GTZ, JBIC, UNDP, USAID and the World Bank.

Nevertheless, coordination across this disparate group of agencies had proved difficult, even after a Decentralization Support Facility was established by the World Bank in 2005 to help coordinate work across the group.

---

[20] Emphasis in the original.
[21] Planned activities of the Secretariat were set out in Wismana, nd, *Sharing Experience*. See also Riyadi, 2009, *Aid Accountability and Transparency: Indonesia's Experience*.
[22] Winters, 2010, *Paper Prepared for June 2010 Meeting.*

Coordination of partner activities across regions also continued to be somewhat uneven. In 2010 Winters observed that:[23]

> Australia has worked predominantly in Eastern Indonesia, whereas USAID has had a larger role on Java and Sumatera. CIDA has taken an extensive interest in Sulawesi. GTZ's local-government work has been concentrated in five provinces—Central Java, Kalimantan, Nusa Tenggara Barat, Nusa Tenggara Timur and Yogyakarta. The Dutch pay particular attention to Papua and Maluku.

This "geographic sorting," however, did not necessarily reflect development priorities. Donors sometimes preferred to work in parts of Indonesia which reflected the strategic interests of the donors themselves. In other cases development partners may have preferred to work in areas where there had been past successes.

A second issue which arose following donor support for the Jakarta Commitment concerned arrangements for financial flows to Indonesia. Looking to the future, in terms of the principles set out in the commitment, it seemed that a movement away from project-based lending by international agencies toward program lending would have advantages. ADB, Japan, and the World Bank had been providing program lending through the Development Policy Support Program (ADB) and the Development Policy Loan series (World Bank) since 2004. From the Indonesian point of view, more program loans of this kind would help streamline financial flows to Indonesia. Indonesian policymakers also indicated that an increasing use of multidonor trust funds would be welcome. The hope was that by concentrating international support for agreed activities into a single pool, it would be easier to monitor flows and to record them as an on-budget item in Indonesia's budget accounts.

In 2011, two years after the Jakarta Commitment had been signed, the OECD released a survey of Indonesia's progress toward the Paris Declaration.[24] Although the results of the survey were too early to be a measure of the long-term impact of the Jakarta Commitment, the conclusions provided an overview of the way that donor operations in Indonesia had changed in response to the principles set down in the Paris Declaration in 2005. Not surprisingly, the overall conclusions were mixed. The OECD emphasized that efforts to achieve the goals of the Paris Declaration

---

[23] Ibid., 12.
[24] OECD, 2011, *Aid Effectiveness.*

(and, by implication, the objectives of the Jakarta Commitment) were a collective endeavor which depended on the work of both the international community and developing partner governments. At the broadest level, the OECD concluded that "while aid effectiveness challenges remain for Indonesia, significant progress is being made."

At a more detailed level, the OECD pointed to encouraging trends which had strengthened aid effectiveness. To improve strategic objectives, all eight of the key Millennium Development Goals (Mdgs) had been mainstreamed into Indonesia's RPJMN. There had also been active community participation in the development policy process:[25]

> Participation in the formulation of the development strategy and budget process includes civil society and the public through the media. The Parliament is extensively consulted and has the final say in budget approval. Civil society organisations are involved on a routine basis alongside the government and the private sector in development planning consultations. Civil society and the media are also taking active roles in dialogue and reporting on government affairs. Government documents are available to the public through the internet and in printed form.

Against other OECD measures of effectiveness, aid delivery and coordination had improved as well. The OECD observed that[26] "alignment of aid flows to national priorities has been achieved with 95% of dispersed aid accurately reflected in the budget…the majority of bilateral donors now report that their aid is fully or almost fully untied." On the other hand, arrangements for the harmonization of the costs of managing aid were varied. There were marked differences between donors in the use of streamlined program-based approaches (PBAs) to deliver aid:[27]

> The use of PBAs varies greatly among donors. Ten out of 24 donors…made no disbursement through PBAs. Three donors, Asian Development Bank, Global Fund and Islamic Development Bank, channelled all their aid through PBAs.

---

[25] Ibid., 4.
[26] Ibid., 4.
[27] Ibid., 13. The Global Fund to Fight AIDS, Tuberculosis and Malaria (often called the Global Fund) is one of the world's largest financiers of AIDS, tuberculosis and malaria prevention, treatment and care programs. It is largely supported by governments but also receives support from non-government organizations. It was established in 2002 and maintains a secretariat in Geneva.

The 2011 OECD review, in looking at the details of aid delivery, pointed to areas where further efforts to improve cooperation were needed. But at the broader level, the review endorsed the changes made in Indonesia to improve the quality of the management of aid.

In the meantime, Bappenas worked with international partners to implement the approaches outlined in the Jakarta Commitment. In carrying on their agreed programs, international agencies often needed to liaise with many different Indonesian departments and agencies. However, Bappenas took the lead in coordinating overall relations between Indonesia and international partners.

One key role for Bappenas was to foster the involvement of stakeholder organizations across Indonesia in dialogue about the development process. To this end, Bappenas held many meetings at provincial and local levels with community groups such as village-level gatherings and with non-government organizations. Bappenas also issued many documents reporting on the development process in Indonesia, both describing sectoral programs and providing information on activities at provincial and local levels.[28] Many of the documents were prepared in cooperation with international partner agencies.

Measures were taken to strengthen the institutional capacity of Bappenas following an agreement with partner countries to the Jakarta Commitment. In October 2009, in announcing the Indonesian Cabinet for his second five-year term in office, President Yudhoyono appointed one of Indonesia's most senior academic economics, Professor Armida S. Alisjahbana from Padjadjaran University in Bandung, as the minister for national development planning and head of Bappenas. Following her appointment, Alisjahbana promoted a program for the revitalization of Bappenas which, she said, would need to focus on:[29]

> ...steps to renew a positive view of Bappenas as a strategic agency by introducing sustained efforts to improve the quality of planning and to ensure that Bappenas always takes the lead in addressing development issues. In this way, Bappenas will position itself as a credible and respected agency. If this is done, there will be appreciation of the quality and dedication of the role of Bappenas based on the agency's achievements rather than on work undertaken

---

[28]   See, for example, Indonesia, 2013, *Data dan Informasi*.
[29]   Alisjahbana, 2011, Ministerial message: Revitalisi Bappenas, 3 (translated by author).

merely in response to artificial regulatory goals. With planning efforts such as these, and with the establishment of institutional links with shareholders involved as voluntary and well-informed participants, Bappenas will secure its place as a strategic and valuable agency in the eyes of shareholders.

As part of this approach, Alisjahbana encouraged Bappenas to promote attention to international targets such as the MDGs and to raise awareness of the implications of the MDGs for Indonesia.[30]

A comprehensive history of Bappenas and of planning in Indonesia since 1945 was also prepared. The study, *Bappenas dalam Sejarah Perencanaan Pembangunan Indonesia 1945–2025* (Bappenas and the History of Development Planning in Indonesia 1945–2025) was launched in 2012.[31] The constellation of senior policymakers who contributed introductory comments to the history included Boediono, Jusuf Kalla, Alisjahbana, J.B. Sumarlin, and Ginandjar Kartasasmita.

In 2014, when Widodo took office as the seventh president of Indonesia, the status of Bappenas as an agency within the government was upgraded. Formerly, Bappenas had reported to the president indirectly through the coordinating minister for the economy. Under the new arrangements, Bappenas reported directly to the president and held a status equivalent to that of the State Secretariat Ministry. President Widodo then adjusted appointments to the post of minister of national development planning several times before announcing, in July 2016, that Professor Bambang Brodjonegoro from the Economics Faculty at the University of Indonesia was appointed to the role. As minister, Brodjonegoro quickly moved to further strengthen the role of Bappenas within the government and with international partners.

Place of ADB

The bank's activities in Indonesia at the beginning of the fifth ADB decade in 2007 reflected the key priorities of the time—support for the large post-tsunami reconstruction program in Aceh, and for efforts to promote decentralization across Indonesia (Table 8.1). The broader outlines of the bank's work were guided by the priorities set out in the two country strategic plans (CSPs) for 2006–2009 and for 2012–2014.

---

[30] Alisjahbana, 2013, Ministerial message: Capaian MDGs Kita, 3.
[31] Mustopadidjaja, 2012, *Bappenas.*

Table 8.1: Notable Events, 2007–2018

Item	Comment
2007	
Consultative Group on Indonesia dissolved	Full ownership of the coordination of international assistance was taken over by Indonesia
2008	
Multidonor assistance package of $5 billion prepared to bolster economic stability	ADB committed to provide $1 billion for a Public Expenditure Support Facility as part of the package
2009	
Jakarta Commitment agreed to by Indonesia and partners	The commitment set out a road map to help implement international principles for aid effectiveness in Indonesia
ADB annual meeting in Bali	42nd Annual Meeting of ADB was held in Indonesia
2010	
ADB and ILO economic study prepared	A diagnostic study on *Indonesia: Critical Development Constraints* discussed key constraints on growth
2011	
Priority to program lending continued	Program loans were designed to support policy and institutional reforms
2012	
ADB Precautionary Financing Facility approved for Indonesia	The PFF was part of ADB's participation in a contingent $5 billion donor package to provide liquidity support
2013	
International "taper tantrum" in global financial markets	Indonesia requested access to the $5 billion contingent package prepared in 2012
2014	
Stepping Up Investments for Growth Acceleration Program (SIGAP) loan	The first of several SIGAP loans designed to strengthen investment-led growth
2015	
ADB's first results-based loan approved for Indonesia	To support transmission investment in Sumatra provided by the State Electricity Company (PLN)
2016	
Further program loans approved	Two large loans to support public financial management

continued on next page

Table 8.1   *continued*

Item	Comment
2017	
First Indonesia rupiah-linked bond issued	ADB raised about $74 million from a new issue of offshore Indonesian rupiah-linked bonds
2018	
Major response to natural disasters	ADB provided assistance following large-scale disasters in Lombok and in Palu, Sulawesi
Private sector lending	ADB lending to the private sector in Indonesia reached a record lending level

ADB = Asian Development Bank, ILO = International Labour Organization.

In Aceh, ADB remained closely involved in the reconstruction and rehabilitation effort. The post-tsunami Aceh and Nias support program was one of the largest aid-supported reconstruction efforts ever seen in the developing world.[32] Total reconstruction support at the end of the program was estimated at $7.2 billion. Of this, around $5.2 billion was made up of grants from the government and aid agencies including ADB, about $1.6 billion from nongovernment organizations, and $400 million from multilateral and bilateral agencies.[33]

The bank's main contribution to the tsunami response effort in 2005 had been through the provision of a grant, the Earthquake and Tsunami Emergency Support Project, a $320 million program approved in April 2005. But delivery of the agreed programs sometimes ran into delays. One main problem in providing the assistance was that the initial plans to provide aid within a three-year period turned out to be too optimistic. ADB's 2011 Completion Report suggested that "ADB should review its time frame for completing emergency assistance following major disasters. Project experience suggests that a 3-year time frame for such substantive support is too short."[34] The Completion Report also summarized some of the main experiences for bank operations in assisting with disaster relief in seven main lessons (Box 8.3).

---

[32] ADB, 2009, *Indonesia: Aceh-Nias Rehabilitation*. This document provides a useful review of the overall reconstruction program in Aceh and Nias.

[33] ADB, 2011, *Indonesia: Earthquake and Tsunami*, 1.

[34] Ibid., 18.

Box 8.3: Seven Lessons for Disaster Reconstruction

(1)   **Needs assessment.** Disaster management support should be based on a needs assessment that should identify and address such implementation problems as the lack of government staff, regulations, and design standards for physical works.

(2)   **Selective intervention.** Reconstruction support should be selective and adopt a realistic time frame, with ADB focusing on areas that are unlikely to receive support from other partners.

(3)   **Phases of response.** Phasing of reconstruction assistance may be considered, clearly distinguishing the needs of initial emergency response from those of subsequent reconstruction.

(4)   **Coordination.** Proper institutional arrangements and central coordination by one agency are essential. The effectiveness of post-disaster reconstruction depends on the willingness and collaboration of relevant government agencies.

(5)   **Financial sustainability.** Off-budget activities may expedite implementation; however on-budget implementation ensures sustainability by establishing an extensive outreach program and building capacity for future reconstruction programs.

(6)   **Flexibility.** Flexibility in implementation is essential, as it facilitates the design of need-based reconstruction projects through simplified documentation

(7)   **Decentralization.** Decentralization is essential in effective disaster management. Adapting to emerging needs is desirable in disaster reconstruction.

Source: ADB, 2011, *Indonesia: Earthquake and Tsunami Emergency Support Project.*

A second focus of ADB's work was continued support for Indonesia's ambitious decentralization program.[35] The bank, along with numerous other international partners, had been providing assistance for decentralization activities since the first main laws had been approved in May 1999. However, the speed and complexity of the changes had created

---

[35]   Nasution provides an overview of Indonesia's decentralization program in Nasution, 2016, *Government Decentralisation.*

numerous inconsistencies in policies and in service delivery. In late 2003, the government had suggested that ADB might provide support, on a flexible basis during the period 2004–2009, to help facilitate the design of reforms. A major step in ADB's program was the Local Government Finance and Governance Reform Sector (LGFGR) Development Program, approved in October 2005.[36] The main objective of the loan program was to improve the effectiveness of the delivery of basic public services and help develop the capacity of local governments in Indonesia.

ADB continued to support these activities in 2007–2009 and beyond. Nevertheless, despite the efforts of both the government and of international partners, there was growing concern about the problems that had arisen in management in the public sector following decentralization. A major stocktaking report on *Decentralization 2009* prepared by the US Agency for International Development (USAID) Democratic Reform Support Program with the support of Bappenas described the situation as follows:[37]

> …a policy and legal tangle is being created in [decentralization/ local government] that is characterized by conflicting regulations; relations that are sometimes overly idealistic, or unworkable, or mired in old paradigms.

The result, according to the USAID report, was that:[38]

> There are now sufficient signals, on the ground, and in the public discourse, to suggest that decentralization is not delivering what is expected. The democratic wave of the last decade has brought political changes, but has yet to bring the more concrete changes expected of decentralization. Disappointment is now often expressed on the ultimate impact. Prominent national figures regret the meagre results from regional autonomy, passing harsh judgement in cases: "We have seen no improvement in prosperity between the era prior to decentralization and a decade later"; regional heads believe that "…few significant developments are experienced with respect to the goal of improving people's welfare"; or [Regional Representatives Council] DPD members opine "…regional autonomy that gave new hope, in reality has not brought meaningful change."

---

[36] ADB, 2005, *Local Government Finance*.
[37] USAID, 2009, *Decentralization 2009*, 9.
[38] Ibid., 9. This source provides references for the quotes cited in the extract above.

Against this background, in 2010 the Independent Evaluation Department of ADB released a study, *Asian Development Bank Support for Decentralization in Indonesia*, which provided a detailed review of the bank's work to strengthen the decentralization program.[39] The study noted that since 1998, the bank had provided four core decentralization support loans for $1.04 billion, $1.27 billion for sector-based decentralization support loans, and a further $2.93 billion for public sector management support loans with decentralization components (Table 7.2). In addition, ADB had provided a considerable amount of technical assistance for decentralization activities and had participated in numerous policy dialogue discussions.

The conclusions set out in the evaluation study of this sustained effort by the bank reflected the concerns of both the government and the international community at the time. In terms of relevance, the study judged that ADB's work had been "variable":[40]

> Effectiveness has been influenced by the way in which assistance has been provided. ADB's core decentralization loans and supporting TA projects have been effective in supporting required policy reforms. However, they have been less effective in developing the institutions and processes needed to implement the required policies.

In terms of impact, the report concluded that the effects of the bank's work had been "modest." And summarizing the overall results of ADB's program over the decade since 1998, the evaluation study judged that the outcome had been "partly satisfactory":[41]

> Irrespective of the urgent need for assistance, interventions taking place during periods of rapid economic, political, and administrative transitions face the risk of becoming irrelevant and ineffective, with short-lived outputs and unsustainable outcomes. In terms of ADB performance, this has meant finding a difficult balance between the need to ensure the effectiveness and efficacy of deploying scarce TA resources, and the need to support important policy processes during a period characterized by risk and uncertainty. ADB responded promptly to a rapidly changing situation, but the very nature of the situation precluded detailed analyses and programming.

[39] ADB, 2010, *Asian Development Bank Support*.
[40] Ibid., ii.
[41] Ibid., iii.

The study set out recommendations which were expected to be reflected in ADB's forthcoming CSP for Indonesia for 2012–2014. And although it was clear that the bank's experience in supporting decentralization in Indonesia had yielded some mixed results, the study recommended that the bank should continue support for the large decentralization program because "The government is increasingly assertive in policy development and has welcomed support that is facilitative."

ADB Activities

The bank's broader strategic approach during this period reflected the priorities set down in the CSP for 2006–2009.[42] At the time that the 2006–2009 CSP was prepared, the investment climate in Indonesia was still seen as somewhat discouraging for both domestic and foreign investors. The country also seemed to be losing competitiveness. The CSP had therefore been framed with the aim of supporting the government's hopeful goal of moving toward a growth rate of 7% by 2009, of reducing poverty and unemployment, and of promoting good governance through combating corruption. These objectives had been set down in the RPJMN for 2005–2009. As themes, the RPJMN emphasized policy and institution reform. The CSP, in turn, was also drawn up to reflect ADB's own strategic objectives set down in three documents—a Poverty Reduction Strategy, a Medium-Term Strategy, and Strategy 2020.[43]

The 2006–2009 CSP balanced these strategic priorities by setting out five areas of engagement for ADB:

    (i)   improved infrastructure and infrastructure services;

    (ii)   deepened financial sector;

    (iii) improved decentralization;

    (iv) accelerated achievement of the MDGs; and

    (v)   strengthened environment and natural resource management.

---

[42] ADB, 2006, *Indonesia 2006–2009*; see also ADB, 2011, *Final Review Validation.*
[43] See, ADB, 2004, *Review*; ADB, 2006, *Medium-Term Strategy*; and ADB, *Strategy 2020.*

To implement this program, the CSP suggested that a pipeline of loans was needed consisting of a balance of some program lending and increased amounts of project lending.

As things turned out, the balance of ADB's lending during the next few years shifted markedly toward program rather than project lending (Table 8.2). Partly, the change reflected evolving preferences on the Indonesian side for program rather than project loans. But partly, too, the shift toward program loans took place because as the unexpected global financial crisis

Table 8.2: Disbursements by Sector during the 2006–2009 CSP Period

Sectors	$ million	%	Activities
Public Sector Management	1,650	43	Support was provided to link improvement of regulations and building financial and public management capacity for macrostability, private investment, and decentralized service delivery.
Infrastructure	940	24	Activities were aligned with the National Medium-Term Development Plan and supported a government-led policy reform program to encourage an enabling environment and encourage public–private partnerships.
Finance	600	16	Attention was focused on capital market development and financial market governance with the aim of encouraging greater domestic resource mobilization.
Education	580	15	Interventions were designed to help expand access, quality and governance of basic education, and to improve the allocation of Special Allocation Funds for education. Improved *madrasah* (Islamic school) education was supported.
Environment	83	2	Support was provided for improved water resources, coastal and marine resource management, and reduced flood risk. During the 2006–2009 period, the focus widened to include other issues such as renewable energy use.
Total	**3,854**	**100**	

CSP = country strategic plan.

Source: ADB, 2012, *Indonesia: Country Partnership Strategy, 2012–2014*, Manila.

unfolded in 2007–2008, it became urgent for Indonesia to have access to international sources of funds to draw upon if needed.

In response to these changing circumstances, ADB made adjustments in the way that its activities were delivered in Indonesia. There was a move away from the approach set out in the 2006–2009 CSP. In 2007, proposed projects in energy and finance were dropped. There was, rather, a focus on economic management and public policy interventions along with projects in the social protection and nutrition sectors (Table 8.3). A Third Development Policy Support Program (DPSP) loan for $200 million was also approved (Box 8.4).

Table 8.3: ADB Lending to Indonesia, 2007–2016[a]

Loan	Sector	$ million	Loan Terms
2007			
Nutrition Improvement with Community Empowerment	Nutrition	50	OCR and ADF
Poverty Reduction and MDG Acceleration Program	Multisector	400	OCR
Capital Market Development Program Cluster	Insurance and savings	300	OCR
Third Development Policy Support Program	Public sector	200	OCR
2008			
Vocational Education Strengthening	Technical Education	80	OCR and ADF
Rural Infrastructure Support to PNPM Mandiri	Multisector	50	OCR and ADF
Infrastructure Reform Sector Development Program	Multisector	280	OCR
Second Local Government Finance and Governance Reform	Decentralizaion	350	OCR
Fourth Development Policy Support Program	Public sector	200	OCR
Integrated Citarum Water Resources Management	Water	50	OCR and ADF

continued on next page

Table 8.3 *continued*

Loan	Sector	$ million	Loan Terms
2009			
Indonesian Infrastructure Financing Facility	Finance sector	100	OCR
Public Expenditure Support Facility	Public sector	1,000	OCR
Countercyclical Support Loan	Public sector	500	OCR
Capital Market Development Program Cluster	Finance	300	OCR
Fifth Development Policy Support Program	Public sector	200	OCR
2010			
Infrastructure Reform Sector Development Program	Multisector	200	OCR
Sixth Development Policy Support Program	Public sector	200	OCR
2011			
Urban Sanitation and Rural Infrastructure Support	Urban sanitation	100	OCR
Second Local Government Finance and Governance Reform	Decentralization	200	OCR
Low-Carbon and Resilient Development	Energy	100	OCR
Regional Roads Development Project	Roads	180	OCR
2012			
Precautionary Financing Facility	Economic affairs	500	OCR
Financial Market Development and Integration	Capital markets	300	OCR
Inclusive Growth through Improved Connectivity	Transport	300	OCR
2013			
Inclusive Growth through Improved Connectivity	Transport	400	OCR
Java-Bali 500-Kilovolt Power Transmission Crossing	Power	224	OCR

continued on next page

Table 8.3   *continued*

Loan	Sector	$ million	Loan Terms
2014			
Neighborhood Upgrading and Shelter	Urban	74	OCR
Metropolitan Sanitation Management	Urban	80	OCR
Stepping up Investments for Growth Acceleration	Public sector	400	OCR
2015			
Financial Market Development and Integration	Finance	400	OCR
Sustainable and Inclusive Energy Program	Energy	400	OCR
RBL: Electricity Grid Strengthening in Sumatra	Power	575	OCR
2016			
Stepping up Investments for Growth Acceleration	Industry	500	OCR
Fiscal and Public Expenditure Management	Public sector	500	OCR

ADB = Asian Development Bank, OCR = ordinary capital resources , RBL = results-based lending.
Note: ᵃ Main loans only; some smaller loans not shown.
Source: ADB annual reports, various years.

Box 8.4: Development Policy Support Loans to Indonesia

The third ADB Development Policy Support Program (DPSP) loan was one of a series of development program loans provided to Indonesia by ADB in cooperation with the World Bank and the Japanese Government between 2005 and 2008 (Table 8.1). The DPSP loans were designed to provide assistance for the Indonesian Government's Medium-Term National Development Plan (RPJMN) for 2004–2009. The loans were intended to support the RPJMN's broad goals of stimulating higher and more sustainable economic growth (with a goal of up to an average of 7% per annum by 2009) and halving the level of poverty (to 8.2% by 2009 from 16.6% in 2004).

continued on next page

Box 8.4 *continued*

To promote these objectives, the Third Development Policy Support Program loan focused on reforms in three main areas:

(a)   improving the investment climate;

(b)   strengthening public financial management and reducing corruption; and

(c)   improving public service delivery.

The loan was structured as a single-tranche operation. Disbursement would be based on completed actions demonstrating satisfactory progress.

An important feature of the DPSP loan approach was the aim of harmonizing cooperation between main development partners in support for policy reform. In discussions with ADB, Indonesian government officials had indicated that the transaction costs of dealing with multiple partners in negotiations over similar issues were often quite onerous. One main objective in adopting the DPSP approach had therefore been to reduce the transactions costs for Indonesia in accessing international development finance. This approach was consistent with the principles set down in the Rome Declaration on harmonizing the procedures of multilateral development banks (February 2003) and the Paris Declaration on Aid Effectiveness (March 2005).

ADB = Asian Development Bank.
Source: ADB, 2007, *Proposed Loan, Third Development Policy.*

The shift toward program loans continued in 2008. The largest activity approved in 2008 was the Second Local Government Finance and Governance Reform (LGFGR) Program loan for $350 million. This was a follow-on loan to the first LGFGR activity approved in 2005. This second LGFGR loan was designed to address major policy issues and to support decentralization. Activities financed through the loan included efforts to improve regional autonomy, strengthen service delivery, and support capacity building through improvements to public financial management. Two other large program loans approved in 2008 were for an infrastructure reform sector activity and a fourth loan in the DPSP series.

But during 2008 it became clear that international economic conditions were quickly deteriorating. In response, the government confirmed to ADB that it preferred to see a shift toward policy-based loans as the main form of borrowing.

The situation, at the time, was a worrying one for Indonesian policymakers. Global instability in financial markets since September 2008 had affected Indonesia's economy in various ways. First, the global credit crunch and elevated banking sector risks in international markets had made it expensive for Indonesia to access international debt markets. There was even a risk, at times, that developing countries such as Indonesia would find their access to international financial markets closed off. Second, US investors were quickly adjusting their balance sheets. Many investors were selling off holdings of financial assets in developing countries. This led to signs of capital flight from Indonesia.

For a time in late 2008, Indonesia's financial markets showed signs of marked stress. During the last quarter of 2008, soon after the collapse of Lehman Brothers in the US, Indonesia experienced a high degree of market instability.[44] Capital flight of around $10 billion took place, the rupiah depreciated by nearly 40%, and the risk premium on foreign borrowing rose by as much as 1,200 basis points. Exports and imports began to decline, as did government revenues. The memory of the Asian financial crisis from a decade earlier was still sharp for senior policymakers, so signs of instability in financial markets of this kind were a matter of the highest concern in economic policy circles in Jakarta.

In response, in late 2008 the international community, joined by ADB, moved quickly to prepare a large multidonor assistance package with the aim of bolstering economic stability in Indonesia. A package of $5 billion designed as a contingent loan—to be drawn on only if needed—was agreed upon. The objective was to send a strong signal to markets of confidence in Indonesia's economic management from major international partners—the World Bank, ADB, Japan, and Australia. ADB made a commitment to provide $1 billion for a Public Expenditure Support Facility.[45] In the event, the funds made available from ADB were not drawn upon and the loan was canceled in December 2010 without disbursement. Nevertheless, the package was judged to have contributed significantly to rebuilding confidence at a difficult time for Indonesia. The announcement in February 2009 that the multidonor package was available illustrates the confidence-building role that international support can play in helping bolster stability in developing countries such as Indonesia when financial markets are under strain.

---

[44]   Details here are taken from ADB, 2011, *Real-time Evaluation*, 32.
[45]   ADB, 2009, *Public Expenditure Support Facility.*

For its part, ADB responded to the uncertain economic circumstances in international markets by revising its lending program to Indonesia. Most of the project loans in the bank pipeline were dropped. A number of program loans were approved instead. One main program loan approved for Indonesia in 2009 was a new countercyclical support facility (CSF) for $500 million. Previously, ADB had used a range of financial instruments to respond quickly to the needs of borrowing countries. However, as it became clear that the economic problems caused by the global financial crisis in OECD countries in 2008 were widening, a number of the bank's borrowing countries indicated that additional assistance from ADB would be welcome. Further, at the Group of 20 (G20) international summit held in London in early April 2009, the G20 member countries urged multilateral development banks (MDBs) to step up their countercyclical efforts in support of fiscal expansion. The G20 also called on MDBs to provide support for social safety nets in developing countries, trade financing, bank recapitalization, and infrastructure investment. Appropriate loans, it was suggested, would make flexible and front-loaded finance available quickly.

In response to the G20's call for action, in June 2009 the bank introduced a new lending product, the CSF, to meet the needs of countries such as Indonesia.[46] The CSF offered time-bound budget support loans with fast-disbursing assistance to address liquidity difficulties. Within a month, there were applications for CSF loans from a number of countries including Indonesia so a decision was taken to cap the amount available to each country at $500 million. By December 2009, five CSF loans had been approved for Bangladesh, Indonesia, Kazakhstan, the Philippines, and Viet Nam. For Indonesia, the approval of the two large program loans for the Public Expenditure Support Facility and the CSF, along with several other program loans, assisted with the country's economic adjustment to the difficult international conditions during 2009.

In the midst of these difficult conditions, Indonesia hosted the 42nd Annual Meeting of ADB in May 2009. The event, held in Bali, was a significant one for Indonesia. It was a reflection of the convening power of Indonesia in regional economic affairs. It was also the first annual meeting of the bank that Indonesia had hosted since the Ninth Annual Meeting in Jakarta in 1976 over three decades earlier. The statements at the bank meeting in

---

[46] ADB, 2009, *Enhancing ADB's Response*, 2. See also, ADB, 2017, *Banking on the Future of Asia*, 313.

Bali reflected international concerns.[47] In his opening address, President Yudhoyono summarized the global outlook:

> It goes without saying that the world economy is facing the worst downturn since the great depression of the 1930s...And we are seeing capital flows from developing to developed countries of amounts never witnessed before. ... We have no clear indication of whether the worst is already behind us or whether there is more bad news around the corner. But we can safely assume that 2009 will be a difficult year for all economies.

Indonesia's minister of finance, Sri Mulyani, reinforced this message, saying "today we are facing an economic slowdown that is rivaling the great depression." ADB's President Haruhiko Kuroda also spoke of the economic difficulties in the region:

> There is no doubt that the global downturn has hit Asian economies hard. Access to finance has tightened. And a sharp drop in export demand seriously affects the region's production networks, bringing factory closings, massive layoffs, disrupted supply chains, and reduced remittances. As a result, growth in developing Asia and the Pacific is expected to plummet to 3.4% this year—the lowest since the Asian financial crisis and a significant drop from the record 9.5% growth in 2007.

As one response to this challenging environment, Kuroda provided details of the new CSF that the bank would be making available to borrowing countries in the region. In addition, in his speech to the Board of Governors, Kuroda also announced the establishment of an ADB advisory panel on climate change and sustainable development. The panel, Kuroda said, would include one of Indonesia's most well-known specialists on environmental issues, Professor Emil Salim, as one of its expert members.

For several years following the global financial crisis of 2007–2008, policymakers in Jakarta were concerned that events in the global economy would bring new problems for Indonesia. ADB's own plans to prepare a strategic program to follow on from the 2006–2009 CSP were delayed by the uncertainties of the time. Annual country operations business plans were drawn up to guide the bank's work until a more detailed strategic program was prepared for the period 2012–2014.

---

[47]   Details here are taken from ADB, 2009, *Bali 2009.*

In the meantime, as a step toward planning the bank's 2012–2014 pipeline of activities, a country diagnostic study was carried out by ADB in cooperation with the International Labour Organization (ILO) and the Islamic Development Bank. The study, *Indonesia: Critical Development Constraints*, was issued in 2010 with a foreword by the vice minister for Bappenas, Lukita Dinarsyah Tuwo.[48] Lukita noted that Indonesia had been able to weather the most recent international economic problems, and was committed to pursuing the MDGs. He also observed that much more needed to be done:

> …growth is still not at par with the rates before the 1997 Asian Financial Crisis. Employment growth has barely been keeping up with the growth in the labor force, and the unemployment levels remain rather high. We are also concerned that the development gaps between the regions and the urban and rural areas remain large.

In this context, Lukita welcomed the diagnostic study as an input for the preparation of Indonesia's RPJMN for 2010–2014.

The *Critical Development Constraints* study provided an overview of Indonesia's recent economic performance with the aim of identifying key constraints on growth. A range of factors holding back growth was discussed, the most important of which were seen to include:[49]

(i)   inadequate and poor quality infrastructure—particularly transport networks and electricity supply, as well as irrigation supply in some provinces;

(ii)   weaknesses in governance and institutions—especially in the prevalence of corruption, poor government effectiveness, and occasional occurrences of terrorism and violence incidents; and

(iii)   unequal access to and poor quality education—particularly secondary and vocational education.

Indonesian policymakers also often pointed to these factors as critical constraints on growth. International development partners were encouraged to expand efforts to address these issues.

---

[48]   ADB, International Labour Organization, and Islamic Development Bank, 2010, *Indonesia*.
[49]   Ibid., 86.

Following the *Critical Development Constraints* study, a further diagnostic country analysis was prepared. This more detailed study, *Diagnosing the Indonesian Economy*, presented the work of a group of 23 scholars coordinated by an ADB team in cooperation with the government, the ILO, and the Islamic Development Bank. Topics discussed included overall development performance in Indonesia, constraints to growth and poverty reduction, macroeconomic management, industrialization and infrastructure, and human capital and labor market issues. The broad conclusions set out in *Diagnosing the Indonesian Economy* reinforced the priorities emphasised in *Critical Development Constraints*.

Meanwhile, in 2010 and 2011, the bank had approved several project loans such as a Rural Roads Development Project. However most lending was for program activities. The aim was to strike a balance between, on one hand, providing program loans to support policy and institutional reforms and provide budget support and, on the other hand, approve investment financing for urgently needed projects. There was also an increasing emphasis on encouraging cofinancing.

A second step in the earlier Local Government Finance and Governance Reform loan was approved in 2011 and three more program loans were agreed to in 2012. The largest of these, for $500 million, was for a Precautionary Financing Facility (PFF), a financial agreement which was essentially a countercyclical support loan with a precautionary financing option attached to the arrangement.[50]

In the same way that the large Public Expenditure Support Facility loan in 2009 was part of a broader international package to support Indonesia, the PFF was approved as ADB's participation in a major package with other partners. The facility was part of a $5 billion contingent financing agreement provided by Japan ($1.5 billion), Australia ($1 billion), the World Bank ($2 billion), and ADB ($500 million).

The aim of the large package—as was the case with the earlier Public Expenditure Support Facility loan—was to bolster confidence in international markets in Indonesia's ability to service government debt. In 2011, when financial stresses intensified in Europe and developed into a eurozone crisis, there were concerns that emerging market countries such as Indonesia might find access to international financial markets

---

[50] ADB, 2012, *Proposed Loan Republic of Indonesia: Precautionary Financing*, and ADB, 2015, *Republic of Indonesia: Precautionary Financing*.

increasingly difficult. The government, therefore, needed to be able to offer assurances to investors that Indonesian debt issued in international markets was sound.

In signing up to the $5 billion package, the government committed to using the funds as an insurance device. It was understood that the support package was a fallback option. It would only be used if official market operations and other measures to meet debt targets were unsuccessful. The expectation was that the announcement of the package would send a positive signal to markets and make it more likely that Indonesia would be able to meets its financing needs in 2012 and 2013 from market sources.

As things turned out, volatility in international markets continued into 2014 and 2015. There was an international "taper tantrum" in financial markets in late 2013 when there were signs of a tightening in US monetary policy. And there was increased capital outflow from emerging markets in 2014 reflecting continued uncertainty about the direction of monetary policy in the US. As a result, in late 2015 the Government of Indonesia asked the World Bank and ADB to allow it to access the loan proceeds of the agreed package. In view of the continuing stresses in international markets, both banks agreed to the government's request.

In the meantime, ADB had prepared a strategy for its work over the 2012–2014 period. As had been the case with the earlier strategic plan for 2006–2009, the bank's CSP for 2012–2014 anticipated a shift from program to project lending. At the time, the change seemed appropriate. The government was aiming to balance its budget and because Indonesia had weathered the 2008 financial crisis well, it was expected that the country would not need significant support from the international financial institutions. On this basis, the bank noted that the government was committed to a "four-pro approach": pro-poor, pro-job, pro-growth, and pro-environment. Responding to this program, ADB set out two pillars for the 2012–2014 CSP—an emphasis on inclusive growth, and on environmental sustainability.

In establishing the two pillars for the 2012–2014 CSP, the bank was responding to concerns about development priorities in Indonesia at the time. The focus on inclusive growth was a commitment to help poor people and poor regions connect to markets. This would be done by upgrading infrastructure and improving the capacity of local governments to provide service delivery. Support for environmental sustainability was to be provided in various ways including by supporting projects designed to promote renewable energy, help manage river basins, and improve the management of marine resources.

In the event, in the same way that plans outlined in the 2006–2009 CSP were overtaken by events, so the 2012–2014 CSP strategy proved difficult to implement because international economic conditions remained challenging. Indonesia's budget financing needs widened during 2012 and 2013. Continuing weaknesses in eurozone countries left Indonesia vulnerable to risks of international contagion because of its relatively open capital market. In response to these uncertain circumstances, the government decided that it was best to continue to borrow for fast-disbursing program loans rather than project loans.

In the lending program in 2013 and 2014, the bank supported both program and project activities. Although approvals for program loans, especially for public sector management (PSM) activities, came to take up a large share of the program, a number of project loans were approved as well. One main project loan agreed to in 2013 was for a power transmission line crossing between Java and Bali designed to improve energy flows. Implementation of the project was delayed because of the need to obtain land permits. Infrastructure activities of this kind remained part of the bank's pipeline. Two more smaller loans were approved in 2014 for urban projects.

During the next few years, the bank's work in Indonesia shifted markedly toward the provision of large program loans, especially to support activities in the public financial management sector. In September 2014, ADB approved the first phase of a series of program loans to support the Stepping Up Investments for Growth Acceleration Program (SIGAP). The objective of SIGAP activities was to strengthen investment-led growth. The first SIGAP loan aimed to improve the investment climate by cutting back on restrictions on foreign equity investments and on introducing electronic procurement. A second phase in 2016 aimed to streamline licensing regulations, support public-private partnerships, and implement reforms to promote infrastructure investment. A third phase was approved in 2018.

In 2015, there were two more large program loans. The Financial Market Development and Integration loan was part of ADB's ongoing efforts to support reform in the financial sector. In fact, the bank had been supporting activities to promote reform in the financial sector since the Asian financial crisis in 1998. In 2002, ADB had helped to establish the

Financial Services Authority (OJK), a new body formed to regulate and supervise the financial sector. As a follow-up to these earlier steps, the 2015 Financial Market Development and Integration loan was designed to strengthen the capital market in Indonesia.[51]

A second large program loan was the Sustainable and Inclusive Energy Program. This activity, too, was part of ongoing ADB involvement in a key sector in Indonesia. During 1967–2014, the bank had financed 21 investment projects in Indonesia's energy sector for a total of over $2.8 billion in loans. The first phase of the Sustainable and Inclusive Energy Program was expected to promote the use of clean energy.

A third large loan agreed to in 2015—for Electricity Grid Strengthening in Sumatra for $575 million—supported ADB's first results-based lending (RBL) activity in Indonesia. The earlier introduction of RBL activities in 2013 into the range of loans which the bank was able to offer to borrowing countries had been an important step for ADB. The aim was to fill a gap between traditional investment (project) lending and policy-based lending. The main aims of RBL activities included supporting agreed final outcomes of programs, relying on country-owned systems for the supervision of project activities, and developing local capacity to manage these activities.[52]

In order to achieve these objectives, RBL programs were designed to have three features which distinguished them from other forms of ADB lending. First, RBL activities financed a share of the borrowing government's programs at a sector (or subsector) level. Second, a key feature of the new RBL programs was that they relied on local country systems rather than ADB guidelines for implementation and risk management. This aspect of RBL programs was consistent with the government's aim of moving toward greater country ownership of the implementation of international activities in Indonesia. Third, RBL was disbursed only when results agreed with the borrowing government and measured by agreed indicators had been achieved.[53] In Indonesia, the first RBL was approved

[51] ADB, 2018, *Indonesia: Financial Market Development*.
[52] For details both of the introduction and operations of RBL activities, and of RBL activities in Indonesia in 2015 and 2016, see ADB, 2016, *Midterm Review of Results-Based Lending*. See also ADB, 2017, *Results-Based Lending at the Asian Development Bank*.
[53] Measurable indicators used included the numbers of new customer connections, residential sales, interruptions to supply, lines reconductored, and installations of distribution transformers and distribution lines.

in December 2015 to support transmission and distribution systems in Sumatra managed by the State Electricity Company (PLN). The total cost of the program in Sumatra was put at $10.8 billion, of which ADB financed $575 million.

In 2016, the final year of ADB's fifth decade of operations in Indonesia, the bank continued to give priority to the provision of program loans. Two large program loans to support work in the public financial management were approved. One funded a second phase of SIGAP activities. The other, the Fiscal and Public Expenditure Management Program (FPEMP), supported the government's aim of reducing inequality in Indonesia.[54] The FPEMP was also the first step in strengthening a commitment between ADB and the government to tackle issues of inequality. The first phase of the FPEMP was expected to be followed up by at least one, and perhaps several, phases. In shifting in this way toward a phase-based and programmatic approach after five decades of work in Indonesia, ADB had, in steps, moved away from project-based activities in the 1970s and 1980s toward a much broader approach relying on program lending and RBL in the two decades after the Asian financial crisis.

Beyond 50 Years: 2017–2019

In early 2017, around midway through President Widodo's first term in office, Indonesian policymakers took stock of the economic prospects and concluded that the outlook was mixed. On the positive side, economic growth had been sustained at about 5% per year for a considerable period and the range of reform measures that had been introduced appeared to be supportive of sustained growth. On the other hand, international economic conditions remained quite uncertain.

One central concern for policymakers was the rate of economic growth. Official policy was to aim for a growth rate of perhaps 6% or 7% per year. However it seemed that there were various barriers holding back an increase in the growth rate. Raden Pardede and Shirin Zahro listed both internal and external factors that numerous commentators suggested were restraining growth.[55] Externally, the end of the commodity boom around 2012 had served to dampen Indonesia's growth prospects. In addition,

---

[54] ADB, 2016, *Proposed Programmatic Approach.*
[55] Pardede and Zahro, 2017, Survey.

slowing growth in the PRC and Europe, along with talk of a policy shift toward more protectionist policies in the US, suggested that Indonesia would need to look to internal policy measures to promote growth.

Domestic steps that Pardede and Zahro pointed to as policies to encourage higher growth included promotion of structural change to shift resources away from agriculture into manufacturing and services, boosting productivity, and finding the right incentives to support reform within a decentralized system of government.

One immediate issue for policymakers was whether measures were need to stimulate demand. Pardede and Zahro suggested that "Indonesia is in a state of weakened demand." The Widodo administration had introduced 16 reform packages since taking office in late 2014 and had boosted spending on infrastructure.[56] Nevertheless, since the international economic environment showed signs of becoming more difficult, it seemed that further steps to stimulate domestic demand might be appropriate.

Concerns about the need to promote growth continued to be a central issue of attention for policymakers into 2018. Three structural issues— education, infrastructure, and institutions—were widely acknowledged to present major challenges.[57] Resosudarmo and Abdurohman asked "Is being stuck with a five percent growth rate a new normal for Indonesia?" and argued that a more focused growth-oriented approach was needed:[58]

> To overcome current growth constraints—i.e. to grow at [an] annual rate of above 5%—or above 6%—the Indonesian government needs to boost growth in investment and net exports, as well as provide an environment for faster consumption growth.

They recommended that steps be taken to promote investment, to introduce a more flexible exchange rate policy to promote competitiveness, and to implement a more expansionary fiscal policy.[59]

Political considerations increasingly affected policymaking during 2018. Nationwide provincial and regional elections were held in April. These elections were both important in reflecting regional priorities and as a

---

[56]   The 16 packages are listed in Resosudarmo and Abdurohman, 2018, Survey, 143.
[57]   Shrestha and Coxhead, 2018, Survey, 2.
[58]   Resosudarmo and Abdurohman, op. cit., 145.
[59]   Resosudarmo and Abdurohman, op. cit., 162.

pointer to issues likely to be taken up in the presidential elections during the following year, in 2019.

As the year drew to a close, both external and internal economic conditions remained challenging. In the US, the Donald Trump administration was calling into question some of the main principles of long-established international economic relations. At the same time, global trade was slowing and in many countries debt levels were high. During the year, Indonesia had been buffeted by fluctuations in capital flows. Internally, policymakers remained concerned with the need to support economic growth. The government's emphasis on promoting investment in the infrastructure sector helped underpin growth. Other measures, it was agreed, that would help promote stronger growth included accelerating export growth and attracting more foreign direct investment.

Relations with Donors

In recent years, Bappenas has been strengthening Indonesia's systems for aid coordination. As part of this approach, Bappenas arranged a wide range of activities in cooperation with development partner agencies in 2017 and 2018. Regular reports on loan and grant programs supported by international partners were provided in the quarterly *Laporan Kinerja Pelaksanaan Pinjaman dan/atau Hibah Luar Negeri* (Performance Report on the Execution of International Loans and Grants).[60]

The government, working through Bappenas along with a wide range of other government departments and agencies, encouraged both domestic stakeholders and international agencies to participate in Indonesia's development program. Government departments such as the Ministry of Public Works and Public Housing, Ministry of Defence, PLN, and the Ministry of Transport implemented a large number of programs with international partners. Bappenas also worked with numerous shareholders from community and academic institutions: Major international development forums, for example, were held in 2018 and 2019, which involved some thousands of participants from across Indonesia in discussions about national development policy.

---

[60] Indonesia, Bappenas, various dates, *Laporan Kinerja*.

Indonesian policy was also to support South-South programs of cooperation, especially with ASEAN partners but also with other developing countries such as nations in Africa.[61] Reflecting this approach, in the annual Indonesian statement on foreign affairs in January 2018, Foreign Minister Retno L.P. Marsudi announced that an Indonesian agency to support South-South cooperation would be established. Marsudi said that the agency would be responsible for the delivery of Indonesia's international assistance and would also strengthen Indonesia's diplomacy, including humanitarian diplomacy.

Nevertheless, in this era of new relations with the international community, the government aimed to encourage international partners to ensure that their programs were consistent with Indonesia's own policies for the delivery of aid. In coordinating the response to the Palu earthquake and tsunami disaster in September 2018, for example, the government set out guidelines for the delivery of international assistance. Foreign partner agencies were asked to observe a range of conditions—such as closely regulating the number of staff actively working in the field—in planning to deliver aid following the disaster. The lesson from international cooperation programs of this kind was that the government preferred the main decisions about how foreign aid was to be provided in Indonesia to be taken by Indonesian policymakers.

ADB Looking Ahead

At the end of 2016, ADB had been operating in Indonesia for 50 years. Looking ahead, the bank's operational plan for 2017–2019 outlined priorities for the next three years.[62] In total, the proposed resource allocation for sovereign lending (including plans for 2016) was expected to be close to $9 billion—slightly over $2 billion per year over the four-year period (Table 8.4).

The bank's plans into the sixth decade of work in Indonesia were tailored to match the priorities of the government: ADB's main lending program

---

[61] Indonesia, Ministry of National Development Planning and United Nations Development Programme, 2014, *South-South and Triangular Cooperation*.
[62] ADB, 2016, *Indonesia 2017–2019*, Country Operations Business Plan. This program is updated annually. For updated plans see ADB, 2017, *Indonesia 2018–2020*, Country Operations Business Plan, and ADB, 2018, *Indonesia 2019–2021*, Country Operations Business Plan.

Table 8.4: Proposed ADB Spending by Sector, 2016–2019

Sector	OCR $ million	Cofinance $ million	Total $ million	%
Energy	2,400	250	2,650	30
Public sector management	1,900	200	2,100	24
Agriculture and natural resources	1,230	250	1,480	17
Finance	950	150	1,100	12
Education	900		900	10
Water, other urban infrastructure, and transport	523	150	673	8
Total	7,903	1,000	8,903	100

ADB = Asian Development Bank, OCR = ordinary capital resources.
Source: ADB, 2016, *Indonesia 2017–2019*, Country Operations Business Plan.

was expected to focus on infrastructure, better economic governance, and human resource development. To deliver these activities, the bank planned to use a flexible mixture of loan arrangements: project approvals, policy-based lending, RBL, and direct lending to state-owned enterprises. The range of different types of loans that the bank could offer had widened greatly in the two decades since the 1990s.

As had been the case throughout all of the time that ADB had worked in Indonesia, the bank's program consisted of a mix of activities. The delivery of the sovereign loans program underpinned ADB's work but numerous technical assistance and other nonlending services, such as seminars and the preparation of research reports, were also part of the bank's program.

An RBL to support Indonesia's irrigation improvement program (IIP) was one of ADB's main loans in 2017 (Table 8.5). Food security remained a key goal of national policy. The loan, which provided finance for improvements in irrigation systems along with better maintenance and water delivery to farmers, supported the objective of strengthening food security. The RBL approach was chosen because there was strong government commitment to the IIP and because the activity was focused on results and systems rather than on a single project.

Table 8.5: ADB Lending to Indonesia, 2017–2018

Loan	Sector	$ million	Loan Terms
2017			
Integrated Participatory Development in Irrigation	Irrigation	500	OCR
Integrated Participatory Development in Irrigation	Irrigation	100	AIF
Eastern Indonesia Electricity Grid Development	Power	600	OCR
Eastern Indonesia Renewable Energy (Phase 1)	Power	56	OCR
2018			
Rantau Dedap Geothermal Power (Phase 2)	Power	177	OCR
Eastern Indonesia Renewable Energy (Phase 2)	Power	12.5	OCR
Maternity and Child Care Hospital	Health	10.0	OCR
Fiscal and Public Expenditure Management	Public sector	500	OCR
Java 1 LNG Gas-to-Power	Power	250	OCR
Emergency Assistance for Disaster Recovery	Public sector	500	OCR
Skills and Knowledge for Sustainable Development	Education	200	OCR
Riau Natural Gas Power	Power	148	OCR

ADB = Asian Development Bank, OCR = ordinary capital resources, AIF = ASEAN Infrastructure Fund.
Source: ADB, *Indonesia 2005–2018*.

The bank's second large activity in 2017 was a results-based energy loan to support improvements in the electricity supply in eastern Indonesia. The government had given priority to the expansion of electricity services in eastern Indonesia where power grids were often of poor quality.

Electrification ratios in some of the eastern provinces were particularly low—74% in West Sulawesi, 59% in East Nusa Tenggara, and 44% in Papua. The Eastern Indonesia Electricity Grid Development Program loan was designed to extend electricity networks across provinces in eastern Indonesia.

The bank was also active in the important activity of helping expand Indonesia's access to financial markets. In late 2017, in an innovative transaction in international markets, the bank raised Rp 1 trillion (about $74 million) in an offshore issue of Indonesian rupiah-linked bonds. The transaction was the first such bond issue from a multilateral bank to raise international rupiah funding to support local rupiah currency loans. The transaction was also designed both to help expand the pool of local currency available to support ADB's loan operations in Indonesia as well as to foster the development of Indonesia's capital market.

Two further large loans were agreed to in 2018. The first was the second phase of the FPEMP. In Indonesia's Development Policy Letter attached to the loan, Finance Minister Sri Mulyani provided details of what the loan would be used for:[63]

> The loan proceeds from Subprogram 2 of FPEMP will be used to support the program-related development spending in the 2018 and 2019 national government budget. This includes implementation of the legislated 5% budget allocation for health, increased spending to increase the number of subsidized beneficiaries of the national health insurance, increased spending for education, health, social protection programs and public infrastructure investments and execution of the new integrated planning and budgeting platform.

Sri Mulyani also noted that Subprogram 1 of the FPEMP approved in late 2016 had supported structural changes and that the second subprogram would "allow the government to sustain our momentum in implementing our reform program."

The other large loan, for emergency assistance and disaster recovery, was for emergency support following major earthquake-related disasters in Lombok in August and Central Sulawesi in September. These disasters took the lives of more than 4,000 people and left at least another 10,000 injured. The damage in the Palu area of Central Sulawesi was particularly severe. The earthquake caused landslides, a tsunami, and liquefication of the soil near Palu that buried more than a thousand people.

The emergency assistance loan was part of a broader response by ADB to the disasters. Earlier, immediately following the Central Sulawesi disaster, the bank approved an emergency grant of $3 million for activities such as the provision of temporary shelters and schools. Later, in June 2019,

---

[63] Appendix 3 to ADB, 2018, *Proposed Policy-Based Loan for Subprogram 2.*

ADB approved an additional loan of $297 million for rehabilitation and reconstruction in Central Sulawesi.

There had also been an expanding emphasis on ADB's support for the private sector. The bank had been involved in direct lending to the private sector since the mid-1980s (Appendix Table A2.7), but in 2012, the CPS for 2012–2014 indicated that the bank's focus on private sector development would be increased by strengthening collaboration between ADB's public and private sector operations. The CPS also pointed to the aim of promoting bankable PPP projects.

This emphasis on the private sector was reflected in ADB's program through to 2019. In the private sector program, the bank supported a range of projects in the energy sector in Sumatra, Java, and West Papua. An ADB loan for $400 million in 2016 supported the large Tangguh liquefied natural gas (LNG) investment in West Papua (Table 8.6). This facility was one of the largest LNG plants in Indonesia.

Table 8.6: Selected ADB-Supported Private Sector Loans, 2013–2018

Date	Project	Location	Details
2013	Sarulla geothermal	North Sumatra	ADB supported a $350 million package for a 320-MW project for a total financing agreement of $1.17 billion in cooperation with private sector investors from Japan and Indonesia
2016	Tangguh LNG	West Papua	The bank approved a $400 million loan for the expansion (third LNG train) of the plant
2016	Muara Laboh geothermal	West Sumatra	ADB provided a $70 million loan to support a total financing package of approximately $590 million for an 80-MW plant
2018	Rantau Dedap geothermal	South Sumatra	ADB signed a loan agreement of approximately $177 million with a joint venture company with Indonesian and Japanese investors for a 90-MW geothermal plant
2018	Jawa-1 LNG combined cycle	Karawang, West Java	An ADB drawdown of funds for $305 million under a private sector financing package was agreed to in support of a 1,760-MW plant
2018	Riau natural gas	Riau, Sumatra	The bank joined a private sector financing package to support a 275-MW combined-cycle gas plant

ADB = Asian Development Bank, MW = megawatt, LNG = liquefied natural gas.
Source: ADB project data and Appendix Table A2.7.

Several years later, in 2018, the bank supported a number of large private-sector projects in the energy sector in Indonesia including the Rantau Dedap geothermal project and a 275-megawatt (MW) combined-cycle power plant in Riau. The bank also provided a drawdown of $305 million under a private sector financing project to support the Jawa-1 combined-cycle gas turbine plant in Karawang in West Java. This plant was one of the first and the largest projects in Indonesia using LNG. These investments, and the others in the ADB private sector pipeline, were directed toward supporting the expansion of environmentally sustainable activities in the energy sector in Indonesia.

These projects, along with others that ADB often partnered with, often involved PPP arrangements. To widen operations in the private sector, the bank looked for ways to expand other PPP activities as well. The several SIGAP loans in 2014 and 2016 had supported a number of PPP activities. SIGAP funding had included, for example, support to revise the PPP legal framework and to establish a PPP unit in the Ministry of Finance. The Sustainable and Inclusive Energy Program loan, approved in 2015, included activities to improve the legal framework for independent power purchase agreements and PPPs in the energy sector.

Steps to prepare individual projects and to provide financing for these projects were also part of the bank's PPP program. The Infrastructure Reform Sector Development Program loans approved in 2008 and 2010 (Table 8.2) supported a facility which helped with the preparation of the 2,000-MW Central Java power plant in Batang to the west of Semarang. Projects such as the geothermal plants at Sarulla and Rantau Dedap were also part of ADB's Private Sector Operations Department program.

Other changes were occurring during this time as well. One change was that ADB aimed to move away from the program-based lending (PBL) and RBL approaches in providing assistance to Indonesia. ADB management indicated that the share of these types of loans should be reduced from a high level of around 80% in the several years to 2018 to less than 30% in the next few years.

A second main change—reflecting increasing attention to country ownership—was the move toward the use of country safeguard systems (CSSs). International safeguard systems have received greater attention across the international community in recent decades. The systems are usually set out in operational guidelines that aim to minimize negative environmental or social impacts of development programs. Particular emphasis has been given to the need to protect the rights of groups such as indigenous peoples.

In a further step toward country ownership, in late 2013 the government asked ADB to consider the use of Indonesian CSSs for use in ADB activities. After a review, ADB found that agencies in Indonesia (including in such sectors as energy, water, resources, and roads and transport) had varying capacities to adopt safeguards. PLN, the lead implementing agency in the energy sector, seemed to be the most effective agency. The government and ADB then agreed to consider the possibility of using CSSs in ADB-financed projects with PLN.

The implementation of safeguard arrangements—which is a form of regulation, and which involves the formation of numerous guidelines and monitoring systems—can become quite complex. In Indonesia, detailed consultations took several years. Consultations involved Indonesian government agencies, ADB, and Indonesian civil society groups. A first round of consultations involving focus groups was conducted in Jakarta in 2014–2016. Further discussions were held in 2017 and 2018.[64] It took until 2019 for ADB and PLN to reach an agreement on arrangements for the bank to support PLN-level use of CSSs in Indonesia. Nevertheless, although the process took time, the agreement between ADB and PLN on the implementation of CSSs was a significant step toward greater country ownership in the relationship between Indonesia and the bank.

A third change was that steps were taken to expand ADB's relations with civil society in Indonesia. These steps were a further move in the direction of strengthening country ownership. An Indonesian civil society advisory forum was established with members representing Indonesian civil society and ADB staff. The forum met for the first time in mid-2019. It was expected to discuss various issues including providing advice on bank strategies, operations with environmental and social implications, and ways for ADB to work with civil society.

Policy and knowledge oriented activities were also part of ADB's program. One example was the major report *Indonesia: Enhancing Productivity through Quality Jobs* released in 2018. This was a study on the challenges of job creation in Indonesia. The report argued that Indonesia faces both old and new job challenges as the nation moves toward a new industrial model

---

[64]   ADB, 2019, *Indonesia: Perusahaan Listrik Negara.*

("Industry 4.0") during the coming decade.[65] A second study published in 2019, which also considered the implications of changes in structure in the Indonesia economy, discussed *Policies to Support the Development of Indonesia's Manufacturing Sector during 2020–2024.*[66] The report was a joint Bappenas-ADB study which analyzed Indonesia's growth prospects during the 2020–2024 period and considered whether annual growth rates of 6% and above were realistic. The study concluded that higher growth rates were quite possible, but only if important policy reforms were implemented.

Reviewing the Decade

The fifth decade of ADB's work in Indonesia from 2007 was one of continuous adjustment. The beginning of the decade was marked, finally, by clear signs of economic recovery from the Asian financial crisis of 1997–1998. A boom in international commodity prices assisted growth in the early part of the decade but later, falling commodity prices fed through into lower growth in the non-resources sectors of the economy. Policymakers searched for new sources of growth but found it difficult to nudge the economic growth rate significantly above 5% per annum.

Nevertheless, although the aim of achieving an average annual growth rate of around 7% per annum proved beyond reach, the economy was being transformed in other ways. One dramatic change was the rapid expansion in the use of smart cellular phones and the internet in Indonesia. In 2007, around 38% of households possessed a cell phone; by 2019, over 75% of Indonesians (excluding young children) were actively using cell phones. Internet use expanded quickly too. In 2007 only 8% of households accessed the internet at home. By 2019, nearly 48% of Indonesians (over the age of five) had regular access to the internet. A second key transformation was the expansion of investment in infrastructure. In the electricity sector, priority was given to moving toward the universal provision of electricity for households. As a result, the proportion of households using electricity for lighting rose from 91% in 2007 to 99% in 2019. In the railways sector, a striking example of the priority being given to infrastructure was the construction of the mass rapid transit system in Jakarta. President Widodo launched work on the project in October 2013. The modern transport

---

[65]   Ginting, Manning and Taniguchi, 2018, *Indonesia: Enhancing Productivity.*
[66]   ADB, 2019, *Policies to Support.*

project, a combination of underground and overhead rail facilities, opened for service in March 2019.

There were also important gains in reducing poverty and promoting improvements in social indicators during the decade. In 2007, around 37 million Indonesians (nearly 17% of the population) had incomes below the official poverty line. By 2016, the number had fallen to below 28 million (less than 11% of the total population). The maternal mortality ratio fell from 359 per 100,000 live births to 305 between 2010 and 2015, and infant mortality rates improved as well. Adult literacy rose from 93% to nearly 96% between 2010 and 2018, and the share of the population using at least basic sanitation services rose from 60% (2010) to 73% (2017).

Indonesia's relationship with ADB and other international organizations evolved over the decade. Following the dissolution of the CGI in 2007, Indonesia began to play an expanded role in international organizations. In 2010, President Yudhoyono approved Finance Minister Sri Mulyani's move to the senior post of managing director of the World Bank in Washington, DC. She took up the position in June 2010. And then, in 2015, during the administration of President Widodo, Indonesia nominated Bambang Susantono, formerly the acting minister for transportation, as a candidate for a vice-president position in ADB. Soon after, in July 2015, Susantono took up his post as ADB's vice-president for knowledge management and sustainable development. He is the first Indonesian ever to hold this senior position in ADB.

For its part, as in the earlier periods of its work in Indonesia, ADB aimed to be client-oriented in designing its portfolio of activities. The annual program of the bank was regularly adjusted in response to Indonesia's changing needs. At the beginning of the decade, the strategic planning for ADB's work in Indonesia suggested that there should be a shift in the focus of operations toward infrastructure activities and a move back from program lending toward delivering assistance through project loans. However, as things turned out, ADB's approach in Indonesia during the decade was quite different. Reviewing the 2005–2018 period, the Independent Evaluation Department's (IED) Country Assistance Program Evaluation (CAPE) 2019 observed that:[67]

---

[67] ADB, 2019, *Indonesia, 2005–2018*, xii.

> PBL [policy-based lending] remained ADB's and the Government's preferred lending modality over the evaluation period. ... PBLs accounted for 69% of total sovereign lending volume during 2005–2018, much higher than in any other of ADB's developing member countries ... All of this went against the continuously stated objective of infrastructure development.

These observations reflected the fact that the bank's lending program in Indonesia had continued to rely on various forms of program lending to promote reforms in the financial and capital market development areas, and to support changes in public sector management.

One view is that since ADB's operations had moved away from the guidelines set out in the early plans such as the 2006–2009 CPS, the original planning process must have been flawed. An alternative view was set out in the 2019 CAPE:[68]

> ADB's flexibility in providing much more PSM [public sector management] financing than anticipated in CPSs [country program strategies] was seen as defensible in a very difficult and quickly changing environment. ADB, along with other development partners provided the necessary budget support and the necessary incentives for the government to undertake the needed structural reforms. ADB's policy-based support helped the government persist with the reforms.

The operating environment in Indonesia was changing rapidly during this period so the IED assessment presents a useful summary of the way that the bank and other development partners showed flexibility in responding to Indonesia's needs.

Looking back over the decades since the late 1960s when the international community entered into a remarkable effort to support Indonesia's development, it can be seen that Indonesian policymakers and partner agencies cooperated closely. As circumstances changed, so the responses of both Indonesian policymakers and international aid partners changed with the aim of tailoring policies and responses to circumstances.

The next chapter will summarize the changes over the decades since the late 1960s and set out some main challenges ahead.

---

68   Ibid., xv.

Students gather after school on a road in Siak, Riau, which was financed through the Rural Infrastructure Support to the PNPM Mandiri Project (2008).

Leaders pose together at the opening of 42nd Annual Meeting of ADB in Bali in May 2009.

ADB President Takehiko Nakao (*center, wearing white*) meets with local community members in a neighborhood in Surabaya, East Java, where improvements to toilet facilities were financed through the Urban Sanitation and Rural Infrastructure Support Project (2011).

Minister of National Development Planning Armida Alisjahbana (*third left, wearing blue*) visits Ujung Pandang State Polytechnic in Makassar, South Sulawesi, which received support from the Polytechnic Education Development Project (2014).

ADB President Takehiko Nakao (*right*) pays a courtesy visit to Indonesia's President Joko Widodo in 2015.

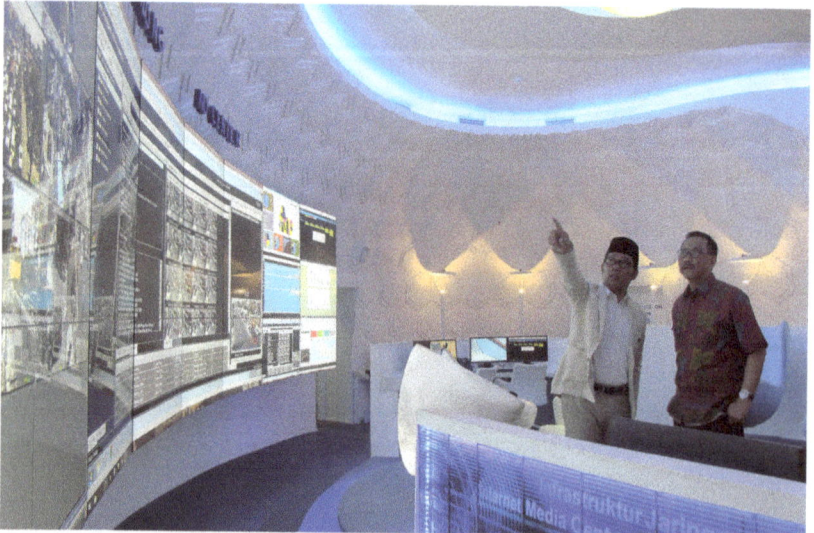

ADB Vice-President for Knowledge Management and Sustainable Development Bambang Susantono (*right*) visits the Bandung Command Center, which received support through the Establishing the Future Cities Program technical assistance activity (2015).

CHAPTER 9

Lessons and Challenges

The development of Indonesia is a work in progress. The account presented here about the Asian Development Bank's (ADB) work in Indonesia is part of a broader story—the story of how the international community joined with Indonesian leaders during the past 50 years to support the goal of building development In Indonesia.

Indonesia and the International Community

Looking back, the long-term international assistance effort that ADB was part of was a remarkable program. During the 50 years from the late 1960s when ADB first joined with the broader international program to support Indonesia's development effort, there has been strong cooperation between leading Indonesian policymakers and international development partners.

To be sure, there were ups and downs along the way, both in the progress of Indonesia's own overall development programs and in the success of activities supported by the international community. The 1997–1998 Asian financial crisis, for example, was a setback for Indonesia that held back the national development effort for close to a decade. And while some programs supported by the international community including ADB were very successful, other schemes sometimes yielded disappointing results: The Green Revolution in Indonesia during the 1970s and 1980s brought a major boost to rice production but transmigration programs in the 1980s were not well planned and ran into major difficulties.

Nevertheless, the overall program of cooperation between Indonesia and the international community in the 50 years from the late 1960s must surely be judged an outstanding success, both in terms of its support at an overall level for good development policy in Indonesia and in terms of the delivery of many thousands of individual projects and activities.[1]

---

[1] One of the few academic studies of the effectiveness of the international foreign aid program to Indonesia until the early 2000s is in Chowdhury and Sugema, 2005.

At the overall level, the international community worked closely with Indonesian policymakers to support good development policy. Perhaps the single most important reason that the international aid program in Indonesia since the late 1960s has been a success is that the partnership between Indonesia and the international community has been an effective one. The lead has always been taken by Indonesian policymakers. Even during the difficult negotiations with international agencies during the Asian financial crisis, the key decisions were taken by Indonesian ministers acting on the recommendations of their advisers.

On the donor side, there has been a well-judged and long-term relationship with senior Indonesian policymakers. Different country members of the donor community have, at times, had their own preferred priorities but the collective approach of the international community, acting through the assistance program, has been to adjust activities to respond to the priorities of the Government of Indonesia. The views of one of Indonesia's most senior policymakers in the 1980s and 1990s, Radius Prawiro, were noted earlier (Chapter 3). Recalling the long period of cooperation between Indonesia and the international community, arranged through the meetings of the Inter-Governmental Group on Indonesia (IGGI) and the Consultative Group on Indonesia (CGI), Prawiro described the IGGI as "perhaps the world's most effective organization in bilateral and multilateral relations" and added that "the CGI retained this spirit and has continued to act as a valued partner to Indonesia."[2] It is flexibility and a willingness to compromise on both sides, then, that have underpinned the success of the long period of cooperation between the government and the international community.

Asian Development Bank

ADB has been a reliable partner in Indonesia's development effort during the past 50 years. The bank's role evolved over the decades. As Indonesia needed to respond to changes in the international environment, so ADB adjusted the forms of assistance that were provided (Table 9.1).

The three key characteristics of the institution as a multilateral development bank—multilateralism, attention to development, and its role as a bank—were discussed earlier in this survey (Chapter 1). Looking back

---

[2]   Prawiro, 1998, *Indonesia's Struggle*, 67 and 77.

Table 9.1: Main Phases in ADB Assistance to Indonesia

Period	Stages in Indonesian development	ADB response
1969–1972	Recovery period; beginning of First Five-Year Development Plan	ADB provided ADF (concessional) funding providing support for individual projects
1973–1974	First oil boom	ADB shifted toward a blend of concessional and market-based (OCR) loans
1975–1984	High oil flows occurred	ADF lending ceased; OCR loans for individual projects were provided
1985–1989	Sharp falls in the oil price	ADB softened the terms of assistance with a greater emphasis on support for local cost finance and for program loans.
1990–1996	Successful economic liberalization	ADB shifted assistance toward OCR loans provided through project and program loans
1997–1999	Asian financial crisis	Emergency assistance provided in cooperation with other main multilateral and bilateral donors
2000–2007	Concerns about the need to reduce the level of national debt	Lending to Indonesia from ADB and other agencies was constrained
2008–2010	Global financial crisis led to uncertainties about Indonesia's access to international financial markets	ADB provided emergency liquidity support, mainly by support for program loans
2010–2016	Continuing uncertainties in global markets.	ADB assistance continued to be provided through program lending
2017–2018	Moving toward upper-income status	Increasing focus on economic competitiveness in Indonesia and economic reform

ADB = Asian Development Bank, ADF = Asian Development Fund, OCR = ordinary capital resources.

over ADB's work in Indonesia, each of these aspects of the bank's activities has been reflected in the programs in Indonesia.

As a multilateral institution that gives special emphasis to regional programs, ADB has supported Indonesia's regional role in a variety of ways. The bank has worked to strengthen regional programs which Indonesia is involved in such as the Brunei Darussalam–Indonesia–

Malaysia–Philippines East ASEAN Growth Area (BIMP-EAGA) and the Indonesia–Malaysia–Thailand Growth Triangle (IMT-GT) and a wide range of ASEAN activities. Further, since the Asian financial crisis, ADB has supported numerous activities designed to strengthen regional financial arrangements including the establishment of the Chiang Mai Initiative (CMI) in 2000 and the expansion of the initiative to the Chiang Mai Initiative Multilateralization (CMIM) in 2010.

Second, in its efforts to fulfil the ADB Charter requirement "to contribute to the acceleration of the process of economic development of the developing member countries in the region," the bank's program in Indonesia since the late 1960s has been designed to be supportive of Indonesia's development effort. Support for Indonesian goals of promoting development and growth runs through all of the programs across the decades of ADB's work in the country. To this end, as circumstances changed in Indonesia, so ADB's approach changed. As an institution, ADB gained much experience from its work in Indonesia through the decades. Drawing, in particular, on lessons set out in the many evaluation reports prepared for its activities in Indonesia (Box 9.1), the bank's aim was to constantly improve the quality of aid delivery and to be responsive to the needs identified by the government.

At the earliest stages of the bank's work in Indonesia in the late 1960s and early 1970s, ADB provided highly concessional finance to support project loans, especially in the agriculture sector. Later, as several successive oil booms came and went, the bank reassessed the terms of its support. In response to the Asian financial crisis, ADB joined with other main multilateral and bilateral agencies to provide rapidly disbursing loans. Following the crisis, the government indicated a preference to continue to borrow for program rather than project loans. The bank adjusted its lending pipeline to respond to these changing needs.

The third role of ADB in Indonesia was as a financial institution. Its work in this area was much broader than its activities as a bank. It was the original goal of the founders of ADB that the new organization would mobilize resources to help finance the growing development needs of Asia. In response to this objective, in the period to December 2018 the bank provided over $37 billion of loans, grants, and other forms of assistance to Indonesia (Table 9.2). But it was also expected that the bank would play a wider role and would help promote, among other things, the development of reliable financial markets across the region.

Box 9.1: Evaluation of ADB's Work in Indonesia

The many references to individual Asian Development Bank (ADB) projects, programs and activities in this study provide an overview of the bank's work in Indonesia. Much additional detailed information is available in numerous publications from ADB's Independent Evaluation Department (IED) which present an extensive survey of the bank's work in Indonesia.

The numerous reports issued by the IED over the years have pointed to both strengths and weaknesses in ADB's work in Indonesia. Many bank activities in Indonesia have gone well and can be judged as successful. Others have run into problems. Many of the IED reports discuss difficulties that have affected ADB's work in Indonesia and provide recommendations for improved performance.

The bank's approach to evaluation has changed over the years. This change is reflected in evaluation reports relating to work in Indonesia. Throughout the 1970s, evaluation reports tended to focus on individual project activities. In the early 1980s, the role of evaluation expanded to begin giving greater attention to issues of effectiveness and to the preparation of impact studies. By the late 1980s, an increased number of special studies at the country and sectoral levels were being carried out. By 2004, eight full country evaluation assistance programs for various borrowing countries had been prepared.

Evaluation reports prepared for activities in Indonesia cover many different types of activities. In addition to many project evaluations, other evaluation studies include sector evaluations and overall country program evaluations. The *Impact Evaluation Study of Asian Development Bank Assistance to the Power Sector in Indonesia*, prepared in 2003, for example, provided a detailed survey of ADB work in the power sector between 1970 and 2001. More recently, the evaluation report on *ADB Support to the Indonesia Finance Sector (2005–2018)* provided an assessment of the performance of the bank's support to the Indonesian financial sector.

Major program evaluations of the bank's overall activities were provided in 2005 in the *Country Assistance Program Evaluation for Indonesia*, and in 2019 in *Indonesia, 2005–2018*, a second country assistance program evaluation. Numerous other references to evaluation reports on ADB's activities in Indonesia can be found in the previous chapters of this study.

Further information, including access to reports on Indonesian activities, can be found at the website of ADB's IED at https://www.adb.org/site/evaluation/overview.

Sources: ADB, 2007, *Independent Evaluation*. ADB, 2003, *Impact Evaluation Study of Asian Development Bank Assistance to the Power Sector*. ADB, 2005, *Country Assistance Program Evaluation*. ADB, 2019, *Indonesia, 2005–2018*.

Table 9.2: ADB Cumulative Lending, Grants, and
Technical Assistance Commitments, 1967–2018
as of 31 December 2018

Sector	Number of projects	Total amount ($ million)	%
Public sector management	116	7,310	19
Energy	102	7,300	19
Agriculture, natural resources, and rural development	278	4,932	13
Finance	69	4,769	13
Transport	90	3,702	10
Education	82	2,656	7
Water and other urban infrastructure	94	2,364	6
Multisector	26	1,789	5
Industry and trade	41	1,664	4
Health	46	1,108	3
Total	944	37,595	100

ADB = Asian Development Bank.
Source: ADB, *Indonesia Factsheet*, July 2019.

Over the years, ADB has supported many activities designed to strengthen financial sectors in developing member countries. At an early stage of its operations, the bank provided loans to development finance institutions such as the Indonesian Development Bank (Bapindo). The bank also prepared numerous loans and technical assistance (TA) activities to help support institutions and improve financial markets, including in Indonesia (Table 5.8 above). Especially after the Asian financial crisis, ADB expanded its financial sector programs in Southeast Asia. In Indonesia, several loans were approved for activities in the financial sector such as the Financial Governance and Social Security Reform program loan in 2002 designed to help establish the new Financial Services Authority (OJK). Partly reflecting these efforts supported by the bank and other international agencies, the financial sector in Indonesia today is much stronger than was the case 20 years ago.

The role of ADB's Indonesia Resident Mission (IRM) has also expanded over time. At first, when the bank began operations in Indonesia, there were no full-time ADB staff in Jakarta. The early activities of the bank in Indonesia in the 1970s were supported through numerous visits by ADB staff on short-term missions. By the mid 1980s, however, it became clear that a sustained local commitment was needed. The IRM was established in Jakarta in 1987. The role of the IRM expanded during the 1990s and after the Asian financial crisis at the end of the decade. Reflecting the increasing emphasis after 2000 on the need for greater country ownership, wider authority was delegated to the IRM from bank headquarters in Manila.

By the end of ADB's fifth decade of operations in Indonesia in 2016, a large degree of operational authority had been delegated from Manila to the IRM. The Jakarta office of the bank had grown into a strong local institution able to both represent the bank's own development priorities and respond to the key priorities set out by the government.

Four Efforts

Another way of gaining an overall view of ADB's work in Indonesia is to consider the bank's contribution to Indonesian development in four main areas: support for capital accumulation; assistance to strengthen economic management; involvement in cross-cutting issues; and involvement in the preparation of knowledge products.

The bank's support for capital accumulation through the provision of project and program loans has been one of its main priorities in Indonesia, especially during the first two decades of operations and into the 1990s. During the first decade of operations, ADB was a project bank; most loans were approved for the specific purpose of providing foreign currency for individual projects. The Tajum Irrigation Project loan, agreed to in June 1969, was ADB's first loan to Indonesia (Box 3.2). However after a time, it became clear that member countries needed to borrow for other purposes—for example, to buy essential equipment or raw materials needed to make better use of productive capacity. Beginning in 1978, the bank began to provide a limited form of program loans for this purpose and during the next decade, a widening variety of new forms of loans was designed in response to requests from borrowing countries.

In 1980, loans began to be approved for activities across specific sectors. This approach had the advantage that a number of small activities in a priority sector could be supported under one loan. Sector lending was particularly useful for agriculture and rural development, water supply and sanitation, and education and health. The first sector loan that ADB approved for any borrowing country was in December 1980 for the Small Towns Water Supply Sector Project in Indonesia. During the succeeding decades, the bank provided many project and program loans which promoted capital accumulation in Indonesia.

As well as expanding its own activities, ADB also promoted a wide range of activities to support the government's own investment programs in infrastructure. Many of the bank's projects and programs included TA and capacity building components such as training designed to strengthen Indonesian institutions. Some loans, for example, provided scholarships for staff in implementing agencies: the Road Rehabilitation Sector Project approved in 2000 included support for the training of 73 staff for advanced degrees at masters and doctoral levels at Indonesian universities. Other ADB loans promoted policy reforms in such sectors as transportation (roads, ports, and air communications), power, urban development, and other subsectors.

In the energy sector, for example, the strategic objectives of ADB programs during the past two decades have included addressing corporate governance issues in lending to state-owned enterprises, the promotion of anticorruption efforts, support for demand-side management, and an emphasis on strengthening accountability and transparency. Numerous bank TA activities have addressed these issues: In recent years the list includes TAs for Implementing Effective Climate Change Adaptation Policy (approved in November 2011), for Scaling Up Renewable Energy Access in Eastern Indonesia (December 2012), and for Supporting the Sustainable Infrastructure Assistance Program (June 2013).[3]

Similarly, many of ADB's lending activities in the energy sector included components for capacity building. The several Sustainable and Inclusive Energy Program (SIEP) loans approved in 2015 and 2017 were accompanied by 12 TA projects to provide capacity building for fiscal sustainability and sector governance, to encourage private participation in power and gas markets, and for regulatory reforms to increase access to clean energy.

---

[3]   Comprehensive details of the program in the energy sector, including of capacity building and policy-oriented TAs, are provided in "Energy Sector Program Assessment," in ADB, *Indonesia, 2005–2018*, Linked Document C.

The bank has given priority to supporting these investment activities because the task of expanding the stock of all types of capital remains a major challenge for Indonesia. A recent study supported by the World Bank estimated that in 2014, Indonesia's stock of capital per person was around one-twentieth of the level in the United States (US): The total stock of capital in the US was estimated at almost $1 million per person compared to around $50,000 in Indonesia (Table 9.3). Clearly, Indonesia, like most other developing countries in Asia, will need to sustain high levels of capital accumulation for decades to come.

A second contribution to Indonesia's development effort has been the way in which ADB's lending has been designed to help strengthen economic management, especially in times of pressure and crisis. During the 1980s, the Government of Indonesia began to give increasing attention to the need to strengthen economic management to promote structural adjustment. In response, ADB, along with other international partners such as the World Bank and the Government of Japan, began to provide program loans to assist with policy reform. The Non-Oil Export Promotion Program loan to Indonesia was the first ADB program loan to be approved after a new bank

Table 9.3: Capital Stock Per Capita, Selected Countries, 2014
($000 per capita, market exchange rate)

	Types of Capital				Total	
	Produced	Natural	Human	Foreign	$ '000	Index
Selected Asian countries						
Singapore	186	..	466	123	775	79
Malaysia	30	29	181	..	239	24
People's Republic of China	29	15	63	1	108	11
Indonesia	15	9	24	–1.5	47	5
India	5	5	9	..	19	2
Comparator countries						
United States	216	24	766	–32	983	100
Germany	237	8	468	17	729	74
Japan	179	4	365	24	572	58

Source: Lange, Woden and Carey, 2018. *The Changing Wealth.*

policy was approved for program lending in late 1987.[4] A Financial Sector Program loan was approved the following year. In 1990 a Food Crop Sector Program loan was agreed to. These loans were designed to provide quick-disbursing budget funds to assist with the implementation of reforms.

The Government of Indonesia again found it useful to access program lending from ADB during the Asian financial crisis and beyond, especially after 2007 and when the difficulties caused by the global economic crisis led to uncertainties in financial markets. As seen earlier (Chapter 8), on several occasions the international financial packages agreed to by major partners such as the World Bank, ADB and the Government of Japan were judged to have contributed significantly to bolstering market confidence when there were signs of pressure in financial markets.[5] Many of these program loans were accompanied by policy dialogue designed to help promote structural adjustments.

ADB's work in Indonesia strengthened economic management in other ways as well. Following the implementation of the crisis-response programs after the Asian financial crisis in 1997–1998, the bank designed a range of activities to support the central processes of government economic management. ADB's finance sector program focused on strengthening the stability of the sector. Activities included helping set up a unified regulatory agency for financial services (the OJK), improving regulation in the nonbank financial sector, and taking steps to deepen capital markets.[6]

ADB also supported activities to improve governance in the public sector. The loan for State Audit Reform approved in 2004, for example, assisted in expanding state audit operations. The loan was approved because "an effective public audit function was essential for good governance in Indonesia" and the existing "transparency, accountability, and overall performance of the audit sector suffered from unclear legal and regulatory frameworks." After the project was completed, ADB's validation report issued in 2012 concluded that the project had been effective and efficient in achieving the intended outcomes of the activity.[7]

---

[4] See ADB, 2001, *Special Evaluation Study on Program Lending*, paragraph 58.
[5] More recent pressures on Indonesia's financial markets resulting from uncertainties in international markets have often been discussed by Basri. See, for example, Basri, 2018, *Waspada*. See also Basri, 2018, *Twenty Years*.
[6] In total, ADB's support to the Indonesian financial sector in the period 2005–2018 totaled around $2 billion. A detailed evaluation survey of the program is in ADB, 2019, *ADB Support to the Indonesia Finance Sector*.
[7] ADB, 2012, *Indonesia: State Audit Reform*.

A third main approach which underpinned ADB's work in Indonesia has been support for cross-cutting issues. Activities of this kind have included attention to disaster response efforts, measures to improve governance, decentralization, and to numerous social issues such as poverty alleviation, the needs of women and children, and health and education reform programs. To help address these issues, the bank has drawn on all of the main forms of assistance that it offers including project and program lending, grant funding, and numerous TA activities.

One example of ADB's approach to cross-cutting issues is the bank's response to disasters: in 1993 the first major disaster-related loan for Indonesia was provided following an earthquake in Flores; in 2005, a major assistance program was provided following the devastating December 2004 tsunami in Aceh; and in 2006 and 2018 assistance packages were quickly prepared following the major earthquake-related disasters in Bantul in Yogyakarta, and in Palu in Sulawesi. Another example of the bank's approach to cross-cutting issues is the package of programs designed to promote decentralization: Beginning with loans provided in 1998 and 1999, ADB aimed to support the priority that the government gave to decentralization (Table 7.2 above).

The bank's involvement in the preparation of many knowledge products is a fourth way in which ADB has aimed to contribute to Indonesia's development efforts. Much of this work was financed through TA programs in Indonesia. Other knowledge activities were carried out by bank staff teams from headquarters in Manila or from the ADB Institute in Tokyo. The first TA project that the bank sponsored for any borrowing country was the grant-financed activity in Indonesia in 1967 for a study of ways to improve food supplies (Table 3.1). Since 1967, ADB has approved TA loans and grants to support a very large number of policy-oriented studies in Indonesia. Recent examples include the study on *Diagnosing the Indonesian Economy* (2012) and the survey of employment and productivity issues in *Indonesia: Enhancing Productivity through Quality Jobs* (2018).[8]

The bank has also sponsored many other economic, sectoral and social studies about regional changes in Asia which have encouraged discussion about development policy in Indonesia; early examples include the two major surveys of agricultural issues in Asia produced in 1968 (*Asian*

---

[8]   Hill, Khan, and Zhuang, 2012, *Diagnosing the Indonesian Economy*, and Ginting, Manning, and Taniguchi, 2018, *Indonesia: Enhancing Productivity*.

Agricultural Survey) and 1978 (*Rural Asia: Challenge and Opportunity*).[9] The ADB-sponsored study prepared by Hla Myint in 1972, *Southeast Asia's Economy: Development Policies in the 1970s*, was also an influential contribution to the evolution of thinking about development policy in Asia in the 1970s.[10] The export-oriented strategy of development discussed in the study was adopted by a number of countries across Asia including Indonesia in the 1980s.

During the following decades, ADB staff and bank-sponsored research teams prepared a large number of reports and publications on policy-oriented development issues in Asia. Following the Asian financial crisis in 1997–1998, the bank sponsored numerous studies of financial challenges in developing countries in Asia and of ways to strengthen regional resilience. Throughout this period, much attention was given to issues of regional development and cooperation, supporting the priority that Indonesia has given to regional institutions such as ASEAN and a variety of subregional programs. The major bank study on *Meeting Asia's Infrastructure Needs* issued in 2017 took up many issues which were relevant for infrastructure policy in Indonesia.[11]

In Indonesia, ADB expanded its work on knowledge-based activities following the adoption of a bank-wide knowledge management program in 2013 known as "Finance ++."[12] Steps toward implementing the Finance ++ program in Indonesia were reflected, among other things, in the provision of policy advisory services, sector surveys, and country diagnostic studies. Various bank papers were prepared on Indonesian issues including studies designed to support the national planning process in the National Development Planning Agency (Bappenas). Papers in this series included sectoral surveys, studies of constraints to growth, and assessments of issues in the financial and private sector.[13] More recently, ADB knowledge work in Indonesia has focused on such issues as the implications of technology and automation, climate change, urbanization, aging, and the need to boost the competitiveness of Indonesia's manufacturing sector.[14]

---

[9]   ADB, 1968, *Asian Agricultural Survey*, and ADB, 1978, *Rural Asia*.
[10]   Myint, 1972, *Southeast Asia's Economy*.
[11]   ADB, 2017, *Meeting Asia's Infrastructure Needs*.
[12]   ADB, 2013, *Knowledge Management Directions*.
[13]   Relevant papers include ADB, 2015, *Summary of Indonesia's Agriculture*, ADB, 2015, *Summary of Indonesia's Energy*, ADB, 2015, *Constraints*, ADB, 2015, *Summary of Indonesia's Finance*, and ADB, 2015, *Summary of Indonesia's Private Sector*.
[14]   ADB's most recent study of the prospects for the manufacturing sector is in ADB, 2019, *Policies to Support the Development*.

ADB will need to strengthen its own work as well. The bank's approach for the next 10 years was set out in Strategy 2030 issued in July 2018. The emphasis on the goal of supporting infrastructure development listed in Strategy 2030 is consistent with the focus on investment in infrastructure which President Joko Widodo has frequently referred to. In addition, in 2017 ADB's President Takehiko Nakao pointed to three areas where the bank needs to strengthen its work: providing a combination of finance and knowledge for developing countries, promoting good policies, and expanding programs of regional cooperation.[15]

Challenges Ahead

Looking ahead, Indonesia faces numerous development challenges. The list is long but perhaps the central challenge for the next decade is how to move into the middle-income stage of transformation and growth.

The priorities set out by President Widodo in July 2019 for his second administration point to several of the most pressing middle-income issues.[16] The president emphasised the need for expanded investment in three main areas—infrastructure, human capital, and job creation. He also urged reform of the bureaucracy to develop "an adaptive, productive, innovative, and competitive Indonesia." The fifth priority that the president mentioned was effective fiscal management to ensure that the annual budget is focused and targeted.

President Widodo emphasized these issues once again in his inaugural speech at the beginning of his second term in October 2019. He listed five priority initiatives that his incoming administration would focus on. The five initiatives pointed to the need to improve the quality of the workforce, continue infrastructure development, simplify regulation, reform the bureaucracy, and transform the economy from one dependent on natural resources to one that is competitive in modern manufacturing and services. If significant progress toward achieving these goals can be made during the next five years, Indonesia will be well placed to establish its position as one of the successful middle-income countries in the Asian region.

---

[15] McCawley, 2017, *Banking on the Future*, 358.
[16] Joko Widodo, We can be One of the Strongest Countries in the World, 14 July 2019.

BIBLIOGRAPHY

Note: In preparing this study, a very large number of sources of many kinds were consulted. Items cited in the text are listed in this bibliography. In addition, a number of other studies about development issues in Indonesia not cited directly but which were used to help prepare this study are included.

Abimanyu, A. 2011. *Refleksi dan Gagasan Kebijakan Fiskal*. Jakarta: PT Gramedia Pustaka Utama.

Abonyi, G. 2005. *Policy Reform in Indonesia and the Asian Development Bank's Financial Sector Governance Reforms Program Loan*. ADB Economics and Research Department Working Paper No. 76, December.

Arndt, H.W. 1966. Survey of Recent Developments. *Bull Indonesian Ec Stud*, No 5, October.

———. 1968. Survey of Recent Developments. *Bull Indonesian Ec Stud*, No 10, June.

———. 1968. Survey of Recent Developments. *Bull Indonesian Ec Stud*, No 11, October.

———. 1974. Survey of Recent Developments. *Bull Indonesian Ec Stud*, 10, (2), July.

———. 1983. Survey of Recent Developments. *Bull Indonesian Ec Stud*, 19 (2), August.

Arsjad Anwar, Thee Kian Wie and Iwan Jaya Azis. 1992. *Pemikiran, Pelaksanaan, dan Perintisan Pembangunan Ekonomi* [Thinking, Implementing, and Pioneering Economic Development]. Jakarta: PT Gramedia Pustaka Utama.

Asian Development Bank (ADB). 1968. *Asian Agricultural Survey*. Manila.

———. 1978. *Rural Asia: Challenge and Opportunity*, New York: Praeger Special Studies.

———. 1980. *Sector Lending*. R52-80. Manila.

———. 1983. *Study of Operational Priorities and Plans of the Asian Development Bank for the 1980s*. Manila.

———. 1989. *Asian Development Outlook, 1989*. Manila.

———. 1992. *Asian Development Outlook, 1992*. Manila.

———. 1992. *Annual Report*. Manila.

———. 1994. *Indonesia Country Operational Strategy*. Manila.

———. 1994. *Asian Development Outlook*. Manila.

———. 1994. Box 1.2: Emerging Capital Markets and Development in Asia. *Asian Development Outlook 1994*. Manila.

———. 1997. *Asian Development Outlook 1997–1997*. Manila.

———. 1997a. Box 1.1: Strong Private Capital Flows. *Asian Development Outlook 1997 and 1998*. Manila.

———. 1997b. Box 2.2: *Financial Problem and Response. Asian Development Outlook 1997 and 1998*. Manila.

———. 1999. *Asian Development Outlook 1999*. Manila.

———. 2000. *Annual Report*. Manila.

———. 2000. *Special Evaluation Study Interim Assessment of ADB's Lending to Thailand during the Economic Crisis*. Manila.

———. 2000. Corporate and Financial Sector Reform: Progress and Prospects. *Asian Development Outlook 2000*. Manila.

———. 2001. *Special Evaluation Study of the Asian Development Bank's Crisis Management Interventions in Indonesia*. Manila. August.

———. 2001. *Special Evaluation Study on Program Lending*. Manila. November.

———. 2002. *Country Strategy and Program 2003–2005 Indonesia*. CSP: Indonesia 2002–13. Manila.

———. 2003. *Impact Evaluation Study of Asian Development Bank Assistance to the Power Sector in Indonesia*. IES: Ino 2003-13. Manila.

———. 2004. *Second Development Finance Project (Loan 1223-INO)*, Project Performance Audit Report. Manila.

———. 2004. *Review of the Asian Development Bank's Poverty Reduction Strategy*. Manila.

———. 2005. *Local Government Finance and Governance Reform Sector Development Program*, Manila.

———. 2005. *Proposed Loan Republic of Indonesia: Tangguh Liquefied Natural Gas Project*. Project No 38919. Manila.

———. 2005. *Country Assistance Program Evaluation for Indonesia*. Operations Evaluation Department. Manila.

———. 2006. *Medium-Term Strategy II, 2006–2008*, Manila.

———. 2006. *Indonesia 2006–2009*. Country Strategy and Program. Manila.

———. 2006. *Program Performance Evaluation Report Financial Sector Program (Republic of Korea) (Loan 1601-KOR) and Institutional Strengthening of the Financial Sector (Republic of Korea) (Loan 1602-KOR)*. Manila.

———. 2006. *Indonesia: Gas Transmission and Distribution Project*. Completion Report Project No 22023, October. Manila.

———. 2007. *Asian Development Outlook 2007: Growth amid Change*, Manila: Asian Development Bank.

———. 2007. *Proposed Loan: Republic of Indonesia: Third Development Policy Support Program*. Manila.

———. 2007. *Independent Evaluation at the Asian Development Bank*. Operations Evaluation Department. Manila.

———. 2008. *Strategy 2020: The Long-Term Strategic Framework of the Asian Development Bank 2008–2020*. Manila.

———. 2008. *Support for Financial Intermediation in Developing Member Countries*. ADB Evaluation Study. Manila.

———. 2008. *Emerging Asian Regionalism: A Partnership for Shared Prosperity*. Manila: Asian Development Bank.

———. 2009. *Indonesia: Aceh-Nias Rehabilitation and Reconstruction*. Project No. 39127. August. Manila.

———. 2009. *Bali 2009: 42nd Annual Meeting Board of Governors*. May. Manila.

———. 2009. *Enhancing ADB's Response to the Global Financial Crisis—Establishing the Countercyclical Support Facility*. Manila.

———. 2009. *Proposed Loan Republic of Indonesia: Public Expenditure Support Facility Program*. Manila.

——. 2009. *Indonesia: Community Empowerment for Rural Development Project*. Manila.

——. 2010. Box 1.3.3 Responding to surging capital flows. *Asian Development Outlook 2010*. Manila.

——. 2010. *Indonesia: Industrial Competitiveness and Small and Medium Enterprise Development Program*. Independent Evaluation Department. Reference Number: PCV: INO 2010-76. Manila.

——. 2011. *Indonesia: State Audit Reform Sector Development Program*. Completion Report, Project No 35144-013, October. Manila.

——. 2011. *Indonesia: Earthquake and Tsunami Emergency Support Project*. Project No 39127. February. Manila.

——. 2012, *Proposed Loan Republic of Indonesia: Precautionary Financing,* and ADB, 2015, *Republic of Indonesia: Precautionary Financing*.

——. 2012, *Proposed Loan Republic of Indonesia: Precautionary Financing Facility*. Manila.

——. 2012. *Indonesia: State Audit Reform Sector Development Program*. Manila.

——. 2013. *Knowledge Management Directions and Action Plan (2013–2015): Supporting "Finance ++" at the Asian Development Bank*. Manila.

——. 2013. *Decentralized Health Services Project in Indonesia*. Independent Evaluation Department. Reference Number: PPE: INO 2013-21. Manila.

——. 2013. *Indonesia: Local Government Finance and Governance Reform Sector Development Program*. Independent Evaluation Department. Reference Number: PVR:-296. Manila.

——. 2015, *Republic of Indonesia: Precautionary Financing Facility*. Manila.

——. 2015. *Summary of Indonesia's Agriculture, Natural Resources, and Environment Sector Assessment*. Manila

——. 2015. *Summary of Indonesia's Energy Sector Assessment*. Manila.

——. 2015. *Constraints to Indonesia's Economic Growth*. Manila.

——. 2015. *Summary of Indonesia's Finance Sector Assessment*. Manila

———. 2015. *Summary of Indonesia's Private Sector Development Assessment*. Manila.

———. 2016. *ADB Through the Decades*. Volumes 1–5. Manila. https://www.adb.org/publications/series/adb-through-the-decades

———. 2016. *Midterm Review of Results-Based Lending for Programs*. Manila.

———. 2016. *Proposed Programmatic Approach and Policy-Based Loan for Subprogram 1 Republic of Indonesia: Fiscal and Public Expenditure Management Program*. Manila.

———. 2016. *Indonesia 2017–2019*. Country Operations Business Plan. Manila.

———. 2017. *Indonesia 2018–2020*. Country Operations Business Plan. Manila.

———. 2017. *Results-Based Lending at the Asian Development Bank: An Early Assessment*. Manila.

———. 2017. *Meeting Asia's Infrastructure Needs*. Manila.

———. 2018. *Proposed Policy-Based Loan for Subprogram 2 Republic of Indonesia: Fiscal and Public Expenditure Management Program*. Manila.

———. 2018. *Indonesia: Financial Market Development and Integration Program*. Reference Number: PVR-534. Manila.

———. 2018. *Indonesia 2019–2021*. Country Operations Business Plan. Manila.

———. 2018. *Strategy 2030*. Manila.

———. 2019. *Indonesia: Fact Sheet*. Manila.

———. 2019. *Policies to Support the Development of Indonesia's Manufacturing Sector during 2020–2024*. A joint ADB-Bappenas Report. Manila.

———. 2019. *ADB Support to the Indonesia Finance Sector (2005–2018)*. Manila.

———. 2019. *Indonesia: Perusahaan Listrik Negara (PLN) Agency-Level Use of Country Safeguard Systems: Summary of Consultations*. Manila. October.

——. All years. *Annual Report*. Manila.

——. All years. *Asian Development Outlook*. Manila.

ADB, Independent Evaluation Department. 2010. *Asian Development Bank Support for Decentralization in Indonesia*. Special Evaluation Study SES: INO 2010-15. Manila.

——. 2011. *Real-time Evaluation of Asian Development Bank's Response to the Global Economic Crisis of 2008–2009*. Manila.

——. 2011. *Indonesia: Country Strategy and Program, 2006–2009 Final Review Validation*. FRV: INO 2011-10. Manila.

——. 2019. *Indonesia, 2005–2018*, Country Assistance Program Evaluation. Manila.

——. 2019. *ADB Support to the Indonesia Finance Sector (2005–2018)*. Manila.

ADB, International Labour Organization, and Islamic Development Bank. 2010. *Indonesia: Critical Development Constraints*, Manila, Geneva, and Jeddah.

ADB and Korea Capital Market Institute. 2014. *Asian Capital Market Development and Integration: Challenges and Opportunities*. New Delhi: Oxford University Press.

Alisjahbana, S.A. 2011. Ministerial message: Revitalisasi Bappenas. *Kabar Bappenas*, 9 (1), April–Mei.

——. 2012. Ministerial message: Capaian MDGs Kita. *Kabar Bappenas*, 13 (4), Desember.

Ashcroft, V., and D. Cavanaugh. 2008. Survey of Recent Developments. *Bull Indonesian Ec Stud*, 44 (3), December.

Aswicahyono, H., H. Hill, and D. Narjoko. 2012. Industrialization: Patterns, Issues, and Constraints. In Hill, Khan and Zhuang, *op. cit.*

Baird, M., and M. Wihardja. 2010. Survey of Recent Developments. *Bull Indonesian Ec Stud*, 46 (2), August.

Basri, M.C. 2017. India and Indonesia: Lessons Learned from the 2013 Taper Tantrum. *Bull Indonesian Ec Stud*, 53 (2), August.

Basri, M.C. 2018. Waspada [On Guard], *Kompas*, 15 August.

Basri, M.C. 2018. Twenty Years After the Asian Financial Crisis, in L.E. Bruer, J. Guajardo, and T. Kinda (eds.), *Realizing Indonesia's Economic Potential*. Washington, DC: International Monetary Fund.

Blustein, P. 2001. *The Chastening: The Crisis that Rocked the Global Financial System and Humbled the IMF*. Cambridge MA: The Perseus Books Group.

Boediono. 1980. Survey of Recent Developments. *Bull Indonesian Ec Stud*, 16 (2), July.

———. 2002. The International Monetary Fund Support Program in Indonesia: Comparing Implementation under Three Presidents. Chapter 26 in Ikhsan, M., C. Manning and Hadi Soesastro.

———. 2005. Managing the Indonesian Economy: Some Lessons from the Past. *Bull Indonesian Ec Stud*. 41 (3), December.

———. 2009. *Ekonomi Indonesia, Mau Ke Mana? Kumpulan Esai Ekonomi* [The Indonesian Economy: Where Should it Go? A Collection of Essays]. Jakarta: KPG (Kepustakaan Populer Gramedia).

Bondan, W. 2012. *J.B. Sumarlin: Cabe Rawit yang Lahir di Sawah* [J.B. Sumarlin: The Chilli born in a Rice Field]. Jakarta: Penerbit Buku Kompas.

Booth, A. 1986. Survey of Recent Developments. *Bull Indonesian Ec Stud*, 22 (3), December.

———. 1999. Survey of Recent Developments. *Bull Indonesian Ec Stud*. 35 (3), December.

———. 1986. *Economic Change in Modern Indonesia: Colonial and Post-colonial Comparisons*. Cambridge, UK: Cambridge University Press.

Booth, Anne and Peter McCawley (eds). 1981. *The Indonesian Economy during the Soeharto Era*. Kuala Lumpur: Oxford University Press.

Cameron, L. 1999. Survey of Recent Developments. *Bull Indonesian Ec Stud*. 35 (1), April.

Chia, S.Y. 2013. The ASEAN Economic Community: Progress, Challenges, and Prospects. ADBI Working Paper Series, No. 440, October.

Chowdhury, A. and Iman Sugema. 2005. How Significant and Effective has Foreign Aid to Indonesia Been? *ASEAN Economic Bulletin*. 22 (2), August.

Daroesman, R. 1981. Survey of Recent Developments. *Bull Indonesian Ec Stud*, 17 (2), July.

Djiwandono J.S. 2000. Bank Indonesia and the Recent Crisis. *Bulletin of Indonesian Economic Studies*, 36 (1), April.

———. 2005. *Bank Indonesia and the Crisis: An Insider's View*. Singapore: Institute of Southeast Asian Studies.

Feith, H. 1962. *The Decline of Constitutional Democracy in Indonesia*. Ithaca and London: Cornell University Press.

Gillis, M. 1994. Dr. Ali Wardhana: Finance Minister Par Excellence. In Pangestu ,M., *op. cit.*

Ginting, E., and P. Aji. Macroeconomic Management. In Hill, Khan and Zhuang, *op. cit.*

Ginting, E., C. Manning and K. Taniguchi. 2018. *Indonesia: Enhancing Productivity through Quality Jobs*. Manila: Asian Development Bank.

Glassburner, B. 1978. Political Economy and the Soeharto Regime. *Bull Indonesian Ec Stud*, 14 (3), November.

———. 1986. Survey of Recent Developments. *Bull Indonesian Ec Stud*, 21 (1), April.

Goeltom, M.S. 2008. Reassessing the IMF Programme in Indonesia. In Miranda S. Goeltom, 2008, *Essays in Macroeconomic Policy: The Indonesian Experience*. Jakarta: PT Gramedia Pustaka Utama Publisher.

Gray, C. 1982. Survey of Recent Developments. *Bull Indonesian Ec Stud*, 18 (3), November.

Grenville, S. 1974. Survey of Recent Developments. *Bull Indonesian Ec Stud*, 10, (1), March.

———. 2004. The IMF and the Indonesian Crisis. Washington: IMF, IEO Background Paper. http://www.ieo-imf.org/ieo/files/completedevaluations/BP043.pdf accessed 30 December 2015.

Gyohten, T. 2007. The Future of Asia. In I. Gill, Y. Huang, and H. Kharas, eds. *East Asian Visions: Perspectives on Economic Development*. Washington, DC: The World Bank and the Institute of Policy Studies.

Hill, H. 1992. Survey of Recent Developments. *Bull Indonesian Ec Stud*, 28 (2), August.

——. 1996. *The Indonesian Economy since 1966*. Hong Kong, China: Cambridge University Press.

Hill, H., M.E. Khan, and J. Zhuang (eds.). 2012. *Diagnosing the Indonesian Economy: Toward Inclusive and Green Growth*. London and Manila: Anthem Press and Asian Development Bank.

Hobohm, S. 1987. Survey of Recent Developments. *Bull Indonesian Ec Stud*, 23 (2), August.

Hollinger, W. 1996. *Economic Policy under President Soeharto: Indonesia's Twenty-Five Year Record*. Washington: Background Paper Number 2: The United States-Indonesia Society.

Hull, T.H. and Ida Bagus Mantra. 1981. Indonesia's Changing Population. Chapter 9 in Booth and McCawley, *op. cit.*

Ikhsan, M., C. Manning and Hadi Soesastro. 2002. *80 Tahun Mohamad Sadli: Ekonomi Indonesia di Era Politik Baru* [Mohamad Sadli at 80: The Indonesian Economy in the New Political Era]. Jakarta: Penerbit Buku Kompas.

Indrawati, S.M. 2007. Developing Broader Regional Financial Integration. In Sri Mulyani Indrawati, 2008, *Turning Words into Action: Advancing Reform and the Economic Agenda*. Jakarta: Ministry of Finance, Fiscal Policy Office.

International Monetary Fund. 1998. Indonesia—Memorandum of Economic and Financial Policies. Jakarta, January, 15. www.imf.org/external/np/loi/011598.htm accessed 20 December 2015.

——. 2003. *The IMF and Recent Capital Account Crises: Indonesia, Korea, Brazil.* Washington, DC: International Monetary Fund.

Indonesia, Government of. 2003. *Instruksi Presiden No 5/2003 tentang "Paket Kebijakan Ekonomi Menjelang dan Sesudah Berakhirnya Program Kerjasama dengan International Monetary Fund"* [Package of Economic Policies Approaching and at the Conclusion of the Program of Cooperation with the International Monetary Fund], Jakarta, 15 September.

Indonesia, Republic of. 1994. *Repelita VI: Indonesia's Sixth Five-Year Development Plan (1994/95–1998/99: A Summary*. Jakarta: Perum Percetakan Negara RI.

Indonesia, Government of, and its Development Partners. 2009. *Jakarta Commitment: Aid for Development Effectiveness, Indonesia's Road Map to 2014*. Jakarta.

Indonesia, Republic of, Bappenas. 2013. *Data dan Informasi Kinerja Pembangunan 2004–2012*. Jakarta: Bappenas. https://www.bappenas.go.id/id/data-dan-informasi-utama/publikasi/evaluasi-perencanaan-pembangunan/

Indonesia, Republic of, Coordinating Ministry for Economic Affairs. 2011. *Masterplan for Acceleration and Expansion of Indonesia*, Jakarta.

Indonesia, Bappenas and United Nations Development Programme (UNDP). 2014. *South-South and Triangular Cooperation (SSTC) Stocktaking and Strategic Review*. Jakarta. https://www.undp.org/content/dam/rbap/docs/dg/dev-effectiveness/UNDP-IDN-DG-2014-SSTC-Strategic-Review-of-Indonesia.pdf

Indonesia, Republic of, Bappenas. Various dates. *Laporan Kinerja Pelaksanaan Pinjaman dan/atau Hibah Luar Negeri* [Performance Report on the Execution of International Loans and Grants]. Jakarta: Bappenas.

Jayasuriya, S. and P. McCawley. 2010. *The Asian Tsunami: Aid and Reconstruction after a Disaster*. Asian Development Bank Institute and Edward Elgar Publishing. Cheltenham, UK: Edward Elgar.

Joesoef, D. 1977. Bantuan Luar Negeri: 'Keharusan Baja'. Prisma, 6 (4), April, reprinted in Hadi Soesatro, Aida Budiman, Ninasapti Triaswati, Armida Alisjahbana and Sri Adiningsih, 2005, *Pemikiran Permasalahan Ekonomi Indonesia dalam Setengah Abad Terakhir Buku III 1966–1982* [Thinking about Indonesian Economic Problems during the past Half-Century Book III 1966–1982]. Yogyakarta: Percetakan Kanisius for the Ikatan Sarjana Ekonomi Indonesia.

Joko Widodo. 2019. We Can be One of the Strongest Countries in the World. Speech at Sentul International Convention Center. *The Jakarta Post*, 15 July.

Kementerian Perencanaan Pembangunan Nasional, Badan Perencanaan Pembangunan Nasional. 2003. *Keberadaan dan Peran Consultative Group for Indonesia (CGI): Kajian dan Rekomendasi Kebijakan* [The Position and Role of the Consultative Group for Indonesia (CGI): Study and Policy Recommendations]. Jakarta.

Kompas. 2005. *Bencana Gempa dan Tsunami Nanggroe Aceh Darussalam & Sumatera Utara* [Earthquake and Tsunami Disaster in Nanggroe Aceh Darussalam and North Sumatra]. Jakarta: Penerbit Buku Kompas.

Kramer, C. 2006. Asia's Investment Puzzle. *Finance and Development*, 43 (2).

Kong, T., and A. Ramayandi. 2008. Survey of Recent Developments. *Bull Indonesian Ec Stud*, 44 (1), April.

Lange, G., Q. Wodon, and K. Carey (eds.). 2018. *The Changing Wealth of Nations 2018: Building a Sustainable Future*. Washington, DC: World Bank. doi:10.1596/978-1-4648-1046-6.

Lewis, B. 2007. On-lending on Indonesia: past performance and future prospects. *Bull Indonesian Ec Stud*, 43 (1), April.

Lindblad, J. 1997. Survey of Recent Developments. *Bull Indonesian Ec Stud*, 33 (3), December.

Lindblad, J. and Thee Kian Wie. 2007. Survey of Recent Developments. *Bull Indonesian Ec Stud*, 43 (1), April.

Lee, H. and C. Rhee. 2012. Lessons from the 1997 and the 2008 Crisis in the Republic of Korea. *ADB Economics Working Paper Series*. No 298. Manila: Asian Development Bank.

Mackie, J. 2005. *Bandung 1955: Non-Alignment and Afro-Asian Solidarity*. Singapore: Editions Didier Millet.

Mackie, J., and Sjahrir. 1989. Survey of Recent Developments. *Bull Indonesian Ec Stud*, 25 (3), December.

Manning, C. 1992. Survey of Recent Developments. *Bull Indonesian Ec Stud*, 28 (1), April.

Marsudi, L.P. Retno. 2018. Indonesia: Partner for Peace, Security, Prosperity. *The Jakarta Post*, 11 January.

Menon, J. and C. Lee. (eds.) 2019. *An Evolving ASEAN Vision and Reality*. Manila: Asian Development Bank.

McCawley, P. 2015. Infrastructure Policy in Indonesia, 1965–2016: A Survey. *Bull Indonesian Ec Stud*, Vol 51, No 2. August.

——. 2017. *Banking on the Future of Asia and the Pacific: 50 Years of the Asian Development Bank*. Manila: Asian Development Bank.

McLeod, R. 1997. Postscript to the Survey of Recent Developments on Causes and Cures for the Rupiah Crisis. *Bull Indonesian Ec Stud*, 33 (3), December.

Mears, L. and Sidik Moeljono. 1981. Food Policy. Chapter 2 in Anne Booth and Peter McCawley (eds.), *The Indonesian Economy During the Soeharto Era*, Kuala Lumpur: Cambridge University Press.

Muir, R. 1991. Survey of Recent Developments. *Bull Indonesian Ec Stud*, 27 (3), December.

Mustopadidjaja, A.R. (editor). 2012. *Bappenas dalam Sejarah Perencanaan Pembangunan Indonesia 1945–2025* [Bappenas in the History of Development Planning in Indonesia 1945–2025]. Jakarta: LP3ES.

Myint, H. 1972. *Southeast Asia's Economy: Development Policies in the 1970s*. Harmondsworth, England: Penguin Books.

Nasution, A. 1991. Survey of Recent Developments. *Bull Indonesian Ec Stud*, 27 (2), August.

———. 1995. Survey of Recent Developments. *Bull Indonesian Ec Stud*, 31 (2), August.

———. 2016. *Government Decentralisation Program in Indonesia*. ADB Institute working paper series, No 601, October.

Nazara, S., and B. Resosudarmo. 2010. Indonesia: The First Two Years after the Tsunami. Chapter 4 in Jayasuriya, S., and P. McCawley, *op. cit.*

Nugroho, H. 2011. *A Mosaic of Indonesian Energy Policy*. Bogor: IPB Press.

Organisation for Economic Co-operation and Development (OECD). 2011. *Aid Effectiveness 2011: Progress in Implementing the Paris Declaration. Volume 2*. Country Papers: Indonesia. Paris, OECD. https://doi.org/10.1787/9789264125780-en.

———. All years. *GeoBook: Geographic Flows to Developing Countries*. https://stats.oecd.org/Index.aspx?ThemeTreeId=3

———. No date. DAC Glossary of Key Terms and Concepts. http://www.oecd.org/dac/financing-sustainable-development/development-finance-data/dac-glossary.htm

Pangestu, M. 1987. Survey of Recent Developments. *Bull Indonesian Ec Stud*, 23 (1), April.

Pangestu, M. (Ed.). 2015. *A Tribute to Ali Wardhana: Indonesia's Longest Serving Finance Minister from his Writings and his Colleagues*. Jakarta: PT Kompas Media Nusantara.

Pangestu, M., and M. Habir. 1990. Survey of Recent Developments. *Bull Indonesian Ec Stud*, 26 (1), April.

Pangestu, M. and M. S. Goeltom. 2001. Survey of Recent Developments. *Bull Indonesian Ec Stud*. 37 (2), August.

Pardede, R. and S. Zahro. 2017. Survey of Recent Developments. *Bull Indonesian Ec Stud*, 53 (3), December.

Park, D. and G.B. Estrada. 2009. Are Developing Asia's Foreign Exchange Reserves Excessive? *An Empirical Examination. ADB Economics Working Paper Series*. No 170. Manila: Asian Development Bank.

Penny, D., and Dahlan Thalib. 1969. Survey of Recent Developments. *Bull Indonesian Ec Stud*, 5 (1), March.

Prawiro, R. 1998. *Indonesia's Struggle for Economic Development: Pragmatism in Action*. Kuala Lumpur: Oxford University Press.

Prasad, E., R. Rajan and A. Subramanian. 2007. The Paradox of Capital. *Finance and Development*. 44 (1).

Posthumus. G.A. 1972. The Inter-Governmental Group on Indonesia. *Bull Indonesian Ec Stud*, 8 (2), July.

Rahadiana, R., and J. Thatcher. 2013. Indonesia says 2014 budget to focus on raising domestic demand. *Reuters Business News*, 14 August.

Resosudarmo, B. and A. Yusuf. 2009. Survey of Recent Developments. *Bull Indonesian Ec Stud*, 45 (3), December.

Resosudarmo, B.P. and Abdurohman. 2018. Survey of Recent Developments: Is Being Stuck with a Five Percent Growth Rate a New Normal for Indonesia? *Bull Indo Econ Studies*, 54 (2), August.

Riyadi, D. M. M. 2009. *Indonesia's Endeavour for Aid Accountability and Transparency*. Paper presented at the High-level Symposium in Vienna, 12–13 November. https://www.un.org/en/ecosoc/newfunct/pdf/riyadi.pdf

Rosendale, P. 1984. Survey of Recent Developments. *Bull Indonesian Ec Stud*, 20 (1), April.

Sadli, M. 2001. Hardening Attitudes of the IMF and the World Bank. *Bull Indonesian Ec Stud*, 37 (1), April.

Sambodo, M.T. 2016. *From Darkness to Light: Energy Security Assessment in Indonesia's Power Sector*. Singapore: ISEAS Publishing.

Sastromihardjo, S. 1990. Indonesia's Foreign Investment Policy: Towards a More Relaxed Posture. In Hal Hill and Terry Hull, 1990, *Indonesia Assessment 1990*, Canberra: Research School of Pacific Studies.

Sayogyo. 1975. *Usaha Perbaikan Gizi Keluarga: ANP Evaluation Study 1973* [Efforts to Improve Family Nutrition: ANP Evaluation Study 1973]. Bogor: Lembaga Penelitian Sosiologi Pedesaan, Institute Pertanian Bogor.

Shakow, A. 1964. *Foreign Economic Assistance in Indonesia 1950–1961*. Tokyo: Ministry of Foreign Affairs, Economic Cooperation Bureau.

Shrestha, R., and I. Coxhead. 2018. Survey of Recent Developments, *Bull Indo Econ Studies*, August, 54 (1).

Sigit, H., and S. Surbakti. 1999. *The Social Impact of the Financial Crisis in Indonesia*. Working Paper No. 1, Economics and Development Resource Center. Manila: Asian Development Bank, December.

Simandjuntak, D. S. 1989. Survey of Recent Developments. *Bull Indonesian Ec Stud*, 25 (1), April.

Soedjatmoko. 1978. National Policy Implications of the Basic Needs Model. *Prisma*. March.

Soeharto. 1976. Address by the President of the Republic of Indonesia His Excellency General Soeharto. *Summary of Proceedings, Ninth Annual Meeting of the Board of Governors*, Manila: Asian Development Bank.

Soesastro, H., and M.C. Basri. 1998. Survey of Recent Developments. *Bull Indonesian Ec Stud*, 33 (2).

Susantono, B. 2013. *Transportasi dan Investasi: Tantangan dan Perspektif Multidimensi* [Transport and Investment: Multidimensional Challenges and Perspectives]. Jakarta: Penerbit Buku Kompas.

———. 2015. *Infrastructure and Regional Development in Indonesia*. Delft, The Netherlands: Delft Academic Press.

Sussangkarn, C. 2010. The Chiang Mail Initiative Multilateralization: Origin, Development and Outlook. *ADBI Working Paper Series*, No. 230. Tokyo: ADB Institute.

Sutton, M. 1982. *Indonesia 1966–70: Economic Management and the Role of the IMF*. ODI Working Paper No 8, London: Overseas Development Institute. https://www.odi.org/sites/odi.org.uk/files/odi-assets/publications-opinion-files/6837.pdf

Takii, S., and E. Ramstetter. 2007. Survey of Recent Developments. *Bull Indonesian Ec Stud*, 43 (3), December.

Thee, K.W. 2012. *Indonesia's Economy since Independence*. Singapore: ISEAS Publishing.

Uning, D, M. 2003. Pemerintah Tak Akan Perpanjang Kerjasama Dengan IMF [Government Not Extending Cooperation With the IMF], *Tempo.com*, 25 August.

van der Eng, P. 2015. International Food Aid to Indonesia, 1950s–1970s, in Alicia Schrikker and Jeroen Touwen (ed.), *Promises and Predicaments: Trade and Entrepreneurship in Colonial and Independent Indonesia*. Singapore: NUS Press, Singapore.

Villafuerte, J., and J.T. Yap. 2015. Managing Capital Flows in Asia: An Overview of Key Issues. *ADB Economics Working Paper Series*. No 464. Manila: Asian Development Bank.

Wanandi, J. 2012. *Shades of Grey: A Political Memoir of Modern Indonesia*. Singapore: Equinox.

Wardhana, A. 1989. Structural Adjustment in Indonesia: Export and the "High-Cost" Economy. In Pangestu, *op. cit.*, 2015.

———. 1994. Financial Reform: Achievements, Problems, and Prospects. In Pangestu, *op. cit.*

USAID, Democratic Reform Support Program (DRSP) with support from the Donor Working Group on Decentralization. 2009. *Decentralization2009: Stock Taking on Indonesia's Recent Decentralization Reforms Update 2009: Main Report*. Jakarta.

Watanabe, T. 1977, reprinted 2010. *Towards a New Asia*. Manila: ADB.

Wells, L. 2007. Private Power in Indonesia. *Bull Indonesian Ec Stud*, 43 (3), December.

Wihtol, R. 1988. *The Asian Development Bank and Rural Development*. Oxford: Macmillan Press.

Widjojo Nitisastro. 2011. *The Indonesian Development Experience: A Collection of Writings and Speeches of Widjojo Nitisastro*, Singapore, Institute of Southeast Asian Studies. Also published as Widjojo Nitisastro, 2010, *Pengalaman Pembangunan Indonesia: KumpulanTulisan dan Uraian Widjojo Nitisastro*, Jakarta, PT Kompas Media Nusantara.

Wilson, D. 1987. *A Bank for Half the World: The Story of the Asian Development Bank 1966–1986.* Manila: ADB.

Winters, M.S. 2010. *Paper Prepared for June Meeting of the Informal Development Partners Working Group on Decentralisation and Local Governance (DPWG-DLG).* 4 June. http://siteresources.worldbank. org/EXTDSRE/Resources/IndonesiaCountryProfile.pdf

Witoelar, W. 2002. *No Regrets: Reflections of a Presidential Spokesman.* Jakarta: Equinox Publishing.

Wismana, A.S. nd. *Sharing Experience on Implementing Paris Declaration: The Jakarta Commitment and Aid for Development Effectiveness (A4DES).* PowerPoint presentation, Jakarta. http://www.oecd.org/ development/evaluation/dcdndep/47080421.pdf

World Bank. 1981. *Indonesia: Development Prospects and Policy Options,* Washington: World Bank. 6 April.

———. 1984. *Indonesia Policies and Prospects for Economic Growth and Transformation.* Report No. 5066-IND. April 26. Washington: World Bank.

———. 1993. *The East Asian Miracle: Economic Growth and Public Policy.* New York, NY: Oxford University Press.

———. 1993. *Second Meeting of the Consultative Group for Indonesia: Chairman's Report of Proceedings.* IND 93-3. Washington. November 16.

———. 1996. 'Donors Reaffirm Strong Support for Indonesia'. Press release, 20 June.

———. 1996. *Consultative Group for Indonesia: Chairman's Report of Proceedings.* CG 96-52. Washington. September 27.

———. 1997. *Indonesia: Sustaining High Growth with Equity.* Report No. 16433-IND. May 30. Washington: World Bank.

———. 1999. *Indonesia: Country Assistance Note.* Report No. 19100. Operations Evaluation Department. Washington: World Bank.

———. 2001. *Indonesia: The Imperative for Reform.* Report No. 23093-IND. Brief for the Consultative Group on Indonesia. November 2. Washington: World Bank.

———. 2010. *Indonesian Economic Quarterly.* March.

World Bank, Independent Evaluation Group, 2012, Transmigration in
    Indonesia, at http://lnweb90.worldbank.org/oed/oeddoclib.nsf/Doc
    UNIDViewForJavaSearch/4B8B0E01445D8351852567F5005D87B8,
    accessed 15 September 2018.

Yoshitomi, M., and ADBI Staff. 2003. *Post-Crisis Development Paradigms
    in Asia*. Tokyo: Asian Development Bank Institute.

Zhuang, Z., and M. Dowling. 2003. Lessons of the Asian Financial
    Crisis: What Can an Early Warning System Model Tell Us? *Asian
    Development Review*. 20 (1).

APPENDIXES

1. **Indonesia: Overview Charts and Tables**

   A1.1   GDP Annual Growth 1968–2019
   A1.2   Total Net Official Flows as % of GDP, 1968–2016

2. **Asian Development Bank and Indonesia: Charts and Tables**

   A2.1   ADB Loan Approvals for Indonesia, 1969–2016
   A2.2   Indonesian Governors and Alternate Governors to ADB
   A2.3   Indonesian Directors to ADB
   A2.4   Indonesia Resident Mission Country Directors
   A2.5   The Inter-Governmental Group on Indonesia (IGGI), 1967–1991
   A2.6   The Consultative Group on Indonesia, 1992–2006
   A2.7   Private Sector Lending to Indonesia, 1985–2019

1. Indonesia: Overview Charts and Tables

Figure A1.1: GDP Annual Growth 1968–2019

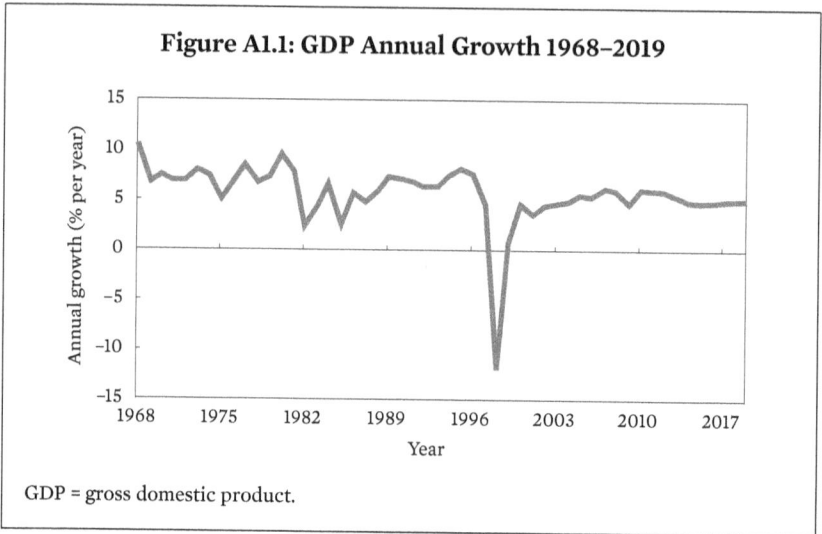

GDP = gross domestic product.

Figure A1.2: Total Official Net Flows as % of GDP, 1968–2016

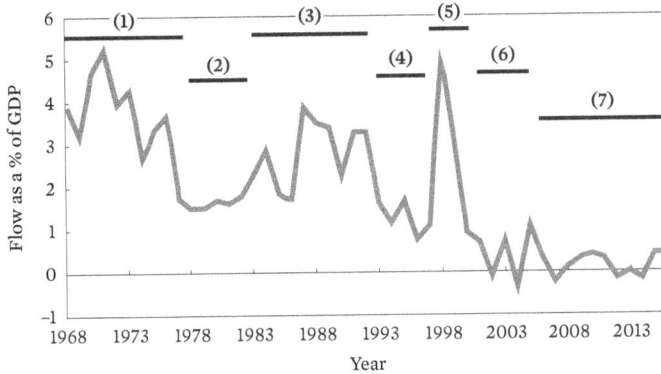

GDP = gross domestic product.

Note: Stages shown in figure are as follows:

(1)   High assistance flows in the early 1970s.

(2)   Lower flows following the two oil price increases in the early and late 1970s.

(3)   Support for structural adjustment in Indonesia during the 1980s.

(4)   Post Berlin wall: international flows fell reflecting Indonesia's high growth and apparent need for less reliance on official international finance.

(5)   Asian financial crisis; sharp increase in international support

(6)   Reduced borrowing by Indonesia reflecting the priority given to reducing public debt after the Asian financial crisis. There was a surge in international flows around 2005 following the tsunami in Aceh in 2004. Indonesia took over aid coordination from the CGI in 2007.

(7)   Move toward graduation.

Source: Organisation for Economic Co-operation and Development, *GeoBook: Geographical Flows to Developing Countries*.

2. Asian Development Bank and Indonesia: Charts and Tables

Table A2.1: ADB Loan Approvals for Indonesia, 1969–2016

Year	ADF $ million	OCR $ million	Total $ million	% of Government consumption	GDP
1969	3		3	0.6	0.04
1970	13		13	1.6	0.13
1971	32		32	3.6	0.32
1972	22		22	2.2	0.19
1973	29	12	41	2.4	0.24
1974	14	64	78	3.9	0.28
1975		78	78	2.6	0.24
1976		109	109	2.9	0.28
1969–1976	113	263	377	2.5	0.20
1977		136	136	2.7	0.28
1978	24	175	199	3.3	0.36
1979	25	210	235	3.9	0.43
1980		285	285	3.8	0.37
1981		338	338	3.7	0.37
1982		371	371	3.6	0.39
1983		426	426	4.8	0.49
1984		587	587	6.6	0.65
1985		502	502	5.1	0.55
1986		319	319	3.6	0.37
1977–1986	49	3,349	3,398	4.1	0.40
1987	135	441	576	8.0	0.71
1988	80	507	587	7.7	0.65
1989	105	675	780	8.7	0.78
1990	130	809	939	9.8	0.83
1991		1,211	1,211	11.3	0.98
1992	55	1,156	1,211	9.9	0.89

continued on next page

Table A2.1 *continued*

Year	ADF $ million	OCR $ million	Total $ million	% of Government consumption	GDP
1993	62	1,224	1,286	9.0	0.76
1994	44	705	749	5.2	0.40
1995	57	999	1,056	6.7	0.49
1996	68	852	920	5.3	0.38
1987–1996	735	8,579	9,313	8.2	0.70
1997	30	1,079	1,109	7.4	0.48
1998		1,839	1,839	33.6	1.81
1999		1,020	1,020	11.1	0.68
2000	165	635	800	7.4	0.46
2001	100	400	500	4.5	0.29
2002	131	636	767	5.4	0.37
2003	74	187	262	1.4	0.10
2004	25	200	225	1.1	0.08
2005	111	1,035	1,146	4.9	0.38
2006	110	685	795	2.5	0.20
1997–2006	746	7,716	8,462	7.9	0.50
2007	50	995	1,045	2.9	0.23
2008	160	925	1,085	2.5	0.20
2009		2,224	2,224	4.3	0.39
2010		785	785	1.2	0.10
2011		580	580	0.7	0.06
2012		1,233	1,233	1.5	0.13
2013		1,014	1,014	1.2	0.11
2014		554	554	0.7	0.06
2015		1,375	1,375	1.6	0.16
2016		1,727	1,727	1.9	0.19
2006–2016	210	11,412	11,622	1.8	0.20

ADB = Asian Development Bank, ADF = Asian Development Fund, OCR = ordinary capital resources, GDP = gross domestic product.
Source: ADB.

Table A2.2: Indonesian Governors and Alternate Governors to ADB

Year	Governor	Alternate Governor
1967	Frans Seda	Radius Prawiro
1968	Ali Wardhana	Radius Prawiro
1969	Ali Wardhana	Radius Prawiro
1970	Ali Wardhana	Radius Prawiro
1971	Ali Wardhana	Radius Prawiro
1972	Ali Wardhana	Radius Prawiro
1973	Ali Wardhana	Radius Prawiro
1974	Ali Wardhana	Rachmat Saleh
1975	Ali Wardhana	Rachmat Saleh
1976	Ali Wardhana	Rachmat Saleh
1977	Ali Wardhana	Rachmat Saleh
1978	Ali Wardhana	Rachmat Saleh
1979	Ali Wardhana	Rachmat Saleh
1980	Ali Wardhana	Rachmat Saleh
1981	Ali Wardhana	Rachmat Saleh
1982	Ali Wardhana	Rachmat Saleh
1983	Radius Prawiro	Arifin M. Siregar
1984	Radius Prawiro	Arifin M. Siregar
1985	Radius Prawiro	Arifin M. Siregar
1986	Radius Prawiro	Arifin M. Siregar
1987	Radius Prawiro	Arifin M. Siregar
1988	J.B. Sumarlin	Adrianus Mooy
1989	J.B. Sumarlin	Adrianus Mooy
1990	J.B. Sumarlin	Adrianus Mooy
1991	J.B. Sumarlin	Adrianus Mooy
1992	J.B. Sumarlin	Adrianus Mooy
1993	Mar'ie Muhammad	J. Soedradjad Djiwandono
1994	Mar'ie Muhammad	J. Soedradjad Djiwandono

continued on next page

Table A2.2 *continued*

Year	Governor	Alternate Governor
1995	Mar'ie Muhammad	J. Soedradjad Djiwandono
1996	Mar'ie Muhammad	J. Soedradjad Djiwandono
1997	Mar'ie Muhammad	J. Soedradjad Djiwandono
1998	Bambang Subianto	Syahril Sabirin
1999	Bambang Sudibyo	Syahril Sabirin
2000	Bambang Sudibyo	Syahril Sabirin
2001	Prijadi Praptosuhardjo	Syahril Sabirin
2002	Boediono	Syahril Sabirin
2003	Boediono	Burhanuddin Abdullah
2004	Jusuf Anwar	Burhanuddin Abdullah
2005	Sri Mulyani Indrawati	Burhanuddin Abdullah
2006	Sri Mulyani Indrawati	Paskah Suzetta
2007	Sri Mulyani Indrawati	Paskah Suzetta
2008	Sri Mulyani Indrawati	Paskah Suzetta
2009	Sri Mulyani Indrawati	Armida Alisjahbana
2010	Agus D.W. Martowardojo	Armida Alisjahbana
2011	Agus D.W. Martowardojo	Armida Alisjahbana
2012	Agus D.W. Martowardojo	Armida Alisjahbana
2013	Muhamad Chatib Basri	Armida Alisjahbana
2014	Bambang P.S. Brodjonegoro	Andrinof Chaniago
2015	Bambang P.S. Brodjonegoro	Sofyan Djalil
2016	Sri Mulyani Indrawati	Bambang P.S. Brodjonegoro
2017	Sri Mulyani Indrawati	Bambang P.S. Brodjonegoro
2018	Sri Mulyani Indrawati	Bambang P.S. Brodjonegoro
2019	Sri Mulyani Indrawati	Bambang P.S. Brodjonegoro

ADB = Asian Development Bank.
Source: ADB annual reports.

Table A2.3: Indonesian Directors to ADB

Year	Director	Year	Director
1967	B. Kharmawan	1994	Soegito Sastromihardjo
1968	R.A. Kartadjoemena	1995	Soegito Sastromihardjo
1969	Abdul Wahab Haider[a]	1996	Soegito Sastromihardjo
1970	Abdul Wahab Haider[a]	1997	Soegito Sastromihardjo
1971	R.A. Kartadjoemena[b]	1998	Soegito Sastromihardjo
1972	R.A. Kartadjoemena[b]	1999	Soegito Sastromihardjo
1973	R.A. Kartadjoemena	2000	Soegito Sastromihardjo
1974	R.A. Kartadjoemena	2001	Jusuf Anwar
1975	R.A. Kartadjoemena	2002	Jusuf Anwar
1976	R.A. Kartadjoemena	2003	Jusuf Anwar
1977	R.A. Kartadjoemena	2004	Jusuf Anwar
1978	R.A. Kartadjoemena	2005	Agus Haryanto
1979	R.A. Kartadjoemena	2006	Agus Haryanto
1980	R.A. Kartadjoemena	2007	Ceppie K. Sumadilaga
1981	Soesilo Sardadi	2008	Ceppie K. Sumadilaga
1982	Soesilo Sardadi	2009	Marwanto Harjowiryono
1983	Sofjan Djajawinata	2010	Marwanto Harjowiryono
1984	Sofjan Djajawinata	2011	Maurin Sitorus
1985	Sofjan Djajawinata	2012	Maurin Sitorus
1986	Sofjan Djajawinata	2013	Bhimantara Widyajala
1987	Sofjan Djajawinata	2014	Bhimantara Widyajala
1988	Sofjan Djajawinata	2015	Bhimantara Widyajala
1989	Sofjan Djajawinata	2016	Bhimantara Widyajala
1990	Sofjan Djajawinata	2017	Syurkani Ishak Kasim
1991	Sofjan Djajawinata	2018	Syurkani Ishak Kasim
1992	Sofjan Djajawinata	2019	Syurkani Ishak Kasim
1993	Sofjan Djajawinata		

ADB = Asian Development Bank.

Notes:

[a] Abdul Wahab Haider from Afghanistan was director of the ADB constituency which Indonesia was part of in 1969 and 1970.

[b] R.A. Kartadjoemena was an alternate director for two years.

Source: ADB annual reports.

Table A2.4: Indonesia Resident Mission Country Directors

No.	Name	Period
1	Richard M. Bradley	July 1987–December 1991
2	Eiji Kobayashi	December 1991–September 1993
3	Theodore C. Patterson	October 1993–June 1997
4	Robert C. May	March 1998–October 2000
5	Johannes P.M. van Heeswijck	June 2000–July 2003
6	David J. Green	August 2003–August 2005
7	Edgar A. Cua	October 2005–August 2007
8	James A. Nugent	October 2007–2 August 2011
9	Jon D. Lindborg	10 October 2011–23 September 2013
10	H.G. Adrian Ruthenberg	18 December 2013–14 December 2014
11	Steven R. Tabor	9 June 2015–30 September 2016
12	Winfried F. Wicklein	13 March 2017–present

Source: Asian Development Bank records.

Table A2.5: The Inter-Governmental Group on Indonesia (IGGI), 1967–1991

Meeting No.	Dates		Place	Chair	Leader Indonesian Delegation
	Year	Days			
1	1967	22–24 February	Amsterdam	Th. H. Bot	H.A. Pandelaki
2	1967	18–21 June	Scheveningen	Th. H. Bot	H.A. Pandelaki
3	1967	20–22 November	Amsterdam	B.J. Udink	Widjojo Nitisastro
4	1968	21–24 April	Rotterdam	B.J. Udink	Widjojo Nitisastro
5	1968	21–23 October	Scheveningen	B.J. Udink	Widjojo Nitisastro
6	1969	14–15 April	Scheveningen	B.J. Udink	Widjojo Nitisastro
7	1969	8–19 December	Amsterdam	B.J. Udink	Widjojo Nitisastro
8	1970	20–21 April	Rotterdam	B.J. Udink	Widjojo Nitisastro
9	1970	15–16 December	Rotterdam	B.J. Udink	Widjojo Nitisastro
10	1971	19–20 April	Amsterdam	B.J. Udink	Widjojo Nitisastro

continued on next page

Table A2.5 *continued*

Meeting No.	Year	Days	Place	Chair	Leader Indonesian Delegation
11	1971	13–14 December	Amsterdam	C. Boertien	Widjojo Nitisastro
12	1972	25–26 April	Amsterdam	C. Boertien	Widjojo Nitisastro
13	1972	21–22 December	Amsterdam	C. Boertien	Widjojo Nitisastro
14	1973	7–8 May	Amsterdam	C. Boertien	Widjojo Nitisastro
15	1973	11–12 December	Amsterdam	J.C. Pronk	Widjojo Nitisastro
16	1974	7–8 May	Amsterdam	J.C. Pronk	Widjojo Nitisastro
17	1975	12–13 May	Amsterdam	J.C. Pronk	Widjojo Nitisastro
18	1975	25 November	Amsterdam	G.A. Posthumus	Rachmat Saleh
19	1976	9–10 June	Amsterdam	J.C. Pronk	Widjojo Nitisastro
20	1977	5–6 April	Amsterdam	J.C. Pronk	Widjojo Nitisastro
21	1978	22–23 May	Amsterdam	J. de Koning	Widjojo Nitisastro
22	1979	3–5 April	Amsterdam	J. de Koning	Widjojo Nitisastro
23	1980	7–8 May	Amsterdam	J. de Koning	Widjojo Nitisastro
24	1981	12–13 May	Amsterdam	J. de Koning	Widjojo Nitisastro
25	1982	8–9 May	Amsterdam	C.P. van Dijk	Widjojo Nitisastro
26	1983	13–14 June	Den Haag	E.M. Schoo	Widjojo Nitisastro
27	1984	4–5 June	Den Haag	E.M. Schoo	Widjojo Nitisastro
28	1985	4–5 June	Amsterdam	E.M. Schoo	Ali Wardhana
29	1986	18–19 June	Den Haag	E.M. Schoo	Ali Wardhana
30	1987	17–18 June	Den Haag	P. Bukman	Ali Wardhana
32	1988	14–15 June	Den Haag	P. Bukman	Radius Prawiro
33	1989	13–14 June	Den Haag	P. Bukman	Saleh Affif
34	1990	12–13 June	Den Haag	J.P. Pronk	Radius Prawiro
35	1991	11–12 June	Den Haag	J.P. Pronk	Radius Prawiro

Source: Bappenas files.

Table A2.6: The Consultative Group on Indonesia, 1992–2006[a]

Meeting No.	Dates		Place	Chair	Leader Indonesian Delegation
	Year	Days			
1	1992	16–17 July	Paris	Gautam Kaji	Radius Prawiro
2	1993	29–30 June	Paris	Gautam Kaji	Saleh Afiff
3	1994	7–8 July	Paris	Gautam Kaji	Saleh Afiff
4	1995	18–19 July	Paris	Russell Cheetham	Saleh Afiff
5	1996	18–20 June	Paris	Russell Cheetham	Saleh Afiff
6	1997	16–17 July	Tokyo	Jean-Michel Severino	Saleh Afiff
7	1998	29–30 July	Paris	Sven Sandstrom	Ginandjar Kartasasmita
8	1999	27–28 July	Paris	Sven Sandstrom	Ginandjar Kartasasmita
9	2000	1–2 February	Jakarta	Jean-Michel Severino	Kwik Kian Gie
10	2000	17–18 October	Tokyo	Jemal-ud-din Kassum	Rizal Ramli
11	2001	7–8 November	Jakarta	Jemal-ud-din Kassum	Dorodjatun Kuntjoro-Jakti
12	2003	21–22 January	Bali	Jemal-ud-din Kassum	Dorodjatun Kuntjoro-Jakti
13	2003	10–11 December	Jakarta	Jemal-ud-din Kassum	Dorodjatun Kuntjoro-Jakti
14	2005	19–20 January	Jakarta	Jusuf Kalla; Aburizal Bakrie	[b]
15	2006	14 June	Jakarta	Jusuf Kalla; Boediono	[b]

Notes:

[a] Meetings shown here were the main meetings of the Consultative Group on Indonesia. A number of informal and interim meetings were also held from time to time.

[b] Meetings chaired by representatives of the Government of Indonesia.

Source: Kementerian Perencanaan Pembangunan Nasional, 2003, *Keberadaan*, ADB records and World Bank archives.

Table A2.7: Private Sector Lending to Indonesia, 1985–2019

Sector	Subsector	Company	Investment ($ million)	Date approved
Industry and trade	Large and medium industries	Indonesian Development Bank (Bapindo)	1.0	June 1985
Agriculture and natural resources	Agricultural production and markets	PT Kratama Belindo International	0.4	June 1985
Industry and trade	Large and medium industries	PT Gunung Garuda	15.0	September 1988
Finance	Banking systems	PT Bank UPPINDO	1.7	November 1988
Finance	Money and capital markets	Bapindo II	5.0	November 1988
Finance	SME finance and leasing	PT Mediasarana Multi Finance	5.3	October 1989
Finance	Banking systems	PT BBL Dharmala Finance	15.0	October 1989
Finance	Investment funds	PT Asian Development Securities Co.	1.2	December 1989
Finance	Investment funds	PT Indonesia Development Fund Ltd.	6.0	December 1989
Finance	SME finance and leasing	PT Mediasarana Multi Finance	2.0	May 1990
Finance	Banking systems	PT BBL Dharmala Finance	5.0	May 1990
Finance	Banking systems	PT Bakrie Finance Corporation	16.3	August 1990
Industry and trade	Large and medium industries	PT Seamless Pipe Indonesia Jaya	20.0	May 1991
Industry and trade	Large and medium industries	PT Seamless Pipe Indonesia Jaya	56.5	April 1992
Industry and trade	Large and medium industries	PT Wiraswasta Gemilang	18.5	April 1993
Finance	SME finance and leasing	PT Mediasarana Multi Finance	0.3	October 1994
Finance	Housing finance	Secondary Mortgage Facility		June 1998
Energy	Conventional energy	Tangguh Liquefied Natural Gas (LNG)	350.0	December 2005

continued on next page

Table A2.7   *continued*

Sector	Subsector	Company	Investment ($ million)	Date approved
Finance	Money and capital markets	Acquisition and Securitization of Motor Loan Portfolios by Deutsche Bank	10.0	July 2006
Water and other municipal infrastructure	Water supply and sanitation	PT PAM Lyonnaise Jaya (PALYJA)	50.0	Aug 2007
Finance	Banking systems	Bank Mandiri (Persero)	300.0	July 2008
Finance	Money and capital markets	Indonesian Infrastructure Financing Facility	40.0	March 2009
Finance	Housing finance	Housing Finance Program		December 2010
Finance	Trade finance	Indonesia Eximbank	200.0	March 2011
Energy	Renewable energy	Sarulla geothermal	250.0	December 2013
Energy	Conventional energy generation	Tangguh LNG Expansion Project	400.0	December 2016
Energy	Renewable energy generation—geothermal	Muara Laboh Geothermal Power Project	70.0	December 2016
Energy	Renewable energy generation—wind	Jeneponto wind project	56.4	November 2017
Energy	Renewable energy generation—geothermal	Rantau Dedap Geothermal Power	177.5	March 2018
Energy	Renewable energy generation—solar	Vena Energy solar project	12.5	April 2018
Health	Health system development	Hermina Maternity and Child Care Hospital Project	10.0	April 2018
Energy	Conventional energy generation	Jawa-1 LNG-to-Power Project	250.0	August 2018
Energy	Energy utility services	Riau Natural Gas Power Project	229.9	December 2018
Finance	SME finance and leasing	PT Indosurya Inti Finance for SMEs	80.0	October 2019

PT = *perseroan terbatas* (limited liability company), SMEs = small and medium enterprises.
Source: Asian Development Bank records.

INDEX OF NAMES

Boxes, figures, and tables are indicated by "b," "f," and "t" following page numbers.

Abdullah, Burhanuddin, 281*t*
Abdurohman, 230
Abimanyu, Anggito, 200
Abs, Hermann, 29
Afiff, Saleh, 71, 96, 111–112, 285*t*
Alisjahbana, Armida, 208–209, 243, 281*t*
Anwar, Jusuf, 281*t*–282*t*
Arndt, Heinz, 27, 41, 66
Asakawa, Masatsugu, 79

Baird, Mark, 201
Bakrie, Aburizal, 285*t*
Basri, Muhamad Chatib, 198, 281*t*
Boediono, 54, 152, 154–155, 194, 201, 209, 281*t*, 285*t*
Boertien, C., 284*t*
Booth, Anne, 152
Bradley, Richard, 283*t*
Brodjonegoro, Bambang, 209, 281*t*
Brodjonegoro, Soemantri, 25
Bot, Theo, 283*t*
Bukman, P., 284*t*
Bush, George W., 153

Camdessus, Michel, 135, 140
Chaniago, Andrinof, 281*t*
Cheetham, Russell, 285*t*
Chino, Tadao, 173
Clinton, Bill, 131*b*, 157
Cua, Edgar, 283

De Koning, J., 284*t*
Djajawinata, Sofjan, 282*t*
Djalil, Sofyan, 281*t*
Djiwandono, Soedradjad, 132, 280*t*–281*t*, 285*t*
Djojohadikusumo, Sumitro, 4, 27, 70

Fujioka, Masao, 98, 124
Fukuda, Takeo, 22

Gillis, Malcolm, 66
Glassburner, Bruce, 39, 90
Goeltom, Miranda, 152, 158
Green, David, 283*t*
Grenville, Stephen, 38
Gyohten, Toyoo, 128

Habibie, Bacharuddin, 84, 132*b*, 135–136, 152, 157
Habir, Manggi, 85
Haider, Abdul, 282*t*
Hamengkubuwono IX, 16, 24, 49
Haryanto, Agus, 282*t*
Harjowiryono, Marwanto, 282*t*
Hobohm, Sam, 83

Indrawati, Sri Mulyani, 17, 190, 201, 223, 235, 240, 281*t*
Inoue, Shiro, 49

Joesoef, Daoed, 89

Kalla, Jusuf, 209, 285*t*
Kartadjoemena, R., 282*t*
Kassum, Jemal-ud-din, 285*t*
Kaji, Gautam, 110, 285*t*
Kartasasmita, Ginandjar, 84, 209, 285*t*
Kasim, Syurkani, 282*t*
Kharmawan, Byanti, 282*t*
Kobayashi, Eji, 283*t*
Kuntjoro-Jakti, Dorodjatun, 164, 285*t*
Kuroda, Haruhiko, 183, 188–190, 223
Kwik, Kian Gie, 285*t*

Lindblad, Thomas, 201
Lindborg, Jon, 283*t*

Mackie, Jamie, 84
Malik, Adam, 16
Mar'ie, Muhammad, 280*t*–281*t*
Martowardojo, Agus, 281*t*
Marsudi, Retno, 19, 232
May, Robert, 283*t*
McNamara, Robert, 27–28
Mears, Leon, 32, 57
Mooy, Adrianus, 280*t*
Myint, Hla, 256

Nakao, Takehiko, 243–244, 257
Nasser, Gamal, 15
Nasution, Anwar, 88, 102, 129, 180
Nehru, Jawaharlal, 15
Nitisastro, Widjojo, 24, 27, 41, 69–70, 84, 283*t*–284*t*
Nugent, James, 283*t*

Okita, Saburo, 98

Pandelaki, H., 283t
Pangestu, Mari, 40, 82, 84, 89, 152, 158
Pardede, Raden, 229–230
Patterson, Theodore, 283t
Posthumus, G., 284
Praptosuhardjo, Prijadi, 281t
Prawiro, Radius, 21, 23–24, 28, 65, 104, 124, 246, 280t, 284t–285t
Pronk, Jan, 38, 109–110, 284t

Ramli, Rizal, 158, 285t
De Rato, Roderigo, 200
Resosudarmo, Budy, 230
Ruthenberg, Adrian, 283t

Sabirin Syahril, 281t
Sadli, Mohammad, 24, 27, 98–99
Saleh, Rachmat, 280t, 284t
Salim, Emil, 24, 99, 223
Sandstrom, S., 285t
Sardadi, Soesilo, 282t
Sastromihardjo, Soegito, 282t
Sastrosoenarto, Hartarto, 84
Sato, Mitsuo, 186
Sayogo, 57
Schoo, E., 284t
Seda, Frans, 1, 22, 24, 280t
Sen, Amartya, 98
Severino, Jean-Michel, 285t
Sjahrir, 84
Shafer, Jeffrey, 128
Siregar, Arifin, 280t
Siregar, Mahendra, 160
Sitorus, Maurin, 282t
Soeharto, 1, 12, 24–25, 39, 44–46, 49, 70, 102–103, 110, 131b–132b, 134–135, 140, 186, 201
Soekarnoputri, Megawati, 135–136, 153–155, 173, 180
Subianto, Bambang, 281t
Subroto, 24

Sudibyo, Bambang, 281t
Sukarno, 15–16
Sumadilaga, Ceppie, 282t
Sumarlin, Johannes, 84–85, 104, 209, 280t
Susantono, Bambang, 240, 244
Suzetta, Paskah, 281t

Tabor, Steven, 283t
Tanaka, Kakuei, 38–39
Tarumizu, Kimimasa, 79, 122
Thee, Kian Wie, 68, 103, 201
Tuwo, Lukita, 224

Udink, B., 283t

Van Dijk, C., 284t
Van Heeswijck, Johannes, 283t
Volcker, Paul, 53

Wahid, Abdurrahman, 135–136, 152, 155, 157
Wardhana, Ali, 2, 25, 40, 53–54, 65–66, 70, 81, 84, 124, 280t, 284t
Watanabe, Michio, 92t, 109
Watanabe, Takeshi, 22
Wells, Louis, 121
Wicklein, Winfried, 283t
Widodo, Joko, 19, 193, 199, 209, 230, 239–240, 244, 257
Widyajala, Bhimantara, 282t
Wihardja, Monica, 201
Winters, M., 205–206
Wolfensohn, James, 157

Yoshida, Taroichi, 45
Yudhoyono, Susilo Bambang, 154, 164, 176, 180, 184–185, 189, 191, 193–194, 198–199, 208, 223, 240

Zahro, Shirin, 229–230
Zhou, Enlai, 15
Zoellick, Robert, 153

.

www.ingramcontent.com/pod-product-compliance
Lightning Source LLC
Chambersburg PA
CBHW041143230326
41599CB00039BA/7149